John S. Hittell

A History of the Mental Growth of Mankind in Ancient Times

Volume II: Heathen Barbarism

John S. Hittell

A History of the Mental Growth of Mankind in Ancient Times
Volume II: Heathen Barbarism

ISBN/EAN: 9783743394001

Manufactured in Europe, USA, Canada, Australia, Japa

Cover: Foto ©ninafisch / pixelio.de

Manufactured and distributed by brebook publishing software (www.brebook.com)

John S. Hittell

A History of the Mental Growth of Mankind in Ancient Times

A HISTORY

OF THE

MENTAL GROWTH OF MANKIND

IN

ANCIENT TIMES

BY

JOHN S. HITTELL

VOLUME II.
HEATHEN BARBARISM

NEW YORK
HENRY HOLT AND COMPANY
1893

CONTENTS OF VOLUME II.

CHAPTER X. BRONZE.

Section.	Page.
159. Barbarism	9
160. Bronze Tools	11
161. Superiority of Iron	16

CHAPTER XI. THE AZTECS.

162. Anahuac	17
163. Crops	18
164. Weaving, etc	20
165. Metallurgy	21
166. Stone Work	23
167. Trade	26
168. Social Condition	27
169. Records	32
170. Astronomy	34
171. A Martial Empire	35
172. Ranks	37
173. Imperial Office	38
174. Laws	42
175. Aztec Gods	43
176. Aztec Temples	46
177. Human Victims	48
178. Aztec Priests	51
179. Burial	52
180. Aztec Ethics	53
181. Aztec Culture	55
182. The End of Anahuac	58

CHAPTER XII. THE QUICHUANS.

Section.	Page.
183. The Quichuan Empire	59
184. Agriculture	60
185. Various Arts	62
186. Buildings	65
187. Mining	68
188. Social Affairs	69
189. Government	72
190. Aggressive Policy	75
191. Quichuan Religion	77
192. Quichuan Temples	80
193. Quichuan Ethics	82
194. Culture and Collapse	84
195. Muyscas	87

CHAPTER XIII. THE CHINESE.

196. China	88
197. Original Arts	92
198. Houses, etc.	94
199. Different Arts	96
200. Manners	97
201. Matrimony	100
202. Music, etc.	102
203. Speech	103
204. Writing	104
205. Imperial Power	108
206. Examinations	110
207. Local Administration	113
208. Person and Property	116
209. Confucius	118
210. No Supernaturalism	121

SECTION.	PAGE.
211. An Honored Sage	123
212. Chinese Ancestors	125
213. China's Place	128
214. Japanese Society, etc.	130
215. Japanese Government	133
216. Japanese Religion	134

CHAPTER XIV. THE ANCIENT EGYPTIANS.

217. Egypt	135
218. Egyptian Agriculture	136
219. Handicrafts	138
220. Egyptian Architecture	141
221. Pyramids	142
222. Egyptian Temples	146
223. Metals in Egypt	150
224. Egyptian Homes	151
225. Hieroglyphics	156
226. Egyptian Books, etc.	159
227. Political Condition	161
228. Egyptian Gods	164
229. Osiris the Mediator	166
230. Sacred Beasts	167
231. Kings and Gods	169
232. Monotheistic Expressions	170
233. Adoration of Ancestors	172
234. The Mummy	174
235. Egyptian Morality	178
236. Egyptian Gospels	180
237. Last Judgment	182
238. Egyptian Priests	187
239. Egyptian Antiquity	189
240. Egypt's Place	194

CHAPTER XV. THE HINDOOS, ETC.

Section.	Page.
241. Primitive Aryans	196
242. Hindostan	199
243. Vedic Hindoos	200
244. Vedic Religion	201
245. Vedic Hymns	204
246. Hindoo Literature, etc.	207
247. Brahminism	210
248. Menu	212
249. Caste	214
250. The Brahmins	217
251. Suttee, etc.	220
252. Brahmin Women	222
253. Brahmin Morality	224
254. Brahmin Henotheism	227
255. Transmigration	228
256. Krishna	230
257. Buddha	233
258. Nirvana	238
259. Bikshoos	240
260. Laymen	243
261. Viharas	244
262. Discourses	247
263. Siddhartha's Death	249
264. Councils	251
265. Asoka	254
266. Growth	256
267. Hindostan's Place	261

CHAPTER XVI. THE ANCIENT PERSIANS.

Section.	Page.
268. Land and People	264
269. Persian Government	267
270. The Avesta	268
271. Ormuzd	271

CHAPTER XVII. THE BABYLONIANS, ETC.

272. Chaldea	277
273. Chaldean Buildings	279
274. Chaldean Learning	280
275. Chaldean Government	284
276. Chaldean Religion	284
277. Assyria	288
278. Assyrian Polity	291
279. Assyrian Religion	292
280. Phœnicia	295
281. Phœnician Commerce	299
282. Phœnician Letters	300

CHAPTER XVIII. THE TEUTONS, ETC.

283. Teutonia	302
284. Teutonic Army	304
285. Teutonic Religion	305
286. The Celts	307
287. Celtic Polity	309
288. Druidism	310
289. Stone Monuments	313
290. Etruria	317
291. Etruscan Industry	318
292. Etruscan Polity, etc.	319
293. Etruscan Religion	320

CHAPTER XIX. HEATHEN BARBARISM.

Section.	Page.
294. Race and Place	322
295. Barbarous Industry	323
296. Barbarous Society, etc	324
297. Great Achievements	325
298. Barbarous Polity, etc	327
299. Religious Growth	328
300. Religious Comparison	331
301. Ecclesiastical Growth	333
302. Natural Causes	336
303. Departmental Values	337
304. Change of Scene	340

APPENDIX	342
Notes	342
List of Authorities	371

A HISTORY OF MANKIND.

Heathen Barbarism.

CHAPTER X.

BRONZE.

SECTION 159. *Barbarism.*—The Aztecs, Quichuans, Chaldeans, Assyrians, Phœnicians, Carthaginians, Etruscans, and the ancient Egyptians, Persians, Jews, Teutons, and Celts were, and the modern Chinese, Hindoos and Mohammedans are, above the level of savagism and yet decidedly below the civilization of the Greeks of the Vth. century B. C., and of the modern Europeans. We need some one word to express the cultural condition of the peoples between savagism and civilization; and we have in English no better term for the purpose than barbarism, which is used in that sense by authors of high authority; though by others it is employed as synonymous with savagism. The word heathen is applied "to all nations except [Jews], Christians and Mohammedans."[1] In preparing this volume for the press, it was found convenient to include in it all the leading barbarous nations save the Mohammedans and ancient Jews; and therefore the subject of this volume is " Heathen Barbarism."

In the first volume we examined the cultural condition of man when his best edge-tools were of stone. We found that he had pottery, cloth, boats propelled by paddles and sails, tillage, herds of ruminant animals, tribal government, despotic chieftainship, slavery, nobility, rudiments of military discipline, and an idolatrous polytheism. He had not advanced to the smelting of metals, to the construction of cut-stone houses, to the building of cities, to the formation of orderly national governments, to the invention of writing, to the organization of well-drilled armies, nor to the adoption of a moral code as a prominent part of his religion. These deficiencies disappear in barbarism.

The study of savagism showed to us a multitude of small communities, each possessing many peculiar customs and institutions. A separate statement of the habits and ideas of each tribe would have required much repetition, which besides tiring would have confused the reader. Under these circumstances, convenience required that the main divisions of the subject should be based on cultural, not on political boundaries, and that the industry, society, polity and religion of the savages should each be treated comprehensively in its own chapter or chapters. But in barbarism a different arrangement is demanded. The political organizations are large and relatively few. The simplicity of savage life has given way to complexity; heterogeneity has succeeded to homogeneity. Arts, governments, and ecclesiastical systems have advanced by many differentiations. There is so much that is original, characteristic, and instructive in Aztec Mexico, Quichuan Peru, China, Egypt and Hindostan that each of those countries must be made the subject of a special chapter.

This volume will be devoted to the examination of the culture of the Aztecs, Quichuans, Chinese, Japanese, ancient Egyptians, Primitive Aryans, Hindoos, Babylonians, Assyrians, ancient Persians, Etruscans, Phœnicians, Celts, and Teutons. The barbarous nations of America are taken first because they were, industrially, in a lower culturestep than any of the others, until their empires were overthrown and deprived of special interest for the studies in which we are now engaged; and also because neither of these empires exercised the least influence on the development of any other nation. An isolation less complete, and yet very remarkable, appears in China, which therefore comes next on our list. For many centuries, Egypt remained in national seclusion; and not until the VIIIth century B. C. did it enter into intimate relations with other countries. Hindostan developed the barbarous arts at a later period, and under circumstances not traceable until it became part of the Persian Empire, which first established an intimate intercourse among many nations, and thus organized an international or general culture. In this empire the provinces of Persia, Babylonia, and Phœnicia occupied central and influential positions. The Etruscans, Celts, and Teutons are introduced to complete the list of heathen nations in the barbarous culturestep.

SEC. 160. *Bronze Tools.*—In portions of Europe, Asia, Africa, and North and South America, stone as the material of the best edge-tools, was succeeded by bronze. Before men made that alloy, however, they had long been familiar with copper, which they found in lumps of the natural metal. Its malleability, luster, and color gave it much value for ornaments. It was used for centuries east of the Mississippi, and perhaps in other parts of the world, by savages who had no other metal. By hammering and grinding, they shaped it into plates, rings, pendants, and other articles. But its use had no perceptible influence on industry. It gave no superior efficiency to any important tool or weapon.

In the course of ages, when men learned to make fires hot enough, they discovered the fusibility of copper and its ores. Then they found that by mixing it with tin, they obtained an alloy which possessed the combination of hardness with elasticity, needed for knives, chisels, axes, swords, awls, hoes, and sickles. Bronze gave a highly-increased efficiency to their toil in many directions. It supplied facilities, previously unapproached, for digging up the soil, chopping down trees, shaping wood, and quarrying and cutting stone. By stimulating tillage, it increased the supply of food and made population more dense. It enabled men to build houses of cut-stone; it cheapened the construction of boats. It improved arms and military discipline. It elevated men from savagism to barbarism.

When discovered by the Europeans in the XVIth century, the Aztecs and Quichuans had bronze and no iron. In Switzerland, Denmark, Sweden, England, France, Belgium, Italy, Spain, Portugal, Greece, Asia Minor, and Mesopotamia, the strata deposited and the sepulchers constructed, in the period next after the stone culturestep, contain tools, weapons, and ornaments of bronze but not of iron. The supposition that articles of iron once existed in these places, but have been destroyed by oxidation, does not account satisfactorily for the lack of that metal; first because there are no traces of the rust, and second because many of the implements in bronze would never have been made of that alloy if iron had been known. In some prehistoric strata, bronze is found with stone shaped by art; in other strata, it is found with iron; but traces of both the stone and the iron industries are not numerous in strata of the same period. There are abundant evidences that in many countries the age of iron was separated from the age of stone by an intervening age of bronze.

In the Swiss lake villages of the bronze age, we find no coins, no inscriptions, no glazed tiles, and no articles of silver; but all these things appear on a higher stratum when iron was in common use. The early monuments of Egypt had pictures of warriors with red swords and spear-heads as if the material were not iron.[1] In the Iliad, the swords, spear-heads, shields and helmets are of bronze. Hesiod tells us that "men wrought in bronze when iron did not exist." The poets and historians of Greece, writing in historical times, said their ancestors fought with weapons of bronze. That was the material of a spear preserved in the temple of Phaselis, as the spear of Achilles.[2] Euripides wrote of the bronze-speared Trojans, and according to Virgil the companions of Æneus had bronze swords, and the reapers of the Carthaginian territory had bronze sickles. In the time of Herodotus, the Massagetæ of Central Asia had metallic weapons, but none of iron or steel. About a century before the Christian era, the Greek Agatharcides wrote that some bronze chisels had recently been found in an Egyptian gold mine that had been abandoned for many centuries. The Greek word for smith is "chalkeus," that is bronze worker, a survival of a time when bronze was the only material wrought in the smithy.[3] Most of the Aryan tongues have the same name for bronze and different ones for iron, showing that the former metal was known and the latter was not before the Aryan nations separated from one another.[4]

After iron had come into use, bronze, because of its greater antiquity, had a character of sacredness. In the time of Hesiod, the Greek priests used only bronze knives for sacrificial purposes, and in the last century of the republic the same custom prevailed at Rome. In the Pentateuch, iron is mentioned only four times and bronze (brass in the English translation) more than six times as often. In the construction of the tabernacle, the only metals to be used were gold, silver, and bronze. When an altar was to be erected by the Israelites after crossing the Jordan, the stones were not to be touched with "any iron tool," and yet the ten commandments were to be written, that is engraved on them.[5] The engraving must then have been done with chisels of bronze.

The manner in which the forms of tools changed indicates that iron appeared after bronze. The shapes of stone implements were imitated by the early workers in bronze, and the shapes of bronze tools were copied by the early workers in iron.[6] After iron came into use, blades of it were mounted on handles of bronze as if the latter were the more abundant and less costly material.

The Tinière River, which flows into the Lake of Geneva, has brought down from the mountains and deposited in the plain, a large mass of gravel, sand, and loam, in strata which belong respectively to the ages of iron, bronze, and stone, the last being the lowest in position, and earliest in date, of the three layers. The iron stratum includes glazed tiles and Roman coins, and began presumably about 500 B. C., when the inhabitants of Switzerland first traded with the Romans. The comparison of the thickness of the strata leads to the inference that the bronze period lasted three thousand or four thousand years.⁷

Of the cultural condition of the Europeans, Chinese, Egyptians, and Western Asiatics in their age of bronze, we have no definite information. Nearly all our knowledge of these peoples comes to us from the iron culture-step, or from times in which iron may have been in use among them. We have great numbers of bronze tools, weapons, and ornaments from various countries, but these convey little instruction to us. In one hundred and ten British burial barrows, nearly fifteen hundred articles of bronze were found, and of these more than half were tools, a third were weapons, and the remainder were mostly ornaments. Of chisels, flanged celts, socketed celts, and palstaves (these celts and palstaves might be classed as small hatchets) there were nearly six hundred; of swords more than a hundred; of lumps of metal ready for the founder eighty-five, and of moulds ten.⁸ The Dublin Museum has eleven hundred weapons of bronze. The Swiss lake villages of Nidau, Cortaillod, Estavayer, and Corcelettes produced nearly four thousand articles of bronze, three-fourths of them ornaments.⁹ The museums of Denmark have 20,000 prehistoric articles of bronze, and those of Switzerland as many. In the bronze age it seems that bronze was shaped exclusively by casting, but afterwards by forging also.¹⁰ The moulds were of clay, stone, or bronze, and they have been found in England, Scotland, Ireland, Denmark, and Switzerland.¹¹ The crucibles were of clay, mixed with other substances, the material being the same as that used in our time.¹² Soldering was unknown, but the art of burning bronze on bronze, akin to welding, was practiced.¹³

The forms of tools continued to improve. Thus the

plain celt or small hatchet blade was succeeded by a celt with flanges which grasped a handle; a transverse stop ridge was put between the flanges to prevent the handle from slipping too far; then a socket was made for the handle, and finally an eye was cast on the socket for tying the celt to its handle.[14]

SEC. 161. *Superiority of Iron.*—As compared with iron, bronze is greatly inferior for general use in the industrial arts, and is more difficult to shape and temper, besides being, in our century, thirty times more costly. Moreover the ores required for its production are relatively rare, and the heat required to smelt them must be twice as great.[1] Tin is found in few countries and iron in nearly all. The latter metal can be welded, shaped under the hammer, and mended when broken, with little delay, heat, and labor, and without deterioration in quality. Not so bronze. It requires melting heat, a recasting for the repair of any break; and at every fusion, the proportion of tin is reduced and the hardness and elasticity of the alloy changed. Besides, in these qualities bronze is so far inferior to steel, that knives, axes, chisels, and swords would never have been made of the former metal if the latter had been equally cheap, abundant and manageable. The art of tempering and welding iron, which are of immense importance, may not have been discovered until after the metal had been familiar to men for many centuries.

CHAPTER XI.
THE AZTECS.

SECTION. 162. *Anahuac.*—In the beginning of the XVIth century the highest culture of North America was found on the high table-land of Mexico between the 14th and 22nd degrees of latitude. Though within the tropics, this region has an equably warm climate, with a mean temperature at the city of Mexico, of 52 degrees in January and 65 degrees in July, leaving a difference of only 13 degrees between the two characteristic months; whereas London, which has the most equable climate among the capitals of Europe, has a difference of 25 and New York one of 45 degrees. The moderation of both summer and winter in the valley of Anahuac is highly favorable to physical and mental activity and perhaps contributed to give to its inhabitants a higher culture than that developed in the basins of the Mississippi, St. Lawrence, Columbia and Sacramento.

When Cortes first landed at Vera Cruz, this high plain was occupied by about half a dozen nations of the Nahua blood, including the Aztecs, Acolhuans, Tepanecs, Chichimecs, Tarascos, and Tlascalans. Southward and southeastward of them, between the isthmuses of Tehuantepec and Panama, were the Maya nations, who were, as is supposed, of the same ethnological family with the Nahuas and yet were different from them in their dialect and in some of their institutions. The Mayas had invented alphabetic signs and in this respect were decidedly superior to the Nahuas; but in many respects, we know less about them. The name of Aztecs will be used here to include the Acolhuans and the Tepanecs, who were their allies and subordinates, in the most powerful and wealthy of the Nahua nations.

Before the Spanish conquest, the country was more populous than at present. When the city of Mexico was taken by Cortes it had as many inhabitants as it has now, about 300,000. The neighboring city of Tezcuco, the capital of the Acolhuans, then had as many people and now has only four thousand. In 1520 the valley of Anahuac had many other towns with more than 15,000 inhabitants and now has none. Clavigero[1] says that after the conquest there was a decrease of ninety per cent in the population, and according to one statement there were thirty great Aztec nobles each of whom could call out more than a hundred thousand soldiers; or 3,000,000 for all.[2] Waitz[3] tells us that "the conquest of the capital led here, as later in Peru, to the destruction of the irrigating ditches, and thereby a large part of the country was converted into a desert. With the overthrow of the nobility and priesthood, all the higher knowledge and culture of the Aztecs disappeared; by the destruction of the chief city and the enslavement of the people, the useful and ornamental arts were ruined; and with the dissolution of the political and social systems, came a general demoralization of the people."

Sec. 163. *Crops.*—A great majority of the people devoted themselves to tillage. Maize was the chief article of cultivation, and after it came beans, pumpkins, maguey or American aloe, red pepper, tomato, cotton, nopal, plum, cherry, lettuce, chian, cress, onion, tobacco, and in the warm districts, cacao, plantain, manioc, and cochineal cactus. A wooden spade, pressed into the soil by the foot, was used in loosening the ground. Irrigation was employed extensively and ashes were used for purposes of fertilization. Fields were inclosed with lines of stone or of maguey plants. In the lakes of Anahuac floating islands, each about three hundred feet long and twenty feet wide, were made by covering an interlaced frame of poles, first with reeds and then with soil. Such an island would support a garden, several small trees, a thatch hut, and sustain a small family. These floating homes might be moved about by pushing with poles or towing with boats, and as "an archipelago of wandering islands," so Prescott calls them, they made a lively impression on the minds of the Spanish conquerors.

The root of the maguey was roasted for food. Its sap was boiled down into a syrup or into sugar, or was fermented into an intoxicating drink. Its leaves yielded paper, thread, cord, cloth, and thatching material. Its thorns served as pins, awls, and needles. Prescott[1] remarks that it supplied the Aztecs with "meat, drink, clothing and writing material," and he adds that "surely never did nature enclose within so compact a form so many of the elements of human comfort and civilization." Valuable as the maguey was to the Aztecs and as it is to the Mexicans of the present time, the plant is cultivated in Europe and in California exclusively for ornament so far as my observation and information go. It is only in Mexico that people like the taste of its fermented and distilled juice, and its roasted root, and find a valuable fiber in its leaves.

Maize was eaten green, in hominy, in porridge, in thin

cakes or tortillas, and in bread. It was the staff of life to the Nahuas and Mayas. It was also used with or without honey to make a kind of beer; and the sap of its green stalk was boiled down into a syrup. The cacao was made into a palatable and nutritious drink which has now been adopted in all civilized countries. The Aztecs drank their chocolate cold; the Mayas took theirs hot. Red pepper occupied a prominent place in the fields and kitchens of the Aztecs as it does in those of their Mexican descendants. The vanilla collected from wild plants was prized for its flavor.

The people had no large ruminant animal, but they had tame dogs, deer, hare, rabbits, turkeys, pigeons, quails, geese, and ducks. The American buffalo, goat, and sheep ran wild in regions not far from the territory of the Nahuas, but were never domesticated. Fish were kept in ponds or brought by runners for the tables of the nobles from the Gulf of Mexico.

SEC. 164. *Weaving, etc.*—The garments of the poor were made of maguey fiber; those of the rich of maguey, cotton, skins, furs, and cloth interwoven with feathers. Cotton was spun in threads so thin that the conquerors compared its woven web to silk; and they thought the feather mantles of the Aztecs elegant enough for their Spanish monarch to wear, when he held his court in Madrid or Vienna.

The artisans included miners, smelters, smiths, burnishers, engravers in metal, gilders, quarrymen, stonemasons, stone polishers, cutters of gems, makers of mosaics, sculptors, enamelers, jewelers, knife-makers, lime burners, charcoal burners, brick-makers, potters, plasterers, boat builders, carpenters, dressers of skins, weavers, cacao grinders, bakers, brewers, cigar-makers, barbers, salt boilers, paper-makers, india-rubber workers, and manufacturers of medicines and pigments. The productions of all these artisans were offered for sale not in shops open every day, but in booths open at occasional fairs, and in the capital city on every fifth day. Caoutchouc though known to them[1] was not prominent in their industry and therefore did not attract the attention of the Spanish conquerors.

Pottery was shaped by hand and glazed. It was the common material of vessels for cooking, and for holding the food of the poor at their meals. The rich had dishes and bowls of gold and silver. The patterns of the pottery were usually rude, often grotesque, never elegantly artistic. Lamps and tapers were unknown. The only artificial light was supplied by torches or fires.

SEC. 165. *Metallurgy.*—The Aztecs had an extensive metallurgical industry. They understood how to sink shafts and run tunnels; how to wash gold from alluvial deposits; how to use the bellows and furnace in smelting the ores of copper, tin, lead, and silver; and how to cast metals. They made blow-pipes, crucibles, and moulds. They had a little tin[1] and considerable quantities of copper, silver, gold, and lead. They prized the precious metals for personal ornament, household decoration, and household utensils. The value of the precious metals taken as spoil by Cortes was considered immense, but the sum is not now ascertainable. According to report, after giving one-fifth to the king, and dividing a large part of the treasure among his companions, Cortes went to Spain with $600,000; and we cannot presume that he had retained more than one-tenth for himself.[2]

Among the articles made of the precious metals by

the Aztecs, were vases, plates, mirrors, bells, ear-rings, bracelets, armlets, anklets, cups, bowls, dishes, pots, and kettles, the last with fixed or movable handles. They manufactured figures in imitation of butterflies, birds, quadrupeds, fishes, flowers, and trees. They made parrots with movable heads, tongues, and wings, and monkeys with movable legs. They had scales and could tell the proportion of gold in alloys.[3] They had discovered the principle of specific gravity, which was unknown to the ancient Egyptians and to the Greeks before the time of Archimedes. They had no solder, but they could cast silver and gold so as to unite in a perfect joint while the metals remained separate. They made solid plates, the opposite quarters of which were alternately of silver and gold. They also cast fish the alternate scales of which were of different metals. Las Casas saw many Aztec ornaments of gold sent to Charles V. by Cortes, and he declared them superior in workmanship to any he had ever before seen. Cortes writing to his sovereign about these jewels of gold and silver, feather-work, and gems, said that "in their novelty and strangeness," presumably of design and execution, they were "above all price," and were such as were not possessed "by any other prince in the world."

Cinnabar was mined for use as a pigment, but whether it was sublimated into quicksilver is doubtful.[4] The Spanish accounts, written soon after the conquest, do not mention that metal among the productions of the country. Some recent authors have thought that a knowledge of mercury by the Aztecs would furnish an explanation of the fact that the Spanish goldsmiths could not imitate some of the Aztec jewelry, and that the conquest was followed in 1557 by the use of amalgamation in the reduction of silver ores, a process previously unknown to Europeans.

SEC. 166. *Stone Work.*—Porphyry, basalt, marble, and granite were used extensively in architecture; onyx and brick occasionally. In some of their buildings the blocks of stone were fitted together with such accuracy that their joints were scarcely visible. Stone was often quarried and transported in large blocks. The ruins of Mitla contain rectangular pieces each eighteen feet long, four wide and three and a half thick, and round columns of polished porphyry eighteen feet long and three thick. The famous calendar stone is of porphyry thirteen feet square and three and a half thick. This block weighs twenty-four tons, and its transportation from its original bed thirty miles distant, with some rough country intervening, was no easy task. Onyx was cut in thin slabs to let a dim light in at the windows, but was used in very few houses. Chimneys were unknown to the Aztecs as to all other barbarous heathens before they came in contact with civilization. Floors were paved with tiles, or small blocks of alabaster, marble, or porphyry. The fronts of temples were ornamented with lattice-like and arabesque designs, and carvings of beasts and men in stone. Among the designs copied from animals in Yucatan were heads of elephants which may have been suggested by traditions or drawings of similar beasts seen in the New or the Old World. Lime, mortar, and burned gypsum were parts of walls and stuccoes. The arch was applied in ovens, steam baths, and a few small bridges, but not in dwellings, palaces, or temples.[1] Over doorways, the walls were supported by lintels of stone or wood, or by a gradual approach of horizontal layers of stone. A few streets were paved with stone.

Obsidian or volcanic glass was abundant and was used for many purposes. It was the common material for knives and razors; and pieces of it were fixed in wooden swords to give a cutting edge. It was polished for mirrors. The diamond and ruby were unknown to the Aztecs, but the turquoise, emerald, and amethyst were cut, polished, and bored, and used in mosaics; and these gems as well as pearls were set in rings and in the handles of weapons.

The most notable remains of Aztec architecture preserved to our time are those of mounds or truncated pyramids erected for purposes of worship. The material is earth with walls or casings of stone or brick, burned or unburned. There is usually no chamber or gallery in the mound. A staircase connecting horizontal terraces led to the summit, in such a manner that the person or procession ascending the pyramid must make a complete circuit of the structure on each of several stories. The level top of the pyramid had chapels for idols, and altars for sacrifice.

The largest of the existing Aztec pyramids is that of Cholula. Its base is four hundred and eighty yards, and its summit sixty-six yards square, and it has a height of fifty yards. The material, so far as examined, is unburned brick. Some writers suppose that a considerable part of the mass is a natural hill.[2] Four miles from Otumba is the pyramid of Teotihuacan, which is two hundred and twenty-seven yards square on the ground and sixty yards high. The material is gravel mixed with clay, and was encased with stone. Xochimilco has a pyramid of porphyry laid in mortar thirty-one yards high; Papantla has another of the same material, fitted together with remarkable accuracy and laid without mortar.

The latter structure is nineteen yards high. A pyramid of masonry at Izamal is two hundred and seventy yards square.

Of the palaces and dwellings of the Aztecs in the valley of Mexico, all have been destroyed, but numerous ruins of such buildings are found in Yucatan, the land of the Mayas, and we may presume that the two peoples had similar architecture in their homes. The Maya palaces had walls of cut stone, narrow rooms, many doors, few windows, no arch, and much external decoration, either carved in stone or made with stucco.

The royal palaces of the Aztecs have been entirely destroyed. The main palace of Montezuma, in the capital city, was more extensive than any palace of its time in Europe, and had accommodations for more than five thousand residents, including three thousand women in the seraglio. The palace of Tezcuco had three hundred rooms and covered an area more than half a mile square.

Other remarkable structures of the Aztecs were their aqueducts and dykes. The Chapultepec aqueduct, built to supply the city of Mexico with water, had two pipes or channels each six feet square. One could be cleaned while the other was in use. A stone aqueduct supplied water to the city of Tezcuco. Dykes were built to give access to the city of Mexico from the mainland and to protect it against inundation. One of these, seven miles long and twenty yards wide, was for part of its length covered with stones laid in mortar, and was protected at the side by piles.

We do not read that the Aztecs graded any roads, unless that name could be given to the dykes connecting the insular city of Mexico with the shores of its lake; but there were plainly-marked roads or trails leading to all parts of the empire with stations at intervals of about six miles for couriers who conveyed news and packages, and often sea-fish for the imperial table. The six miles of each runner were to be made in little more than half an hour.

SEC. 167. *Trade.*—The mercantile profession was honorable and was adopted by many nobles without discredit to their rank. When Aztec merchants traveled beyond the limits of their own country, they were regarded by their home government as its agents for the collection of information. Any outrage committed on them was promptly avenged. They had a special divinity, a special ceremonial of worship, special funeral ceremonies, and special courts for the trial of their lawsuits.

So far as we can judge from the remains of their sculpture preserved to our time, the Aztecs had not developed much artistic taste. Their principal idols were rude and grotesque figures, without even an approach to accuracy in proportion of the human form or fidelity to the shape or expression of the human face. Some of the reliefs found in the temples of the Mayas are much truer to nature than anything now existing in the valley of Mexico, but even there the artists showed little originality or felicity of design, and perhaps were compelled by ecclesiastical influence to follow a few stiff conventional patterns. There was no artistic pottery in the country; and of their jewelry none has been preserved, or at least none of those articles which excited the wonder of Europe in the time of Cortes. The Aztec music had no harmony but several voices sang its airs in unison.

At the fairs the stocks of merchandise were spread out on the ground in packages, which could be readily put together for transportation in canoes or on the backs of slaves. Fairs were held at different towns on different days, which were so arranged that the merchants could keep up a constant round of travel. Customers were attracted to these gatherings by dramatic, acrobatic, and sleight-of-hand performances. Every city had its large public square for fairs, and that of the Aztec capital had room for 100,000 persons. Shops were not kept open constantly for the sale of merchandise. The people depended on the fairs for their purchases. Every article had its district or spot in the square, and each vender paid rent in proportion to the space which he occupied. Cotton cloth and salt were the leading commodities. Officials, selected by the merchants, had general supervision of the weights, measures, contracts, and crimes of the fair, and they decided all suits summarily. Many of the payments were made by barter, but cacao beans, small pieces of cotton cloth, quills containing gold-dust and pieces of tin and copper, were mediums of exchange.

SEC. 168. *Social Condition.*—Social life and the household were organized and governed under rules similar to those dominant at the same time in Spain.[1] The treatment of the wife by the husband and of the children by the parents, the system of education, the occupations of men, women and children, the methods of private entertainment and public amusement, the demeanor at meals, and the standards of domestic virtue and social propriety, seemed to the conquerors, like those of their own country in many respects.

Women had more liberty and a nearer approach to social equality with man than in some Christian countries. The wife ate with her husband; she was wedded to him by a priest, sometimes in the temple by a sacred ceremony. She could not be divorced without a judicial decree; the same grounds of divorce were available to her as to him; and though she usually spent her time in the house, she was permitted to be present at certain public festivities. Polygamy and concubinage were permitted but were limited to the nobles or rich.

The new-born child was sprinkled with water to wash away sin and protect it from evil; and at a later day was taken to a temple where a name was given to it by the priest. The boys were educated in the temples where the sons of the nobles remained from their tenth till their fifteenth year; and afterwards these young nobles went to a military school. The temples had nunneries for the education of noble girls, many of whom remained there till they were married.

The children were kept under a strict discipline. Among the poor both sexes were early taught the work that they were to do, and the rules of demeanor they should observe. The boys and girls in the temples were instructed in the art of writing and in the doctrines and ceremonies of religion. The girls of well-to-do parents were kept in the house and trained to be modest and chaste. Marriages were arranged by the parents.

There were traditional speeches which were delivered by noble parents to their children. The father speaking to his daughter said: "I pray God that you may live many years. But you must know how to live, for you will learn, my daughter, my dove, that the path of life is hard. Remember that you are of noble blood, and that your ancestors were princes. Remember that they founded this kingdom and have left you an inheritance of honor and glory. Remember that you have been loved as a precious jewel.

"Lay aside the plays of childhood and act like a woman

of noble blood. Do not lie abed by day. Rise, sweep, wash the mouths of the idols and burn incense before them. Prepare cacao, grind maize, spin, weave, and learn to cook delicate dishes suitable for noblemen. Thus you will be prepared to enjoy love and honor and riches if God should give you a husband. Apply yourself zealously to all womanly tasks, including spinning, weaving, painting, and dyeing. Learn all these things while you are young, while your reason is open and active, while your heart is like a gem and is pure from every sin. We, your parents, have begotten you, according to God's will. It is proper that you should be taught how to live before He calls us away, so that you may live in honor after we have gone. The gathering of herbs and of sticks and the selling of salt at the street corners are not suitable occupations for you. Some man will probably look upon you with favor and seek you in marriage, and if you should be ignorant of womanly work, would we not be blamed for your stupidity? If you are virtuous, you will be praised, and we shall be blessed; if you are wicked, you will be stoned. God knows which of these two results will come to pass.

"Pay attention, my daughter, to what I say. Take care that you do not dishonor your ancestors, that you do not defile their images which indicate their famous achievements. Avoid all dissipation. Do not fall into the mire; choose death in preference. If anyone seeks you in marriage do not reject him; prize the will of God who sends the wooer. Although you are our daughter and of noble lineage, do not consider yourself too good; otherwise you will offend God, who may then permit you to fall into a disreputable career. Do not choose a man as you would a mantle at the fair. Take the one that seeks your hand; do not be governed by beauty; do not let passion run away with your reason. Do not allow the men to deceive you. Do not give yourself to anyone whom you do not know or who does not wish to marry you. Be faithful to your husband; do not leave him while he lives, even if he wishes to leave you, even if he be a poor farmer, or petty official or a common man. If he should be extremely poor do not despise or desert him, for God will provide for you."

The mothers had a traditional address to deliver to their daughters, and in it urged them to keep their dress neat and cleanly without much ornament, to be quiet, modest, polite, kind, and obliging, to avoid the use of paint on the face, to pay no attention to the words of strangers in the street, and to prize chastity as indispensable to the enjoyment of life. A similar traditional address delivered by fathers to their sons advised them to be just, polite, modest, peaceful, truthful, economical, faithful, and considerate of the feelings of others.[2]

At meals, the people sat on the ground or on low seats, round the cloth on which the pots or dishes were placed. Chafing-pans to keep the dishes warm were in general use and were soon copied by the Europeans, to whom they were novel. The wife and children ate with the husband and father, not after him as in most barbarous and some civilized countries. Forks were unknown. Napkins were common and hands and mouth were washed before and after meals.[3]

Human flesh was frequently eaten and was considered palatable, but its use, if it had not been offered in sacrifice to a god, was considered sacrilegious, and wars were never undertaken for the purpose of supplying their tables with such food. The 20,000 human victims offered to their gods every year did not supply a pound of meat annually to each person of the Nahua blood on an average; but relatively few shared in the cannibal feasts, and some persons may have eaten twenty or thirty pounds of such food in a year.

The clothing of the laboring men in warm weather consisted only of a thin loin-cloth. When protection was needed against cold, a large waist-cloth superseded or covered the loin-cloth, and a mantle of cotton, padded cotton, feather-cloth or fur was added. The heads were bare. On the feet the poor wore sandals, the rich sandals or shoes of maguey or cotton. Women wore petticoats attached at the waist and gowns attached at the shoulders. The needle made of fine thorns or of bone was used, but most garments were made by cutting from the woven piece without sewing. Roots and the pulp of fruits were used in washing.

Flowers were cultivated, and were worn as ornaments on festive occasions. Distinguished visitors were welcomed with nosegays, the burning of incense,[4] and the offer of tobacco, which was taken in snuff, and smoked in cigars and pipes.[5] The temple grounds were asylums for the indigent whether well or sick, and charitable attention to these unfortunates was one of the duties of the priests.[6] Mendicants were numerous, and were frequently treated with much kindness by the wealthy people.

In the beginning of the XVIth century, the largest botanical and zoölogical collections to be found anywhere were those of the city of Mexico. Much care had been taken to have specimens of all the most notable species. The menagerie included serpents, carnivorous birds and quadrupeds, and required six hundred men to keep it in order. Among their cultivated plants were ipecac and jalap, which have taken a place in the pharmacopœia of civilization.

Among the common amusements were dancing, singing, games of ball, acrobatic exercises, juggling tricks, and dramatic and pantomimic plays. Dancing was regarded as an enjoyment for the spectators, not for the participants, and sometimes a band of a thousand dancers were employed by a great noble. Ball was played in courts or buildings erected for the special purpose.

SEC. 169. *Records.*—The Aztecs had a system of hieroglyphics so complete that it sufficed for keeping records of laws, land titles, tax payments, judicial proceedings, ecclesiastical rituals, moral precepts, historical events, and household accounts. It included signs for words, syllables, and letters, and the same sign might be interpreted in various ways, so the reader was often puzzled, and a sentence might be read with many different meanings. The name of the god Itzcoatl was written with the hieroglyph for knife "Itzli" (intended in that connection to be read Itz); the sign for a pot "comitl" (to be read in that connection "co"), and the hieroglyph for water "atl," the three signs making the word "Itz-co-atl." In other combinations the sign for "atl" might mean simply the vowel "a" as the sign for "etl" (bean) might mean the vowel "e." Alphabetic signs were relatively rare among the Aztecs, but were common among the Mayas.

Records were kept on coarse paper made of maguey or palm fiber, upon cotton cloth or parchment made of deer-skin. The maguey paper, the most common material, was made in strips ten or fifteen inches wide and many yards long; and such a strip folded together in a square form and an inch or so thick, with board covers, made a book which could not be read without unfolding.

Writings on cotton cloth were sometimes varnished over to protect them against mold. Tablets for reckoning and for notes were kept by merchants and nobles. Among their books were historical annals, periodical records, a criminal code, tribute register, a statement of marriage customs, dream and fortune-telling books, genealogical tables and calendars, with a list of days dedicated to various divinities and explanations of the sacrifices and ceremonies proper for each.

The system of numeration had the score for its basis. There were special words for the first five numerals; for twenty; for its square, four hundred; and for its cube, eight thousand. Other numerals were expressed in speech by combinations of words. In writing, a point meant, one; a flag, twenty; a feather, four hundred; a purse, eight thousand. A quarter, half or three-quarters of twenty could be indicated by drawing a flag and coloring a quarter, half or three-quarters of it; and similar fractions of four hundred and eight thousand could be written in the same way. Thus three-quarters of a purse, a quarter of a feather, and half a flag meant six thousand one hundred and ten. For large sums this method of writing figures was more convenient than that used in ancient Rome. No similar system of expressing numbers is found elsewhere.

Of the Aztec books few are preserved, and the art of reading their hieroglyphics has been lost. As Cardinal Ximenes destroyed the books of the Spanish Moors, so Juan de Zumarraga, first Archbishop of Mexico, gained a detestable fame by collecting all the procurable literary productions of the Aztecs, making a "mountain heap" of them and burning them to ashes.[1] The men familiar with the hieroglyphs were slain or reduced to slavery, and the observance of ancient usages was discredited and discouraged.

SEC. 170. *Astronomy.*—The chronological system of the Aztecs is regarded as the highest evidence of their intellectual development. Their year consisted of eighteen months or chief subdivisions of the year, containing each twenty days, with five surplus days after the end of the last month to make up the three hundred and sixty-five days. Four years were combined in a quadrennial period, and thirteen of these periods made a cycle of fifty-two years, at the end of which they added twelve and a half surplus cycle days to the five surplus annual days. The addition of the half day was made by counting one cycle from noon, and the next from midnight. By this method, they gave to the year an average length of three hundred and sixty-five days and twenty-four-hundredths, which is nearer to the precise figure than the one accepted by the ancient Greek and Roman astronomers.

The month had four weeks of five days each; and thus the calendar, as Prescott remarks, " has the advantage of giving an equal number of days to each month and of comprehending entire weeks without a fraction both in the months and in the year." The first year of the cycle began on the 9th of January, and the last on the 27th of December, and by deducting the five surplus days from the latter day we have the 22nd of December, or approximately the winter solstice, as an original starting point.

One of the most remarkable relics of Aztec industry is the calendar stone, which has a circular face eleven feet in diameter, cut into hard porphyry, with hundreds of figures arranged in half a dozen concentric rings.

The center shows the sun; next to it is a ring supposed by some authors to represent the two solstices and two equinoxes; then a ring with the twenty days of the month; another ring with the fifty-two years of the cycle; and other rings, the meanings of which are not clear. This stone was set in a horizontal position so that the meridian agreed exactly with the line from forehead to chin, through the middle of the sun's face. In the border of the stone there are holes for gnomons to be used in observation of the solstices and equinoxes and perhaps of the times of day.[1]

SEC. 171. *A Martial Empire.*—The Aztec Empire extended from Colima in latitude 21 degrees to Locomazco in latitude 16 degrees. The boundaries were very irregular and excluded much between those parallels. Michoacan to the southwest of the valley of Mexico and Tlascala to the east, the kingdom of the Chichimecs to the north, and the Zapotees to the south, were independent and hostile. The Aztecs, and their confederates and subordinates the Tezcucans and Tlacopans, were always loyal; the conquered provinces sometimes broke out in revolt.

The conquered lands, though divided among the sovereigns of the three allied nations, were governed by native rulers who promised to administer the government in accordance with the orders of the emperor. The people were not disturbed in their local customs except that they were required to erect a temple to Huitzitopochtli, to worship him on certain occasions, to pay tribute, and to furnish soldiers. The native rulers spent several months every year in the city of Mexico, and while absent were represented there by some son, brother, or other near relative as hostage. All the natives of the Nahua blood had elective monarchs, hereditary nobles, numerous slaves, and communal ownership or control of most of the land not held by the nobility.

The Aztecs were a martial and conquering people, and if the career of their empire had not been interrupted by the appearance of the Spaniards with fire-arms, they would probably have brought all the barbarous nations in their vicinity under their dominion. They had an army of about 200,000 men in divisions of eight thousand, each division having its special standard and dress.[1] The common soldiers were armed with slings, spears, bows, and swords or clubs, and, for defensive armor, carried shields and wore quilted corselets, greaves, and helmets. The men were drilled to march in good order, and to keep close together. The standard was carried by the commanding officer, whose place was near the front. Those of his subordinates who abandoned him when he was in the midst of the enemy, were considered guilty of serious crime. Drums, trumpets, and shell-horns gave signals for different movements. Night attacks were frequent. Towns and cities were protected by walls, moats, and permanent garrisons. A defensive wall near Tlascala, crossing a valley from mountain to mountain, was seven miles long, twenty feet thick, and nine feet high. The pyramids and courts of the temples were used for military as well as for ecclesiastical purposes, and the height of the pyramids with their broad tops and narrow, winding staircases made them secure against storm by a relatively large force. When in active service, besides their arms and defensive armor, the soldiers carried cooking-pots, stones for grinding grain, and mats for bedding.

Heralds were treated as sacred characters. War was

not declared until three successive embassies had been sent with explicit demands for satisfaction, and not until the three demands had been refused. Priests accompanied the armies, interpreted the omens, announced the times propitious for battle, kindled new fires for burning incense and offerings to the god of war, prayed to their own god for success and to the god of the enemy to come over to their side, and then gave the signal for attack. Aggressive wars were undertaken to compel aliens to worship the Aztec gods, to obtain victims for human sacrifice, to capture slaves, and to extend the area of the empire.

SEC. 172. *Ranks.*—The people were divided into nobles, freemen, and slaves. Nobility was acquired by inheritance, imperial appointment, or popular election to the office of communal mayor. The hereditary nobles were of two classes, those with and those without estates of land. The appointed nobles were men who had distinguished themselves by eminent courage and ability in war, and had been placed by the king in possession of tracts of the royal domain which they held by life tenure. The highest rank belonged to those hereditary nobles with estates who had been honored by the king as great warriors. The second rank belonged to the appointed nobles; the third, to the mayors; and the fourth, to the hereditary nobles who had no land or no courage. The mayors were necessarily men of some education, for they were required to keep the records of the lands of the communes, with lists of the occupants, the precise situations and boundaries of the different fields, and the amounts of tribute or tax due and paid by each. They also made new assessments of land to the men of the commune, and made contracts on its behalf for additional tracts. These mayors were presumably in many cases landless nobles. Some of the hereditary nobles had very large estates, and perhaps the force of 100,000 soldiers which it was said could be brought into the field by any one of thirty great lords, consisted entirely of tenants.

Slaves were numerous and were either captives taken in war, convicted criminals, children sold by their parents, or insolvent debtors. Many of those of the last class were enslaved for definite periods, at the end of which they regained their freedom. Slavery was not hereditary, and while it existed did not destroy civil rights. The slave could make valid contracts, marry a free person, and own property, including other slaves. Under ordinary circumstances he could not be sold without his own consent, and if he could reach the palace of the king he became free. The master who killed his slave except in self-defense was a murderer.

The country was divided into large estates of land, which were owned by the monarch, the high nobles, and the temples; and were occupied by communes which paid tribute to the owners. The freeman could not obtain land in severalty, but, in the agricultural districts, at least, he could always get the use of a tract for cultivation, by application to the mayor of his commune. Families could not be deprived of land in their possession unless it was left uncultivated for three years.

SEC. 173. *Imperial Office.*—The office of emperor was elective. When the monarch died, his successor was chosen from the imperial family by the four electors, who were members of the imperial council.[1] Military capacity, proved by experience and unquestioned by the army, was the most important qualification, and a brother of the deceased sovereign was often preferred to a son.

The newly-chosen emperor, having been informed of his election, went, followed by his court in procession, to the temple of the god Huitzilopochtli, where his body was painted black and his head was sprinkled with water as a symbol of purification. Then he was clothed with the imperial robes; the emblems of his sovereign authority were given to him; and incense was offered to him in recognition of his divine character. The high priest delivered an address including the following passages: "Receive with humble kindness those who come to you in anxiety and oppression. Neither speak nor act in passion. Hear quietly to the end the complaints made to you. Do not cut the speaker short, for you are the image and representative of God. He has intrusted our welfare to your care. He hears through your ears and speaks through your mouth. Punish no one without cause. Your power is like the claws and teeth of God, not to be used except in doing justice. Do what is right without regard to persons; such is God's command. Do not leave the punishment of evil to God. He has given you the power to do that. Take care that judicial proceedings shall be conducted without disorder or haste, and that nothing shall be controlled by passion. Never say, 'I am master and will do as I please.' Policy based on such an idea would bring ruin to your realm and disgrace to your royal office. Let not your might lead you into pride and arrogance; rather let it remind you of the low position out of which you have been lifted without merit of your own. Do not give yourself up to idleness, nor indifference, nor sensual pleasures. Do not squander the sweat and toil of your subjects. Do not misuse for unholy and foolish purposes the grace which God has given you. God

looks on the rulers of states, and when they go wrong, he laughs at them and says nothing. He holds us all in the hollow of his hand and rocks us to and fro, and amuses himself when we fall to one side or the other."²
"My son, remember that your subjects have conferred this honor on you. Since you have been recognized as ruler, you must provide carefully for their welfare; look on them as your children, protect them from suffering, and shield the weak against the oppression of the strong. Before you are the heads of all your provinces and of all your subjects. Be a father and a mother to them. Guard them against bad government. All eyes are watching you. Command and enforce your commands. Manage military affairs with the closest attention. Discover and punish wrongdoers whether nobles or common people, and chastise all disturbers of the public peace."³

The emperor prayed thus to Huitzilopochtli: "Merciful God, thou hast shown much favor to me. It would be folly for me to believe that my merit has induced Thee to lay the heavy burden of the government on my shoulders. What shall I say for my poor self? How shall I, who am blind and deaf, and cannot rule myself, how shall I rule Thy people? What I deserve is to wander in the dust. I need guidance for myself. Thou hast decided to lift me on high for the scorn of men, and I obey Thy will. Perhaps Thou hast not known me well; otherwise Thou wouldst have found a better person for the place. Or is it only a dream that occurs to me? O God, who knowest all my thoughts and givest all gifts, deign to make clear to me Thy words and Thy wisdom. I do not know the way that I ought to pursue. Show to me the light which should guide me. Let me and those who follow me go not astray. Shield us against war and pestilence. Oh, how ignorant and incompetent I am! What will become of me if I should yield to dissipation and let the state go to ruin, or if I should become idle and careless? My God, I pray Thee, come down often to my house. I will wait for Thee here. With great longing I wait and beg for Thy word, which Thou hast breathed into Thy old friends and chosen servants, that with zeal and justice they may govern Thy state, the seat of Thy majesty and honor."[4]

Having promised to comply strictly with his duties as explained to him, and made an offering of his blood drawn from several parts of his body, and sacrificed some quails, the emperor received the homage of the nobility and people in the court of the temple. This was his installation in office, but it was not until after he had led a victorious expedition into the country of some hostile nation, and had brought back a number of captives suitable for sacrifice, that he was crowned by the king of Tezcuco.

Two ministers, one for political and one for religious affairs, assisted the emperor in the discharge of his duties. Every important question was submitted to a council of state, comprising representatives of four classes of officials, and including the four imperial electors.

The monarch owned a considerable part of the land of the realm. Some of it was tilled for the production of the supplies needed for the royal palace; other portions were given for life to nobles or officials for their support. Some villages supplied the royal palace with a fixed quantity of cotton cloth; others with dogs, turkeys, pigeons, quails, ducks, maize, cacao, pepper, and so on, according to a schedule. All the tilled land was required to pay tribute to some official or noble.

Sec. 174. *Laws.*—The judicial system of the Aztecs was better than that of any other barbarous nation of either ancient or modern times, and indeed better than that of many civilized nations. As has already been stated, there were special courts for the summary trial of civil and criminal cases that had their origin in the fairs, the judges being elected by the merchants. For other cases, there were other tribunals. The commune elected a centurion or justice of the peace for each group of about one hundred families. He had jurisdiction over all their petty civil and criminal cases; and besides he was the collector of their taxes or tribute. The more important cases were tried in a district court, which had two judges; and from that tribunal there was an appeal to a Supreme Court, which had twelve justices and exercised jurisdiction over the whole empire. The judicial proceedings were all public, and records of them were kept. Every case was decided within three months. The judges of the district court and of the Supreme Court were appointed by the emperor to hold during good behavior;[1] and each with his office received an estate in land sufficient for his support. He was not allowed to accept any fee or present from litigants. The people had great faith in the integrity of the judges. Trials for crime were prompt and the punishments severe. Death was a common penalty, even for small offenses, when there was a second conviction. There was no class of professional criminals.

Many provisions of the Aztec law showed much liberality. The freemen or serfs were declared to have equal rights with the nobles in all cases of litigation. Slaves were entitled to judicial protection. Adultery by the husband was subject to the same penalties as that by the wife. The husband could not discard his wife at his pleasure; both parties had equal rights to divorce by judicial decree. Widows, orphans, and helpless persons were fed out of the public stores.

The police regulations seem to have received much attention. The law forbade the throwing of filth into the canals in the capital city. The streets were "cleaned by day and lighted by night."[2] Without special permits the common people were not allowed to drink pulque, except at certain festivals.

SEC. 175. *Aztec Gods.*—The main features of the Aztec religion were the prominence of its moral code, and of the worship of ancestors and of the sun, the multitude of its gods and idols, its assertion of the equality of all men before the gods, and the frequency and number of its human sacrifices. It had a carefully-trained and powerful priesthood, numerous temples, an elaborate ceremonial, and a complete control of the faith of the people. All ranks accepted the sacerdotal fictions of the supernatural with unquestioning faith. They believed in an immortal life after death for all men and for all beasts, with a heaven in the East for the good and a hell in the West for the bad. The happiest future was to be enjoyed by brave warriors slain honorably in battle, by women dying in childbirth, by victims sacrificed to the gods, and generally by those men who, as high officials, had done credit to their station and valuable service to their country.

The number of divinities was estimated by thousands. There was one for every occupation, for every virtue, for every prominent natural object or phenomenon, and for every nationality and district. The soul of every man when he died, became a god; and the deceased father, grandfather, and great-grandfather were the chief objects of worship in every family. In public, and by the priests, devotion was paid to the great gods who had never been human, but with the people, the chief objects of adoration were the minor ancestral divinities.

The divinity who received the most general worship was the sun. When the sun rose the priests said, "He begins his work," and in all the temples, no matter to which divinity dedicated, they saluted him with horn-blowing, incense, prayers, and sacrifices of quails. When the sun set, they said, "He has finished his work." According to a common legend, the gods collected at the beginning of time to decide which of them should govern the world, but as soon as the sun made his appearance all the others died. Fire was considered the sacred earthly representative of the sun, and was addressed by the same title, "Father of all the gods," and as "the oldest of the gods."[1]

No such universality of worship was paid to any other divinity, not even to the deities within the domains of their respective nationalities. Tezcatlipoca was spoken of as the creator, governor, and all-pervading soul of the universe, the author of morality, the god of repentance and forgiveness. He was represented by figures of fire, river, arrow, and snake, as emblems of the four elements which he had created. His idols had four eyes, suggesting that he sees everything, and held four arrows, indicating his justice and the pestilences which he sends in the punishment of sin; and a wreath of smoke ascends to his ear as a symbol of the prayer of the penitent to whom he gives a merciful hearing.[2] At his annual festival sins were confessed to the priests and absolved by them. Flowers and incense were offered in his temples; and also bloody sacrifices occasionally, though, according to some priests, they were inconsistent with the spirit of his worship. Notwithstanding the multitude of divinities, idols, and temples, many of the prayers had a monotheistic phraseology. The god from whom favors were solicited was addressed as if he were the only one whom the worshiper recognized. This habit of treating one, in a great multitude of divinities, as if he were omnipotent and exclusively divine, is common among polytheists.

In every department of life the great influence of their religion on the people was apparent. Their worship was not limited to the temples and to public occasions. It accompanied every important action. Before eating or drinking, a small portion was invariably offered on the hearth to the household god. The people never left their houses without adoring the domestic divinity by touching the earth at the doorway with the hand, which they then kissed. When an Aztec added after an assertion that it was true "as God sees me," he was believed. A very solemn and sacred form of oath was, " By the life of our father the sun and of our mother the earth." A new dwelling could not be occupied until it had been consecrated by a priest.[3] The gods were supposed to attend and watch over human beings at all times and to give them omens indicating the results of every undertaking, great or small; and for these omens the people were always looking under the guidance of fancies which were often potent in proportion to the ignorance on which they were based. Before invading an enemy's country the Aztecs offered sacrifices to the gods of the land, and when they conquered a district they adopted and honored the local divinity. It was their highest duty to conquer all other nations and compel them to worship Huitzilopochtli, their god of war.

SEC. 176. *Aztec Temples.*—Temples were numerous; some of them large and prominent, others small. In the cities and chief towns there was at least one for every thousand of inhabitants. Izcucan, with three thousand houses, had one hundred temples. The court of the great temple in the city of Mexico was four hundred yards square, and it inclosed forty temple pyramids, each dedicated to a different god. Its buildings had accommodations for five thousand ecclesiastical attendants, and for a garrison of ten thousand soldiers, who were to occupy it in time of danger. The largest of the temple pyramids was one hundred and twenty yards square on the ground, with an area of sixty-five by eighty yards on the upper level. Each god had his own set of priests.

The inside of the inclosing wall was lined with cells in which certain nobles and officials stayed while undergoing a regular fast and penance of four days. Rooms, said to number four hundred, served for the instruction of boys and girls and for the shelter of indigent and sick persons. Other rooms were used for storing arms, musical instruments, incense, thorns, and relics of victims sacrificed, including human hides. One building was a lodging-house for guests of the emperor; another was a place for instruction in music. In the courts were a bathing-tank for washing away the sins of penitents after confession; and a large stone to which a prisoner, desirous of fighting for his life, might be chained. If he succeeded in defeating successively six assailants, he was entitled to his life and freedom. When this temple was taken by Cortes the main court, opposite to the western entrance, had a pyramid of 130,000 human skulls, the remains of so many victims there sacrificed to the gods.

SEC. 176. AZTEC TEMPLES.

Every temple or chapel in large temple grounds was consecrated to a special divinity, and had his idol in the most sacred chamber, with an altar before it for offerings. The divine images were generally in the form of men, but also of women, beasts, and monsters, and were of stone, wood, or burned clay, those of the latter material being usually hollow, and some of them so made that a priest could go into the figure and deliver his oracles or declare his auguries through the mouth of the god. Idols were also found at the sides of the streets, so that persons passing in haste could pay their devotions by a brief prayer or an obeisance. When a living sacrifice was offered, the mouth of the idol was always smeared with the blood, which was regarded as especially acceptable to the gods.

Among the temple implements was one called by the Spaniards a drum. It had four metal plates, presumably like gongs, each of which gave out a different tone, and when struck with great force made a noise so loud that it could be heard at a distance of five miles.

Besides the temples, there were other buildings occupied by sacerdotal communities, some of men and others of women, living under vows of chastity, poverty, and obedience to the rules and superiors of their respective orders. The women inmates of these institutions could creditably leave at any time for the purpose of accepting an offer of marriage; and while they remained they spent their time in spinning, weaving, and other household labor, and in ecclesiastical observances.

Religious festivals were frequent and were conducted with much pomp. There was one on the last day of every month, and an important one on the last day of the year. The greatest was at the beginning of the cycle, after several weeks of fasting, penance, and humiliation. According to their mythology, the world was to come to an end at the close of one of their cycles, and they acted as if they feared that each would be the last. Many confessed their sins, swept their houses, put out their fires, destroyed or cleaned their clothing and furniture, threw their millstones and ancestral idols into the water, and when the old cycle had come to an end marched in procession to a sacred hill, where the chief priest undertook to kindle a new fire on the breast of a prostrate slave. So soon as the smoke showed that the experiment would be a success, a glad shout announced that the gods had granted a continuation of life to mankind, and that all the sins of the past had been absolved. The slave on whom the fire had been kindled was burned with the new flame, which was then distributed among the people, so that each could carry it to his own home. Days of general festivity followed.

SEC. 177. *Human Victims.*—A multitude of human victims were sacrificed; the best authorities say about 20,000 annually. We are told that at the consecration of the chief national temple, in 1487, 60,000 persons were slain, and that in each of the great temples there was at least one human victim every day. The customary place of sacrifice was on the top of a temple pyramid, which was visible to a great number of persons. The victims were usually captive enemies, convicted criminals, slaves, and the children of slaves. The most common method of sacrifice was that the person was laid with his back on a convex stone, and while his legs, arms, and head were held by five priests, another cut open his breast, and took out his heart, held it up to the sun, rubbed the lips of the idol with it, and then threw it into a basin which stood on the altar. If the victim was a prisoner of war the corpse was thrown from the top of the temple pyramid to the ground, where it was picked up by the owner, the captor, who took it to his house to be cooked and eaten. If the victim was not a captive, the corpse was carried down the steps and given to the person who had a right to it. The bodies of the victims were generally eaten at feasts in the private dwellings. Besides cutting the heart from the live person, other methods were used in human sacrifices, including drowning, starving to death, burning and flaying alive. When the maize began to sprout a boy and girl of noble blood were drowned; when it began to blossom, four children were starved to death in a cavern.

No sacrifice was more acceptable to the gods of the Aztecs than the life and blood of an enemy of their favorite nation. The offering of a human victim, especially a noted warrior of a warlike nation, proved the devotion of the worshiper, who in taking the captive risked his life and proved his possession of military courage, the highest of all virtues.

The victim was secure of a happy life in the future. From the time when he was selected for sacrifice, he was fed with abundant and delicate food; and for one of the festivals he was instructed in flute-playing and in his demeanor, and during the last month of his life he had four young girls for his companions. On the fatal day he wore the dress of the god to whom he was to be sacrificed, and while mounting the temple pyramid, he broke a flute on every step. At the occasion of the sacrifice, the chapel of the god was elaborately decorated with flowers and garlands, and there was singing, instrumental music, and dancing.

At the chief annual festival of Huitzilopochtli, a large cake mixed with the blood of a child, representing the divinity, was divided among the people, so that they might all eat the flesh and drink the blood of the god, in a holy communion. By participation in the feast, they assumed the obligation of fidelity and tribute. At this festival, water was consecrated, and preserved to be drunk by the commanders of important military expeditions before starting out on their campaigns.

The following is a copy of a prayer spoken at the beginning of a campaign: "Most kind and helpful Lord, invisible and intangible protector, by whose wisdom we are led and by whose power we live! Lord of battles! it is true and certain that a war draws near; the god of war opens his mouth; he is hungry; he wants to drink the blood of those who fall in battle. The sun and the god of the earth want to enjoy themselves. They want to regale the gods of heaven and hell with the flesh and blood of the mortals who will perish in the approaching contest. The gods of the upper and lower spheres are already looking to see who will conquer and who will be conquered, who will slay and who will be slain. They are watching those whose blood they will drink, whose flesh they will eat. But the noble fathers and mothers whose children shall die do not foreknow their misfortune, neither do their other relatives, nor the mothers who nursed them when they were infants, and suckled them with their own milk. Grant, O Lord, that those who fall shall be kindly accepted by the sun and the earth, the loving father and the mother of all. Thou hast not deceived them in requiring them to die in battle. Thou hast given them life that they might feed the sun and the earth with their flesh and blood! O most kind and helpful Tezcatlipoca, O invisible and intangible Lord, we pray that those who may fall in this war shall be received with love and honor in the dwelling of the sun, that they may be gathered to our heroes who have fallen in previous wars, and that, like all the brave who die gloriously on the battle-field, they may forever share the celestial delights, and the perfume of the flowers that never fade, and the intoxication of endless pleasure, and that they may forever sing the praises of our ruler, the sun."[1]

SEC. 178. *Aztec Priests.*—The priests were organized in a hierarchy or disciplined body under a chief whose title was "Lord of Sacred Affairs." They were divided into ranks, and laymen were admitted only into the lowest; and the higher grades could not be reached without a service of several years in each of those below. No amount of favor could obtain a violation of this rule. Promotions were made by imperial appointment. Most and probably all the priests were of noble and some were of princely blood. They wore a peculiar dress, smeared themselves all over every morning with black and red pigments, which they afterwards washed off; and they neither trimmed their finger nails nor cut nor combed their hair. Entrance into the sacerdotal profession did not bind them for life; they could at any time resume the character and occupations of laymen. Some of the priests lived a celibate life; others had wives.

Among their regular duties were the custody, cleansing, and decoration of the temples and temple grounds; the feeding of the sacred fire; the worship of the great gods with prayer, vocal and instrumental music, processions and offerings of incense, flowers, cakes, beer, beasts, and men; the education of the young; the keeping of the temple records; the observation and interpretation of the omens for public and private life; the calculation of nativities; the custody of the calendar; the announcement and supervision of the ecclesiastical festivals; the granting of absolution at confessions; the performance of sacred ceremonies at weddings, funerals, baptisms (at which children were sprinkled and named), and coronations; the practice of frequent penances; and abstinence from dissipation, from jovial amusements, and from a luxurious mode of life.

Among their regular penances were long vigils, a severe fast of eighty days every year, and frequent bloodletting from the tongue, lips, ears, and other organs, which were pierced with thorns. In the blood-letting, as in the sacrifices of animals and men, the main idea was that the gods wished to be fed, and especially with raw blood. At midnight as well as at sunrise, noon and sunset, incense of copal was burned to the sun, the priests turning successively to the four cardinal points of the compass, beginning with the east. The usual sacerdotal dress was a white gown over which was worn a black cloak fastened on the right shoulder. Every priest was devoted to the worship of a special divinity, and on certain occasions he might wear the dress and emblematic ornaments of his god. If a priest was smeared with blood from a sacrifice or grimed with smoke from incense, he did not wash off the smear or grime until nightfall.

SEC. 179. *Burial.*—The usual method of disposing of the bodies of the dead was burial. The grave was dug in the yard of the home, or of a temple; the body was clothed in the conventional attire of the god of his profession, and to his dress were attached pieces of paper, which, as charms, or by their instructions, were to protect him against the dangers that beset entrance into the other world. Among these dangers were those of a great snake, or alligator, and of mountains which stand on opposite sides of his path and rush together. With a man, a sword and shield were put into the grave; with a woman, a spindle, and with both food and drink and a dog as guide and watchful sentinel.

A month after the burial, and again after a lapse of four months, the grave was visited by the near relatives for purposes of mourning; and for four years offerings of food were made to the dead at intervals. When a king or high noble died, he was burned, with his wives and slaves, and on the fourth, twentieth, fortieth, and eightieth days, human victims were sacrificed to him.

SEC. 180. *Aztec Ethics.*—Much of the ethical character of the religion has been indicated in the quotations made from the addresses delivered to the king when installed in office and to boys and girls when becoming young men and women. The priests said, "Keep peace with all; bear injuries with humility; God, who sees all, will avenge you." Again they said, "He who looks too curiously on a woman commits adultery with his eyes."

After giving extracts from the addresses delivered by parents to children and by priests to the emperor at his installation, and after deciding that they are genuine products of Aztec culture, not Spanish inventions, Waitz says that "these speeches are full of irresistible evidences of high social refinement and mild manners. We can accept and commend every sentence. Possibly among the Aztecs, as among us, the practice of common life differed much from the teachings of wise men, whose sublime doctrines the common people admired and impressed on their children; but this divergence is not sufficient to sustain the opinion almost universally accepted hitherto, that the Aztecs, notwithstanding considerable advances in material culture, were lacking in true civilization and moral and spiritual development. The fact that religion and morality were inseparably associated as they were in these addresses, has conclusive weight in this respect, and indeed no indication is more trustworthy and no measure more accurate for the culture in a community, than the degree in which the demands of a fine morality are supported by the popular religion and interwoven with the ecclesiastical teachings."[1]

Waitz[2] adds that "a further evidence of the near relation between religion and morality among the Aztecs is to be found in the confession of all his sins required from every person, once in his life, to a priest. According to the Aztec faith, man came pure as gold from the hand of his Creator Quetzalcoatl. By his own will, which is not entirely free, for he is influenced by the star under which he is born, he defiles himself with sin. If he confesses all honestly to God, who sees the heart and the thoughts of all mortals, and if he promises never to sin in the future, he is pardoned. The pure source of divine mercy washes away the stain of sin, and he is born again to commence a new life. For the confirmation of his veracity, and instead of an oath, the penitent touched the earth with his hand, which he then kissed; and he undressed himself, a symbol of laying aside all concealment. After hearing the confession, the priest turned to the god Tezcatlipoca, to whom he addressed some words, and then he directed the penitent to fast, to draw blood from all his limbs, to be charitable to the indigent and sick, and to make an appropriate sacrifice of a slave if he could afford it. By compliance with the penances imposed, a criminal could escape punishment for a crime, but confession was permitted only once in a man's life, and was usually kept back until he had reached an advanced age. Sins committed after the confession remained without forgiveness."

SEC. 181. *Aztec Culture.*—Considered as a whole, the culture of the Aztecs is wonderful for the inequality in the development of its different departments. They had no iron; and their tools and ornaments of bronze were so few that those preserved to our time are among the rarest of curiosities in the great museums. That alloy was so scarce with them that they did not use it for swords, daggers, or agricultural implements. Their poverty in hard metal fit for edge tools would lead us to infer that when discovered by the Europeans, they had only recently risen from the stone culturestep, and that we should find their general industrial condition, and their social, political, and ecclesiastical institutions, nearly as rude as those of the higher savages. And as a fact, we find them even ruder than the Tahitians, in their lack of shipping, in their cannibalism, and in the frequency of their human sacrifices. They had no domestic animal bred for burden, draft, wool or milk. In all these points they were low in their culture.

On the other hand, in many important points they were superior to any other barbarous nation, and even to many civilized states. Every child was born free. The slave could defend his life against his master, could own property and could make a valid marriage with a free person or a slave. Valor in battle might entitle him to freedom and to admission into the nobility. Marriage was a sacred contract, celebrated before a priest, and it could not be dissolved without a judicial decree, to which the wife was entitled on the same grounds as the husband. There was a privileged nobility, but many of its members held it by life tenure only, and as a reward for distinguished public service. Every commune elected its mayor, who was a noble by virtue of the popular choice. Retaliation was prohibited, and justice was administered by an independent judiciary, with a careful division of original jurisdictions between communal and district courts under a national appellate supreme court. The high judges had adequate pay, held office during good behavior, and kept written records of all their cases. The mercantile profession was pursued by many nobles without discredit. The imperial office was filled by election from the imperial family, and at his installation the emperor was very distinctly told that he was expected not to give way to his caprice, but to protect the traditional rights of all classes of the people. The children of the nobles, girls as well as boys, were educated in the temples and were taught that there was little satisfaction for them in life without honesty and toil. Morality was intimately associated with religion; and the moral tone of the community was far in advance of its ecclesiastical ceremonies. The social system was quiet and orderly. The adoption by the government of a year more accurately measured than that of any other contemporaneous state, must have been based on long-kept records of careful observations of the heavens, records of which nothing is told us by Aztec history or tradition.

When we remember that this remarkable system of popular rights, this excellent judiciary, this superior moral and social tone, and this unequaled calendar, are found in a community which was just commencing to produce bronze, or at least had produced very little of that, its only hard metal, we must conclude that the Aztecs were indebted for many features of their culture, not to their own internal development, but to the instruction of immigrants who had come to them from abroad, and from the other hemisphere. The nearest nation from which they might have received instruction was in the northwestern part of South America; but when we examine the culture of the Quichuans we shall see that there is little in common between them and the Aztecs except in those things which might have been derived by both from savage ancestors.

We may suppose that in the course of thirty centuries before the time of Columbus, many European, Asiatic and Carthaginian ships were driven by winds and carried by currents across the great oceans to the shores of North or South America, against the will of their crews; that among these crews there was now and then a man who survived for many years, and by superior knowledge gained much influence in his new home; that he introduced something of the skill, ideas, and customs of his native land; and that the arts and institutions thus established did not suffice to make an evenly-developed culture.

Under the influence of such presumptions, I follow Latham, Waitz, and Tylor in accepting Humboldt's opinion that Aztec culture was not entirely indigenous. Humboldt found that certain resemblances in the names of the Aztec and Chinese calendars cannot be explained satisfactorily by chance or by the theory of independent development. Tylor calls attention to the Aztec god with the body and limbs of a man and the head or mask of a jackal, reminding us of the Anubis of the ancient Egyptians. The same author observed at Xochicalco the head of a chief wearing a helmet with the neck and head of a serpent projecting out in front, similar to a head-dress or cap represented in Egyptian art. There is a resemblance as to some points, and also a dissimilarity as to others, in the pyramids of the two countries. Those of the Nile Valley rise to a point and are tombs; those of Anahuac are truncated and are foundations for temples. In both countries the sovereign was styled " The Son of the Sun ; " and in both the corpse was consigned to the tomb with a paper giving the soul directions what to say and do, when on trial in the world of spirits. Buildings in Central America were ornamented with carvings of heads of elephants or mammoths; but whether these forms were drawn from animals of the New or Old World we do not know.

SEC. 182. *The End of Anahuac.*—The Aztec Empire, strong as it was in many points, and especially in its military organization as compared with all neighboring states, soon collapsed when it was attacked by Cortes, though he had only four hundred Spaniards when he first entered the valley of Mexico, and had only seven hundred when he took the capital city by storm. He was aided by some thousands of Tlascalans, by the influence of his fire-arms and his horses, by the prophecies that a great national calamity was near at hand, and that one of their gods was to return to earth and reign over Anahuac, by the lack of complete harmony among the different provinces in the empire, and most of all by the success of Cortes in seizing the emperor Montezuma, who then forbade his subjects to resist the invaders. In the boldness of its conception, in the courage and skill of its execution, and in the magnitude of its success as compared with the smallness of its means, the conquest of Mexico is without a parallel in previous history.

CHAPTER XII.
THE QUICHUANS.

SECTION 183. *The Quichuan Empire.*—Four centuries since there was a large barbarous monarchy or empire in South America, south of the equator, extending two thousand miles along the western coast, and inland about three hundred miles. The eastern boundary was on the eastern slope of the Andes and the capital city, Cuzco, is situated on the bank of a tributary of the Amazon.

Several names have been given to the people of this empire. They have been called Peruvians, but this title is objectionable because it confounds them with the citizens of the present Spanish-American Christian state; and because Peru is only a small part of the old empire. The term Incas has also been applied to them, but this was their word for their royal family which included all their high nobility. Their language was called Quichuan and the best name for them as a people is the Quichuans.

Nine-tenths of the area and population were in the torrid zone, but the land rises steeply from the Pacific, and on account of their high elevation, most of the provinces have a genial climate. Indeed the most equably cool temperature on the globe is that of Quito, which has a mean of 58 degrees in January and 59 degrees in July; and those two are the coldest and warmest months in the year.

Quito, only a quarter of a degree south of the equator and nine thousand feet above the sea, was the second city of the Quichuan Empire in population and importance. The capital, Cuzco, nine hundred miles distant to the southward in a direct line and more than twelve hundred by any passable road, is 11,000 feet above the sea and has a temperature similar to that of Quito but not quite so equable.

SEC. 184. *Agriculture.*—The cultivation of the soil was the chief occupation of the people. They used hoes and spades of wood and bronze, and also an implement that may be called a plough, which was drawn through the soil by six or eight men, and was perhaps used mostly on ceremonial occasions, as at an annual festival when the king made a show of participating in agricultural labor. The dryness of much of the territory during a large part of the year, and the abundant supplies of snow in the higher Andes, made a demand, and gave facilities, for irrigation, which the people did not neglect. Great reservoirs were constructed in the mountains, and from them the water was led to the fields in artificial channels, which in some cases were forty or fifty miles long, and in places were cut through the hills or into the sides of steep cliffs, lined with stone in loose soil to prevent seepage, covered to check evaporation, supported on embankments, or taken across ravines in inverted syphons.[1] Some of the subterranean channels made for agricultural and household use by the Quichuans are in good order now, after the lapse of more than three centuries and a half, and after the loss of all tradition of the sources from which the water comes.[2] In districts which could not be irrigated and which had an arid surface with moisture abundant at a depth of fifteen or twenty feet, the dry stratum was taken off from as much as an acre at a place for the purpose of getting a productive field.[3] Fertilizers, including fish and guano, were used, and the latter was brought to the mainland in large quantities from the Chincha islands.[4]

The principal objects of cultivation were maize, potato, quinoa, plantain, manidc,[5] cotton, tobacco, coca, agave, and bamboo. Some of these thrive in the cool, and others in the hot districts. The goose, the dog, an animal similar to the guinea-pig, and the llama were bred for food; and the last was shorn for its wool, and used as a beast of burden. In adaptation to the rocky declivities, stunted herbage, and frequent snows of the high Andes, it is as wonderful as is the camel to the sandy deserts of Arabia. The llama "carries a load of little more than a hundred pounds, and cannot travel above three or four leagues in a day. But all this is compensated by the little care and cost required for its management and its maintenance. It picks up an easy subsistence from the moss and stunted herbage that grow scantily along the withered sides and steeps of the Cordilleras. The structure of its stomach, like that of the camel, is such as to enable it to dispense with any supply of water for weeks, nay, months together. Its spongy hoof, armed with a claw or pointed talon to enable it to take secure hold on the ice, never requires to be shod; and the load laid upon its back rests securely in its bed of wool, without the aid of girth or saddle. The llamas move in troops of five hundred or even a thousand, and thus, though each individual carries but little, the aggregate is considerable. The whole caravan travels on at regular pace, passing the night in the open air without suffering from the coldest temperature, and marching in perfect order, and in obedience to the voice of the driver. It is only when overloaded that the spirited little animal refuses to stir, and neither blows nor caresses can induce him to rise from the ground. He is as sturdy in asserting his rights on this occasion as he is usually docile and unresisting."[6] To prevent any decrease in the stock of these useful animals, a law provided that none should be slain without permission from the government.

Maize was the staff of life, and was ordinarily eaten in bread or porridge. Fish was often eaten raw. Much of the flesh of the vicuñas and huanacos was used in a dry state. The llama, being larger than the goat, might presumably have been bred to yield much milk, but the idea of obtaining that fluid from their herds does not seem to have occurred to the Quichuans. They made fermented drinks with maize, manioc, and other vegetables; they used tobacco only in the form of snuff,[7] and the nobles chewed the leaves of the coca, which were forbidden to the common people.[8]

The crops of grain, cotton, and wool, and the manufactures of cloth and arms, exceeded the requirements of the population in ordinary years; and the surplus was collected in public store-houses, which often contained a stock sufficient for the consumption of ten years. From these stores, any want among the people was supplied, and a tribute was taken by the provincial governor to the imperial capital at every spring equinox.

SEC. 185. *Various Arts.*—Like other work, weaving was done under official supervision. All the wool, cotton, and agave fiber were collected in public store-houses, and thence distributed among families, with orders to produce specified quantities and qualities of cord and cloth. The garments of the common people were coarse and warm; those of the sovereign, priests, and other nobles, were, in many cases, very fine, and were dyed with brilliant colors, some of which were more beautiful than any known, at the time, in Europe.[1] The women did the spinning, weaving, and dyeing.

Their garments were pieces of cotton or woolen cloth, worn, without sewing, as waist-cloths, skirts, or mantles. They had sandals, but no shoes; bands or turbans on the head, but no hats. The people of every department, whether in military service or not, always wore a distinctive color or combination of colors in their clothing; and even if transferred permanently to another department, they and their descendants were required to adhere to their hereditary costume.

The Quichuans dressed skins so as to make them soft, but did not tan with astringent material. Having few trees near navigable water, they built no boats, but they made rafts of logs or reeds, sometimes rendered more buoyant with inflated skins; and they had both paddles and sails for propulsion on the water. Such rafts they used for fishing and for transporting guano from the Chincha Islands to the mainland.

Along the sea-coast, fish were caught in large quantities with net and hook. In the mountains, the wild vicuña and huanaco, animals similar to the llama, were hunted by parties under official supervision. As many as 60,000 men, distributed around a district, gradually approached a common center, where the game was to be caught or killed. At such a hunt 40,000 vicuñas might be captured. All were sheared, and many slaughtered; and then the young females and some of the young males were turned loose. The meat not needed for immediate consumption was dried. Each game district had one such circular hunt in a period of four years.

The Quichuan Empire had no foreign commerce by sea or by land. To the east were savages who had nothing of exchangable value; and with those northern or southern neighbors who might have some products valuable for traffic, there was almost continuous warfare. There was no coined money. All the necessaries of life which they could not produce in their families were supplied to them by the government; all the accumulated surplus of their toil went into the hands of the officials.

Public roads connected all the towns with one another. Two main roads parallel with the coast line, each about two thousand miles long, extended through the empire from north to south, one near the level of the sea, the other high up in the Andes. These roads, which impressed Humboldt as among "the most useful and most gigantic works of human enterprise," were twelve or fifteen feet wide, with a paving of flat stones or of small broken stone laid in cement, which is in some places so hard that it stands as an arch after the soil beneath has been washed away by cross currents of water. Wheeled vehicles being unknown, steep grades and steps were not considered objectionable. Tunnels, bridges, embankments and side-cuts into steep cliffs were used. In crossing streams, the suspension plan of construction was sometimes adopted. For wide streams, cables of osier were twisted to a thickness of ten inches and a length of seventy yards. Such a bridge, the origin of which is attributed by Squier to Quichuan enterprise, crosses the Apurimac at a height of more than a hundred feet above the water, with a span of one hundred and forty-eight feet. On one side it is reached by a tunnel several hundred yards in length. These roads were intended to facilitate the marching of troops, the journeys of officials, and the transportation of supplies.

At intervals of four or five miles on the main road were huts for runners, who carried official messages or packages at high speed, with a fresh man to take up the burden at every station. In this manner, a distance of one hundred and fifty miles was traversed in twenty-four hours. At distances of eleven miles there were large houses for the accommodation of high officials on their journeys.[2]

SEC. 186. *Buildings.*—Houses were built of adobe, stone, and wattle, and roofs were of thatch. Adobe was used in dwellings and temples, and in size and durability was unequaled elsewhere. In Egypt, the thickness never exceeded six inches; in Peru it was often a foot;[1] and if we may trust an engraving in Squier, and it seems to be taken from a photograph, some of the Quichuan adobes were five feet in each of the three dimensions.[2] Adobes of such magnitude made of the material used in Egypt and Mexico would be very troublesome to make and to handle. Perhaps the wall was built solid with adobe mortar deposited in a frame, the lines of separation now visible being the limits of each new lot of mortar. Not less remarkable than the size is the tenacity. In other countries, where there are twenty inches or more of rain annually, adobe walls, if left uncovered, within a few years sink down into a mere heap of dirt; but in Peruvian districts, where the rain sometimes comes in torrents,[3] adobe walls thirty feet high[4] have stood for more than three centuries without a roof, and have not only stood, but have also preserved their cornices and their sharp corners,[5] and their decorations, made in imitation of lattice-work, by letting some adobes project more than others. Such ruins are found from the level of the sea to an elevation of 12,500 feet, and from Quito to Lake Titicaca.

In some cases, a material similar to that employed in the adobes, instead of being shaped in moulds, was built into a house in a moist condition, so that its walls were uniform and continuous in their substance, without layers or mortar. The village of Azangaro, near Lake Titicaca, has such a structure dating from the period of the conquest. Its form is circular; its walls of clay are eleven feet high and fourteen inches thick.[6] Whether the thatch roof be as old as the walls or not (tradition says it is), the durability of these clay walls, so thin and almost without mark of wear by the elements, is wonderful.

Stone cut and uncut was used. Rough stone was laid in a cement which looks like clay and yet holds like stone. Humboldt found a lime mortar in the Quichuan walls in what is now Ecuador. Prescott, accepting the authority of Velasco, Ondegardo, and Ulloa, says that "a fine bituminous glue" held the stones in a solid mass. After examining the walls found in a region extending through more than ten degrees of latitude, Squier, who gave the matter very careful attention, refuses to give credence to "the stories and speculations about some wonderfully binding and impalpable cement which is said to have been used by the Incas." According to him, the Quichuan architects, in erecting buildings of cut stone, "depended, with rare exceptions, on the accuracy of their stone fitting without cement, for the stability of their work."[7] The exceptions which he mentions are the use of metallic dowell pins and clamps, and mortices and tenons cut in the stone.⁸ In many countries barbarian architects who undertook to build of stone before the discovery of mortar, carefully fitted immense blocks in irregular shapes, and trusted to their weight to keep them in place. One of the best specimens of such cyclopean architecture now in existence is in the ruins of the fortress of Cuzco. One of the blocks in that structure is twenty-seven feet long, fourteen wide, and twelve thick; and the weight of another is said to be three hundred and sixty tons.⁹ Stones fifteen feet long, twelve wide, and ten thick, are numerous in the walls of that structure, and are accurately fitted to one another. Such blocks were transported long distances.¹⁰ Tradition said that 20,000 men were employed fifty years on the Cuzco fortress.

In some buildings the stones were cut with plain surfaces and eight rectangular corners; in others, they were cut with irregular corners, or with straight lines of contact and with rough surfaces, or rustic work on the face of the wall. In the best buildings, the stones are fitted together so closely that there is no perceptible mortar, and in most places not sufficient space to introduce a thin knife blade. Squier tells us that in no other part of the world had he seen "stones cut with such mathematical precision and admirable skill."¹¹

The corners and the doors might be of cut stone, while the body of the building was of rough stone laid in clay, and not unfrequently the courses near the ground would be of stone, with those above of adobe. The stone dwellings were usually one story high, with steep roofs and no windows, though there were doorways in the gables to give access by an external staircase or ladder to the attic or garret. Other dwellings had two stories and an attic, so that there were three floors available for domestic purposes. The access to the second and third floors seems to have been from the outside. There were no chimneys. The doorways were closed with curtains.[12] The dwellings of the common people were small and simple, with walls of adobe, or wattle covered with clay.[13]

The Quichuan architecture was plain. As a general rule the buildings showed no large porticoes, cornices, or rows of columns or pilasters, no spires, no colossal statues guarding the door-ways, and few carvings on the outer walls. The principle of the arch was used in a few buildings and on a small scale,[14] but never in making a support for a wall over a door-way in a palace or temple, nor in a vault over a large room. The door-ways were narrower at top than bottom, so that the lintel was short.

The stone used in their temple walls was porphyry, basalt, or granite, much of it very hard. Those kinds of stone and also marble and jasper were made into idols, cups, bowls, vases, and various ornaments for temples and dwellings. According to Waitz[15] some of the Quichuan heads in stone and pottery show correct proportion and good expression. Emerald and turquoise were cut and polished. Pottery shaped by hand or in moulds was abundant.[16] Large vases were made for storing grain under-ground, and for coffins.

Sec. 187. *Mining.*—Gold and silver were abundant, the former obtained by washing from alluvial deposits, the latter by smelting from vein stone. The monarch Atahualpa filled a room twenty-two feet long and seventeen wide to a depth of nine feet with vessels and ornaments of gold, and he promised to give four times as much silver in addition as his ransom, to his Spanish captors, but they slew him before he had time to keep his promise. Silver, copper, and tin were smelted in furnaces built on patterns still in use in Peru and Bolivia. Cinnabar was prized as a pigment and was sublimated for its mercury.[1] Blast was furnished in their furnaces by bellows and blow-pipes. The value of various minerals as fluxes to aid the fusion of ores was understood. Hollow ware, ornamental figures, and tools were made of metal by forging and casting. For the latter purpose, patterns were made of wax and moulds of clay. Among the plunder taken by the Spaniards were ten golden statues of women and four of llamas all in life size. The Quichuans alloyed gold, silver, and tin with copper; their bronze contained from two to ten per cent of tin, according to the various degrees of hardness and elasticity required; and they hardened copper with silica.[2] They made plates and cups of gold, and trees and maize plants of gold with maize ears in silver. They could not gild, but they covered copper and stone with thin sheets of gold. They made plain and concave mirrors of metal, those of concave form being used to obtain fire from the sun. They soldered metals together,[3] and they used scales for weighing metals and other substances.

SEC. 188. *Social Affairs.*—Marriage was compulsory for the man when he reached the age of twenty-four and for the woman when she was eighteen or twenty and was not permitted sooner. On a fixed day all the common people who were unmarried and marriageable met in the public square of every commune, and then and there the couples were wedded in the presence of the communal chief. The books do not tell us what was done in case of an inequality in the numbers of the young men and young women of a commune or province, but in such case presumably the superfluity of another province could be utilized or the widows and widowers could be appropriated for securing an approximate level in the matrimonial market. The parties interested were allowed to choose their spouses, but if they did not agree, the chief chose for them, and refusal to submit to his decision was a crime. The Inca nobles were married in a similar manner in the presence of the emperor. Polygyny was permitted among the high nobles but not among the common people.

The country was divided into communes, each of which had its definite boundaries, and the tillable land in each was divided again by precise limits into three portions, one for the priesthood, one for the people, and the third for the emperor. The common people cultivated all; their labor on the tracts of the priests and sovereign was part of their tribute to the church and state. There was no individual property in land. The people's share was redistributed among them at the beginning of every crop year, when each married man got a share proportioned to the size or working capacity of his family, in about the ratio of two acres of irrigated land for each person capable of doing agricultural work. All children after reaching the age of six or seven were required to have regular employment in contributing to the productiveness of the country. Everybody among the common people who could work, must do his share of toil, but all who were helpless were entitled to support, and kind attention. The blind, the sick, the deformed, and the crippled were not allowed to lack abundant food, comfortable clothing, or shelter; and at least once a month such unfortunates were invited to a public dinner and festival in every district. The government thus manifested its sympathy with suffering.

The cultivation of the imperial field in every commune was the occasion of a festival. On the days designated, the people—men, women, and children—assembled before sunrise in their gayest dresses, and did the work amidst continuous chants, which had the word "hailli" for the chorus, and conveyed the ideas of joy and triumph.

All the adult male subjects of the empire were required to learn the Quichuan tongue; and all the Inca males went to schools in the temples, where they received instruction in the laws, traditions, songs, religion, and quipus of the country. The quipus were cords, which by different knots, colors, and modes of combination, served to keep records of the number of the people, weapons, food measures, pieces of cloth, llamas, and so forth, in every commune, department, and province of the empire, and also of the laws, history, religions, doctrines, and ecclesiastical ceremonies. The knotted cords were of course inferior to writing for recording thought, but wonderful statements are made of the comprehensiveness and precision with which they conveyed ideas to those persons who devoted much time to their study. Instruction in the quipus was given to none save the nobles; the common people were taught that they must never aspire to rise above the condition of the laborer.

The Quichuans had a solar year of three hundred and sixty-five days, including twelve lunar months and some surplus days; and they had vertical columns to enable them to ascertain the solstices and equinoxes. Beyond these points we know nothing certain of their astronomy. They had dramatic performances. Their musical instruments were drums, pans-pipes, trumpets, bells, and lutes with five or seven strings. Waitz says they had no counterpoint. Rivero asserts that they had two parts to their airs which were in the minor key. Their language had abstract words for thought, wisdom, beauty, spirit, and eternity, indicating a considerable degree of intellectual development.[1]

SEC. 189. *Government.*—The government was a hereditary, theocratic, despotic monarchy. The sovereign was the chief priest, the head of the national religion, divine in his character, the terrestrial representative and son of the great national god, the celestial luminary, the sun. He chose his chief wife among his sisters, and her eldest son was the legitimate heir to the throne. In this manner the blood of the imperial family had remained unmixed for at least fifteen generations. The first Quichuan monarch, who was not, on both sides, the descendant of the pair with whom the Inca dominion began, was Atähualpa, and with him the dynasty came to an end. These monarchs, thus bred "in and in," instead of being weak physically and intellectually, as we might have expected to find them, were noted for their career of success uninterrupted for centuries until they encountered the iron civilization of Europe. Besides his chief wife, the Inca sovereign had hundreds of concubines.

Next in rank to the sovereign was the Inca nobility, consisting of persons descended from the imperial family. These Incas filled all the high ecclesiastical, military, and political offices under the emperor. They paid no tribute, owned no land, serfs, nor slaves, and were dependent for everything on the throne. The second order of nobility consisted of the native chiefs of conquered provinces and their descendants. It was the established policy of the empire that such chiefs, if submissive, should be retained in their offices, and that their power should descend to their sons. Usually the office went to the eldest son, but sometimes to one younger who showed superior capacity. Nearly all the inferior offices were held by these nobles of the second rank. They wore a peculiar dress, spoke a peculiar dialect, held all high offices, whether sacerdotal, military, or political, and were the only persons educated to take charge of the imperial offices.

The remainder of the people were serfs. Without the consent of their noble officers, they could not leave their communes even temporarily; they could not change their occupations, nor idle, nor marry, nor refuse to marry. The families were organized into squads of ten, each of which had a decurion whose duty it was to make periodical reports of all births, deaths, marriages, crimes, and other important facts in his jurisdiction to his immediate superior or centurion who was the chief of ten squads; he reported in turn to his immediate superior, the chief of ten centuriates; and he to his superior, an Inca, who was at the head of 10,000 families, and these Incas to the king. The lower officials were also prosecutors and judges, and were held to a strict responsibility for the preservation of peace and the punishment of crime among their respective subjects. This system kept the whole people under a most effective system of surveillance and maintained excellent public order. All the higher crimes were tried by noble judges, who were required to render a final decision in every case within five days. There was no rehearing and no appeal. Noble inspectors went from province to province, at regular intervals, to examine into the administration and see the condition of the palaces, temples, store-houses, and people, and the conduct of the officials. Justice was administered efficiently and cheaply.

The government took charge of the bed and board, the body and soul of everybody. There was no private property. There was no money, the love of which is said to be the root of all evil; that is, for those who are not worried by the lack of it. There were no traders and no hired laborers. There was no idleness, and among the common people no choice of occupation or residence. Every man had his orders what to do, where to live, and how to dress. There were no disreputable classes. There was no professional criminal, no lawyer, no pauper, no millionaire, no prostitute, no politician, no old maid, no old bachelor. It was a happy land! Without the aid of the industrial wonders of the nineteenth century, without railway, steamboat, magnetic telegraph, or electric light, the people lived free from care under a government which prevented all competition among them, which assumed all their responsibilities, guarded all their interests, and was ever watchful of their welfare. Waitz, reviewing the general condition of the Quichuan Empire, says: "By the strong socialistic institutions, poverty and idleness were rendered as impossible as ambition and greed. Obedience to the law was universal, and although the people had not the least prospect of improving their condition by toil and economy, yet on the other hand no one could fall into indigence. All free movement of individuals, all private enterprise, all competition, all effort for further progress, was smothered, and the machine of state was carefully devised by the paternal supervision of the Incas, so that no spark of spiritual life should be kindled among the mass of the people."

SEC. 190. *Aggressive Policy.*—The Quichuans were a warlike, conquering, and consolidating people. No nation succeeded more completely during a comparatively brief career in founding by arms an extensive dominion on a basis of permanence, with a complete absorption of numerous and extensive heterogeneous elements. We have already seen that the chiefs of the conquered tribes were retained in power. Under Quichuan authority their dynasties obtained a permanence which they never had before. The chiefs then, had little to lose by submission to the Quichuan invaders. Nor had the people much to lose. They were protected against the constant warfare, the anarchical disorder, and the frequent famines that beset them in their independent condition. The construction of roads, irrigating ditches, and store-houses, brought advantages to which the majority could not be indifferent. The reduction of the mass of the people and especially of the native nobility to serfdom, with the obligation of regular labor under strict supervision, was probably the cause of some discontent, but under the precautions taken by the Quichuan officials, resistance was unavailing. When the authorities had any doubt about the fidelity of a province, they moved a considerable portion of its people into the midst of some loyal district, and filled up the vacant place with a trustworthy population. Such compulsory migrations by thousands of families were common events, and they served not only to preserve the peace but also to make the Quichuan tongue, arts, and ideas familiar to the whole people. Every department of the empire had its quarter in the capital whither the sons of the nobles were sent as hostages and students.

When the Quichuan troops invaded a country, they

treated it as if they already considered it a part of their kingdom. They did not wantonly destroy the property nor massacre the people. One of the Peruvian princes is quoted as saying, "We must spare our enemies, or it will be our loss, since they and all that belong to them will soon be ours." So soon as their authority was accepted, they gave to the conquered people more protection against injustice and tyranny and foreign enemies, than they had ever had before. The new subjects found themselves placed on a social and political equality with the mass of their conquerors. They were not plundered cruelly nor driven to work in exhausting slavery nor humiliated in any manner. They found that no degrading discrimination was made against them on account of blood or recent subjection. They were fed and clothed as well, and cared for as attentively as their Quichuan neighbors. Compelled to learn the language, to adopt the religion, and to submit to the officials of the Quichuans, they became Quichuans themselves in spirit, within a few generations.

Every monarch was a leader of armies and a conqueror, with no serious interruption in the career of military success, until the reign of the last Inca emperor. Whether all the sovereigns were brave and capable we do not know; but it is certain that their armies marched from triumph to triumph. Their troops were by far the best on the continent. At least twice a month all the healthy adult males, of an active age, were required to participate in a military drill, in a division which had its distinctive sacred standard. At the beginning of the XVIth century, the empire had an army of 200,000 soldiers.

The troops were armed with bows, spears,[1] slings

clubs of copper, and battle-axes of copper and stone; and they wore corslets of padded cotton and helmets. For protection against snow, rain, and wind, they carried tents, and, while in the territory of their enemies, they erected extensive fortifications which indicated their prudence and purpose of staying. They had studied the principles of fortification, and understood it better than any of the barbarous nations of antiquity. All the faces of the fortress of Cuzco are so planned that "they can be covered by a parallel fire from the weapons of the defenders."[2] No other people thus built fortifications before the invention of gunpowder. In their warfare with the Spaniards, after the first surprise had passed, they showed much courage and steadfastness, and, unlike the Aztecs, after capturing the horses and arms of the Europeans succeeded in using them effectively.

It was with the aid of such a policy and within a period which, according to tradition, did not exceed five centuries, that the Quichuans extended their rule from Cuzco a thousand miles to the northward and as far to the southward. They maintained a population much denser than that found in the same region now. Tschudi conveys the impression that in large districts there are not now more than one-fifth as many inhabitants as there were when Pizarro invaded Peru.[3] Rivero says that in one valley the population has decreased from 700,000 to twelve hundred, and that under Atahualpa the kingdom had a population of 10,000,000.[4]

SEC. 191. *Quichuan Religion.*—The religion was polytheistic and idolatrous. It recognized a creator and governor of the universe, variously styled Tupanqui, Pachacamac, or Viracocha, besides an almost infinite number of subordinate divinities, including the spirits of all the heavenly bodies, of many notable topographical features of the earth, many meteorological phenomena, and the souls of all dead men. The chief object of worship was the sun, who alone of all the deities had a temple in every large town, and whose temple in Cuzco was the grandest ecclesiastical building in the empire, and the place where the chief acts of public worship were celebrated, the emperor himself officiating there as chief priest.

There was no incompatibility between the religion of the Quichuans and that of the surrounding nations. The idols of the conquered countries were taken to the temple or temples of Cuzco, and kept there in honor; and the people of the subject provinces were allowed to worship their idols and their ancestors; but they were also required to adore the sun as the divinity of the empire. Many of the divinities had a local character, and their priests were also subordinate priests of the imperial deities.[1]

The ceremonies of worship were prayer with face towards the sun, singing, instrumental music, dancing, processions, offerings of fruits, flowers, incense, and fermented liquors, and sacrifices of llamas and on rare occasions of human beings. In the temples all the offerings were made by the priests; in dwellings every male head of a family made offerings to his household gods. The chief worship was that of the ancestral spirits.

Many llamas were sacrificed, and in Cuzco, on rare occasions six hundred on one day.[2] The sacrifice was followed by a feast, in which the meat of the victim was eaten, and a small portion of the consecrated food was distributed to everybody in the town or city, to the common people as well as to the nobles. All had the same worship, and seem to have been equal before their gods. When a monarch was crowned, an heir to the throne born, or a military expedition sent out, a human victim was sacrificed, but no part of the flesh was eaten.[3]

All the high priests were nobles; and all of the high nobles were priests, but few of them devoted themselves exclusively to the sacerdotal profession. Their ecclesiastical authority was an incident of political rank, and they had no more thought of controlling the sovereign in matters of church than in those of State. Although religious ideas had a great influence over the people, the priests never attempted to get control of the government as they did in Egypt, India, and many other countries.

Some of the priests dressed in white, but there was no costume or sets of costumes distinctive of any grade of the sacerdotal occupation; nor was there any life-long and strictly ascetic monasticism, nor any chance for personal aggrandizement by exciting the admiration of the most ignorant people. The priest had power to absolve from sin after confession, which was required at least once a year from all the people; and he determined by lot whether the confession was truthful and complete. If not he imposed a severe penance.

Burial was the common method of disposing of the dead. The body was bent together in a sitting posture with the knees to the chin, wrapped with cloth, and seated upright in the grave with the face to the west. In some districts, it was sewed up in llama skins, or put into a large vase of pottery. In the Aymara region, peculiar, tower-like tombs, called chulpas, were erected for the dead. Usually these chulpas were of stone, pear-shaped, and largest near the top. Squier[4] gives an engraving of one thirty-nine feet high, nineteen wide near the top, and sixteen at the base. Some of the Aymara dead were buried in arched vaults; and at Ollantaytambo, tomb chambers were cut into the rocky cliffs.[5] The high nobles were buried in vases of precious metal. The emperors were embalmed, and their mummies were preserved in the Cuzco temple. Meat, drink, weapons, tools, clothes, and ornaments of gold, silver, and gems, were put into the graves to feed the dead; and some tombs had pipes leading down from the surface, so that drink could be poured down frequently.[6] At the funerals of the emperors and high nobles, some of their wives and servants were slain to keep them company into the future life. At the funeral of Huayna Capac, the last emperor who died before the arrival of the Spaniards, one thousand persons were sacrificed.

SEC. 192. *Quichuan Temples.*—Temples were numerous, and most of them were dedicated to the sun; a few to Yupanqui, the creator of the universe. The chief temple of the sun at Cuzco, called also the Golden Palace, was three hundred feet long and two hundred wide, and was built with an elegance of masonry for which Sarmiento knew only two equals in Spain. A thick sheet of gold, six inches wide, ran round the outside of the edifice as a frieze; and there was a similar decoration in every apartment. The room of the sun had a large plate of the same metal, shaped and engraved to represent the god of day, and decorated with precious stones, so placed on the western wall that at certain seasons the rays of the rising sun should shine upon it through a large, open doorway. On both sides of the golden luminary were the mummies of deceased emperors, embalmed with gums and spices, sitting on golden chairs. Another room, dedicated to the moon, had a silver plate representing that heavenly body, and numerous ornaments of the same metal. Other chambers were dedicated to the stars, to lightning, and to the rainbow. Attached to the temple was a large garden, containing ornamental plants, and also imitations of trees, bushes, flowering plants, and animals in gold. The vases for fruits and flowers, the ewers to hold water for temple use, the pipes leading water into the temple, and even the tools for cultivating the temple ground, were of precious metal. Among the vases were twelve of silver, each more than eight feet high and ten feet in circumference.[1] The ecclesiastics employed in this building numbered four thousand.[2] The temples occupied the most central and beautiful sites in the towns; they were surrounded with grounds planted with trees, and were ornamented with idols in the form of men and brutes. The temple on Titicaca Island had six hundred men and one thousand maidens within its walls, and that at Guanuco had 30,000 men in its service, perhaps many of them as tillers of its soil.

The larger temples of the sun had convents filled with maidens, nearly all of Inca blood, selected by the high priests. In these convents, they were educated, and were employed in guarding the sacred fires, and in spinning, weaving, and doing other work for the imperial family. Though not priestesses, these virgins of the sun were required, under penalty of death, to preserve their chastity, and were guarded by eunuchs. They could never leave the convents unless to marry an emperor, or some Inca by imperial order, and no man save the emperor could lawfully enter the precincts of the convent. The great temple of the sun at Cuzco had fifteen hundred of these vestals.

6

Ecclesiastical festivals were numerous, and were celebrated with much pomp. Of these the most important, that of the summer solstice, required the participation of the emperor and most of the Incas at the temple of the sun in Cuzco. At dawn, they and a large concourse of people assembled in the great square, the high nobles being under canopies of feather-work supported by numerous attendants, to await the rising of the sun. So soon as his rays became visible on the tops of the buildings, the multitude shouted for joy, and the musicians greeted the beams with vocal and instrumental music. The emperor offered a libation of maize beer to the god of day as soon as he had appeared above the horizon, and all marched in procession to the temple of the sun, where llamas were sacrificed, and the entrails of one were inspected to obtain omens for the coming year; and then with heat from the sun's rays collected in a concave mirror, a fire was lighted and taken to the altars of all the sun temples in the city, to be maintained there until three days before the next solstice, when all were to be extinguished. In case the sun rose behind the clouds so that wood could not be kindled from his rays, the fire was made by friction. The blood of the sacrificed llamas was caught and mixed with meal into dough, which was baked promptly; and the loaves, broken by the emperor, were distributed to all the Incas, those present eating theirs in the temple, and those at a distance partaking of theirs as a solemn communion, soon after its receipt. With it communicants drank consecrated maize beer.

SEC. 193. *Quichuan Ethics.*—Morality had a prominent place in the Quichuan religion. The common salutations of the people were ethical maxims, such as, "Revere the truth," "Be industrious," and, "Respect property." All suffering was regarded as punishment for sin, which might be much diminished by repentance, confession, and absolution, but could not be entirely atoned in this life. The happiness or misery of the soul in the next world depended on its conduct while in the flesh.[1]

Among the companions of Pizarro was a certain Captain Lejesema, who, while among the first in a fight or a frolic, could also, when occasion required, look at life seriously. When the plunder taken in Cuzco was divided, it was the fortune of Lejesema to become the owner of the first prize, the image of the sun taken from the wall of the great temple. This was a large and heavy circular plate of solid gold. The distribution was made in the afternoon, and in the evening the victorious adventurers sat down to try their luck at cards. Before daylight many of them had lost everything, and among these was Lejesema. He could not keep his gold twenty-four hours. His conduct suggested the Spanish proverb, "Juega el sol antes que salga" —"He gambles away the sun before he has risen," that is, he wastes his opportunity before it arrives. When this Lejesema found himself on his death-bed, and looked back upon what he had done and helped to do, he regretted that he had contributed to establish on the ruins of the Quichuan Empire a much inferior social and political system. He left a will which is a very remarkable bit of testimony to the moral condition of the Quichuans. He says:[2] "Before beginning my will, I declare that for many years I have desired to inform his Catholic Majesty King Philip, our lord, knowing how true a Catholic and Christian he is, and how zealous in the cause of God, our Lord, for the purpose of easing my own mind, because I took much part in the discovery, conquest, and settlement of these kingdoms, when we took them from the Incas, who possessed the land and governed it as their own. I wish to inform his Catholic majesty that the said Incas governed in such a manner that in all the land there was not a thief, nor a criminal, nor an idler, nor an adulterous or evil woman. The men had their honest and profitable occupations. The forests, mines, pastures, and game, and all kinds of natural wealth, were governed and divided in such a manner that each one knew and occupied his property without any danger of molestation or lawsuit. The affairs of war, though extensive, did not interfere with traffic, or mechanical work, or agriculture. Everything, the smallest as well as the greatest, had its regular and exact order. The Incas and their officers were respected and obeyed by their subjects as very able and good rulers. I hope that his majesty may understand that I make this statement to ease my conscience for the sin of having taken part in corrupting, by our bad example, such moral people as the Quichuans were. The Indians, both rich and poor, never committed either excesses or crimes. When they left their houses, they never locked their doors."

SEC. 194. *Culture and Collapse.*—Although the Quichuans and the Aztecs were separated by a distance of less than fifteen hundred miles of communication by land and by coastwise navigation, yet neither people seems to have any knowledge of the other. Each had institutions and arts peculiar to itself. The cacao, the turkey, the calendar, the matrimonial equality of the two sexes, the hieroglyphics and independent judiciary in the Aztec Empire, were peculiar to it, as were the llama, the potato,

SEC. 194. CULTURE AND COLLAPSE. 85

the cocao, the quipus, and the paternal control of the people, in the Quichuan Empire. The llama and the potato would have been very beneficial to the people of the north, as would have been the turkey, the cacao, and the hieroglyphics to those of the south. Maize, tobacco, and manioc were common to both.

As it was said of the Aztecs, so it may be said of the Quichuans, that their traditions and the much higher development of their polity than of their industry, are evidences that immigrants from the Old World introduced certain institutions with which they had been familiar, or which had been suggested to them in their native land. It is highly improbable that the rulers of a nation which had recently commenced to produce bronze, and who had a small stock of it, should by their unaided wisdom have devised and enforced the Quichuan system of administration, by which the common people should be relieved from all care for their maintenance, and protected against the great evils of violence, crime, dissipation, idleness, pauperism, famine, and discord.

Wonderful were the constitution and rise of this empire; and its fall was not less marvelous. With a loyal population of 10,000,000, with a faithful army of 200,000 men, with a territory more mountainous and better suited for defense than that of any other large empire known to history, with a capital four hundred miles from the ocean, and 11,000 feet above its level, and behind a mountain ridge 15,000 feet high,—with such defenses we might suppose that the Quichuan Empire would have resisted a great invading army for many years, and that if conquered in its capital, the royal family and their adherents would have established and maintained themselves for generations in some portion of their numerous high mountain fastnesses. We know how the Persians, and Parthians, and Jews, and Gallic Celts, and Spanish Goths, when vanquished, fled into their mountains, and fought and fought again, century after century, and sometimes triumphed, and never yielded save to formidable armies after numerous well-contested campaigns.

But among the Quichuans we find no such strong national vitality. Whether because their subjection to an exceedingly paternal government had rendered them incompetent to manage their own affairs or not, the fact is that their empire was overthrown by one hundred and eighty men. This little force, with which Francisco Pizarro undertook his conquest and secured his most important successes, was not half so numerous as that of the Spaniards at whose head Hernando Cortes marched into the valley of Mexico; and besides this larger force of Spaniards, Cortes was accompanied by six thousand valiant Tlascalan allies, who were of immense service to him. The emperor Atahualpa, imagining that there was no danger from a petty band of white men, allowed them to advance unresisted and then paid a visit to them in camp. Pizarro immediately pounced on him and held him, the head of the empire, a prisoner. Instead of fighting to the death when the Spaniards attempted to seize him, he allowed himself to be taken alive, and thus gave his captors control not only of himself but of his subjects. The only source of all political and military power was afraid to use it, and in the confusion that followed, the empire of the Incas was overthrown forever.

This most pitiful collapse of what seemed to be a strong government and strong national feeling, was due partly to the peculiar position of Atahualpa. His father, the last Quichuan emperor who died in possession of the throne, instead of bequeathing his whole empire to his eldest son by an Inca wife, divided it, giving the larger and southern part to Huascar, his legitimate heir, and the northern division to Atahualpa, who was a younger and illegitimate son by a Quito woman of inferior blood. Between these two monarchs, war soon broke out, and Atahualpa conquered, captured, and dethroned Huascar. The victor, pretending that he was willing to replace Huascar on the throne, invited the Incas to meet for the purpose of consulting about a new division of the empire. They, trusting his word, assembled, and were then massacred. Thus the great majority of the only class familiar with the business of government were destroyed, and the people were left without leaders to whom they felt much attached.

SEC. 195. *Muyscas.*—North of the territory of the Quichuans was that of the Muyscas, or Chibchas, as they were also called. In most of its features, their culture was inferior to that of their southern neighbors, and we know less of it. They had no bronze, no llamas, and no quipus; but they had a better chronological system than that of the Quichuans.

CHAPTER XIII.
THE CHINESE.

SECTION 196. *China.*—We now pass to the study of another people, not less remarkable and original in many features of their culture than the Aztecs and Quichuans, and like them, long isolated from other nations. Although the silk and perhaps other products of China reached Greece in the age of Pericles, Europe does not seem to have felt any noteworthy stimulus from Chinese industry until after the time of Mohammed.

In many respects, China is the most remarkable of nations. It is remarkable for its great age and its vast population; for the permanence of its political institutions; for the preponderance of its civil over its military officials; for the wide spread of education among its people since a remote antiquity; for the large proportion of men devoted to study; for the rule of giving all the high offices to distinguished scholars; for the constitutional and pacific character of the government; for many valuable inventions and discoveries in remote centuries; and for the cessation of such improvements in modern times.

It is a paradoxical nation. Many of its institutions lack the features which seem to be essential parts of similar institutions elsewhere. It has a language without a grammar; words without parts of speech; writing without an alphabet; reading without spelling; type without a type foundry; paper without a paper mill; printing without a press; canals without locks; the mariners' compass without a compass-box or pivot; gunpowder without a gun; metallic money without gold or silver coin; laws without a word for liberty; poetry without meter; music without rhythm; love without a kiss, and religion without a god. As measured by the European standard of taste, the Chinese are perverse in many of their customs. With them white is the color of mourning and of gloom. They use white not black for shoe dressing. In speaking of persons, they mention the name of the family first, that of the individual last. Thus they would say not James Watt, but Watt James. With them the seat of honor is on the left. When friends meet, they shake not each the hand of the other, but each his own. They pay an agreeable compliment to a young man by calling him old. An affectionate son offers a stylish coffin to his aged father as an acceptable present for his birthday or the New Year's day. The men carry fans, play with kites, and wear embroidered petticoats; the women wear trousers and distort their feet not their ribs. They write in lines from top to bottom, not from side to side; they begin on the right not the left; they put their title at what is to us the back of the book, and there begin the numbering of the pages, and their foot-notes are at the top of the page.

The history of China goes back four thousand years. In that time it has undergone less change than any other nation within a thousand years. Egypt, the only other country which has approached China in the permanence of political institutions, disappeared from the map as an independent country two thousand years since.

Something of the great duration of the Chinese monarchy must be attributed to its situation. Along more than two thousand miles of its boundaries, it is protected against invasion by great deserts and high mountain ranges. The frontiers, where not guarded by such strong, natural barriers, are occupied by Siam and Eastern Siberia, which are or were neither rich enough to excite much cupidity, nor formidable enough to compel the maintenance of large armies for defense.

It is fortunate for China proper, as distinguished from the subject provinces, that it has been occupied since the beginning of its history by people having the same blood, tongue, faith, traditions, laws, and culture. Among them there were no such animosities of race or creed as in Europe, set Turk against Greek, Moor against Spaniard, Roman against Gaul, Teuton against Latin, Catholic against Protestant, Saxon against Celt, and Frenchman against Englishman and German. Although, in the course of their long career, they have had bitter experiences in foreign and domestic warfare, they have not been subjected to frequent incursions from abroad, nor to many rebellions at home, and they have been, relatively, the most peaceful of people.

If the maxim be true that those nations are happy whose annals are tiresome, then the Chinese should be counted among the happiest. Their history possesses very little interest. They have had no great military or political revolution. They have never had a republic, never a socialistic rebellion, never a great struggle for popular liberty, never a violent overturn of political or religious institutions, never a hereditary nobility, never extensive serfdom or slavery, never a dominant priesthood, never an inquisition. Twice they submitted to foreign conquerors; to the Mongols in the XIIIth, and to the Manchoos in the XVIIth century; but in permanent influence, on the country, these conquests were little more than mere changes of dynasty. The victors adopted the language, laws, religion, and manners of the vanquished.

Other notable events in the political history of the country are the beginning of official examinations as conditions for reaching high office in the XIIth century B. C.; the increase and consolidation of the imperial power in the IIIrd century B. C.; the establishment of the present system of examinations in the VIIth century A. D.; the recovery, by Tonquin, of its independence in the XVth; the beginning of direct maritime commerce with Europe by way of the Cape of Good Hope, in the XVIth; and the opening of the country to Europeans in the XIXth century.

The area of the country is 7,000,000 square miles, as great as that of the United States. It includes 1,000,000 square miles of moist, fertile soil under tillage, much more than there is in Europe. A long ocean frontage, numerous great rivers, excellent harbors, and the proximity of many islands to the coast, facilitate and stimulate fluviatile and maritime commerce. In the extreme heat of its summers and cold of its winters, it resembles the eastern slope of the United States, and these two regions are similar also in their positions on the western border of a great ocean; in the frequency and violence of their hurricanes; in the abundance of their magnificent rivers; in the wide area of their fertile soil; in the magnitude of their coal deposits, and in the possession of homogeneous populations. Among all the nations of the globe, China comes next to the United States in the abundant resources for agricultural, mining, and manufacturing industry; but there is a vast difference in the culture of the two peoples. One is the type of progress, the other of the stationary condition; one the nation of the future, the other of the past; one is and the other is not in harmony with the spirit of the age; one has and the other has not scholars and business men competent for the task before them.

As the people were laborious, skillful in agriculture, and relatively peaceful, they had become numerous in ancient times, but there is much doubt about their number. After comparing the conflicting figures of different censuses, I estimate the population of China in 1700 at 125,000,000, and in 1880 at 400,000,000.

SEC. 197. *Original Arts.*—We might presume that a populous and toilsome nation, peaceful in their domestic and foreign relations during many centuries, occupying a fertile soil in a temperate clime, would make many improvements in the useful arts. Such improvements have been made by the Chinese, but many of their inventions and discoveries belong to a remote time, though the date of their origin is no longer discoverable. They practiced distillation and silk-weaving twenty-seven centuries before these arts were known in Europe. As early as 1100 B. C. they coined bronze. Sugar was made before 600 B. C. In 100 B. C. they had canals constructed exclusively for navigation; the magnetic needle, pisciculture, artesian wells, natural gas fuel, petroleum lamps, paper and lacquerware. In 600 A. D. they had explosive powder, cannon, porcelain, spectacles, tea as a common beverage, and as early as 1150 A. D. they had invented movable type, cards, and paper money, and had discovered that inoculation was a protection against small-pox.[1] Before the date last mentioned, they had made some important invention or discovery for every century in a period of two thousand years; but since then not one. Why this cessation of their contributions to progress? Their productive originality ended about the time of the Mongol conquest, but that could not have been the cause, for it did not enslave the Chinese people, nor permanently reduce their number, nor impoverish them, nor destroy their national pride, nor materially change their institutions, nor divert their energies into new channels.

More remarkable than this arrest of their progress, in the useful arts, is the incompleteness of many of their industrial achievements, in which they took the first, usually the most difficult step, and then left to others the glory and the profit of the higher advance. It is wonderful that a populous and wealthy nation could coin bronze extensively for thirty centuries without ever coining gold and silver, while possessing those noble metals in considerable quantity and understanding their superior value. For many centuries, the magnetic needle was used in China by putting it on a small piece of wood, in a basin of water; but it had hardly become known to Europeans before their ingenuity poised it on a pivot, in a compass-box, under glass, and over a card divided into equal points, thus giving to the instrument a precision and a convenience previously unknown, and an applicability to many new purposes. In the hands of the Chinese, explosive powder was little more than a plaything, in fire-works, for centuries; in the hands of the Europeans, it led, within a few generations, to a rapid succession of important improvements in arms and the art of war. The Chinese invented sluices to connect the different levels of navigable canals, letting boats slide down not more than five or six feet or drawing them up by capstans. When the Italians, in the middle ages, began to construct navigable canals, they devised the canal lock, which hoists or lowers a heavily-laden boat as much as twenty feet, keeping it in level water. The failure of the Chinese to invent the canal lock cannot be attributed to a lack of experience; they have more and larger canals than Europe and have used them twice as many centuries. Their grand canal is six hundred miles long; for a considerable distance two hundred feet wide; in one considerable stretch, twenty feet above the level of the adjacent country; and in other places it passes through cuts sixty feet deep. They discovered inoculation, and for nine centuries before it was known in Western Europe, applied it extensively, generally putting some of the virus from a small-pox patient on cotton wool in the nostril of a child. The Europeans had scarcely learned this valuable contribution to the science of medicine, before they superseded it by the still more valuable process of vaccination. Natural gas and petroleum were found by artesian wells in China about the beginning of the Christian era, but no such important industries with these subterranean sources of light and heat were developed there as in the United States. After many centuries of experience with type, the Chinaman continued to cut them by hand. After many centuries of experience in printing, he never made a press. He invented cards, but never devised a good game with them. He invented the arch, but never applied it in such magnificent domes, vaults, or bridges as are to be found in many Aryan countries.

SEC. 198. *Houses, etc.*—The houses of the Chinese are mostly of wood, small, low, and simple, without elegance in their plan, construction, or furniture. There is no high artistic taste in any department of life. There is no appreciation of the relative values of size and color; no fine statuary, painting, or architecture. Their carvings have no accurate modeling; their paintings no perspective or fidelity in color to nature. Their house ornaments are fantastic, not tasteful.

The materials used in the dwellings of the poor are bamboo, wood, unburned brick, burned brick, and stone. Matting furnishes the material for many of the partitions. Roofs are of tiles or thatch. In the North, where the winters are severely cold, the people sleep on brick platforms or furnaces in which fires are kept.

The Chinese have never had a great architect, nor have they ever built a great palace, temple, castle, bridge, or tomb. There is a Chinese style of architecture, but it is curious rather than artistic, and finds its highest expression in the pagodas, which are ecclesiastical structures, and yet are useless for public worship, and not well adapted for sacerdotal residence.

Of these structures the most notable was the porcelain tower at Nanking, destroyed by the rebels in 1856. The body of the building was brick, with a facing of white, yellow, green, and red porcelain tiles. The shape was octagonal and the diameter on the ground forty feet, gradually decreasing to the top. The height was two hundred and sixty-one feet, with nine stories, at each of which was a projecting roof, every corner of which in every story had a bell. It was considered the most notable public building of the country, and though not remarkable for architectural beauty, had the merits of being original in its design, and striking in its appearance There are similar buildings in other Chinese cities, but while that of Nanking stood, it was considered superior to all its rivals. The most remarkable product of Chinese industry is the great wall of China, built in the IIIrd century B. C., to protect the Manchoorian frontier against invasion. Its length is fifteen hundred miles; and for long distances its height is from fifteen to thirty feet. The sides are stone; the inner mass is earth. Towers forty feet high, at intervals of a hundred yards, provide elevated stations of observation for watchmen and shelter to soldiers. This wall is not limited to the lowland; it crosses many hills, and in one place reaches an elevation of five thousand feet above the sea.

Their cities are large but not beautiful. Most of the streets are very narrow; and they are neither well paved nor clean. Everything that can enrich the soil is saved and transported through the streets in methods that are often very offensive to the eye and nose of the European.

SEC. 199. *Different Arts.*—Nearly all the land fit for tillage is used to produce food for man. None is reserved for pasture, and little for roads or purposes of ornament. There are no extensive public or private parks, no beautiful gardens about the homes of the poor or the rich. Williams estimates that the area cultivated is 1,000,000 square miles, or about two acres for each inhabitant.[1] The hills are terraced, and much land is irrigated by buckets or by pumps driven by hand.

China has few herds. Sheep, goats, cows, and horses are rare. Animal food is not abundant and consists mainly of fish, fowls, and pigs. Milk, butter, and cheese are unknown to the people; and so are woolen garments. No space is cultivated in grass. There are no coaches or heavy four-wheeled wagons. Freight is transported in boats, on the shoulders of men, in wheelbarrows, and sometimes in carts drawn by asses. The roads are narrow, and never well paved.

The porcelain of China is unsurpassed in its excellence as an industrial production, but in the features of form and color it is surpassed by that of various European nations. The junks are clumsy in appearance but cheap in cost and good in sailing qualities. The aggregate tonnage of the water craft is supposed to be nearly equal to that of any other nation, and a large number of the people make their home in boats that never venture out to sea. It is said that there have been 80,000 boats at one time on the waters near Canton. The largest Chinese junks measure two thousand tons. The Chinese are expert fishermen with the hook and net; and they make much use of the cormorant, which catches fish for them, and, if not well trained, is kept from swallowing its game by a ring on its throat.

Many branches of Chinese industry are not highly developed. Most of the land transportation and loosening of the soil for cultivation is done by human muscle. Beasts of burden and draught, and mills driven by water and steam, were unknown until within recent years. There is no large manufacturing establishment, no complex machinery, no instrument of high precision of Chinese manufacture, no application of superior chemical knowledge to industrial uses.

SEC. 200. *Manners.*—In no other country is there so much social equality as in China. There is no hereditary nobility save that in the family of Confucius; there is no hereditary office save that of emperor. Great wealth and great poverty are extremely rare. Habits of industry are almost universal, and mendicants and loungers relatively few. The necessaries of life are cheap;

and the style of living, with rare exception, simple among the rich and extremely plain among the poor. The Chinese have no magnificent private residences, no spacious parks, no beautiful drives, no elegant wagons, no horses bred with care for carriage or saddle, no luxurious hotel, nor much-frequented pleasure resort on mountain-top or sea-shore, no public gymnastic exercises, no games like cricket or base-ball, no dancing parties for the pleasure of the participants, no elegant galleries of painting or sculpture. In its general features, the life of the Chinese is bare, unpoetical, inelegant, and coarsely utilitarian. It is a continuous strain for the mere necessaries of existence, including an education narrow in its aims and barren in its results.

The Chinese are polite. In all grades of society, children are reared strictly and instructed carefully in their manners. Marked respect is exacted from ignorance to learning, from youth to age, from private to public station, and from child to parent. An elaborate code, under governmental supervision, prescribes the forms with which officials must be approached, and the manner in which they must dress and keep their dwellings and offices. The demeanor of men towards one another is much influenced by rank, which, among scholars and officials, is indicated by dress or cap. They speak of themselves in terms of exaggerated depreciation. A man addressing an equal calls him "my noble master," and calls himself "your stupid slave;" he calls his friend's son "worthy young gentleman," and his own son "little bug;" he calls his friend's wife "the honorable lady," and his own wife "the mean one of the inner apartments." With all their politeness, they have no such phrases as "good-morning," "good-night," and "how do you do?"

At meeting they say "hail! hail!" at parting, "I pray you;" and when inquiring in general terms of a friend about his health, they ask, "Have you eaten rice?"

To many Europeans the ceremonious politeness of all classes of Chinamen, even the poorest, to one another, seems unreasonable and burdensome in its numerous and punctilious observances. Some travelers, however, find that in a comparison between the manners of the Chinese and the European poor the latter appear to a decided disadvantage.[1] Another observer thinks that the servility of the poor in China and the arrogance of the powerful are disgusting to the man who has a proper respect for the dignity of humanity.[2]

In China there are five social ranks based on occupation. First and most honorable are scholars; second, tillers of the soil; third, manufacturers; fourth, merchants; and fifth, the dishonorable, including slaves, jailers, executioners, actors, criminals, and their sons and grandsons. Dishonorable persons cannot be admitted into the class of scholars.

The Chinese show much aptitude for the combination and organization of their forces. They have many associations for business and charitable purposes. They have asylums for lepers, for the blind, for old men, for the sick, for orphans, and for foundlings; they have vaccine dispensaries, stations for the rescue of drowning persons, and soup kitchens for the indigent. Girl children are not unfrequently exposed and left to die by parents who do not feel able to support them, or they are sold as slaves.

The amusements of the people are few and simple. They include acrobatic, juggling, and dramatic performances, boat-races, wrestling-matches, kite-flying, and playing shuttlecock, which last is struck not with a bat, or the hand, but with the foot. There is no gladiatorial fight, boxing-match, bull-fight, dog-fight, or bull or bear-baiting, no dancing-party, no gathering of both sexes for cards, no church fairs, no exhibitions of agricultural or manufactured products, no large picnics or excursions of both sexes. There is no weekly or monthly day of rest; and including those at the new year, there are not a dozen holidays in the twelve-month.

Fermented and distilled liquors, though known to the Chinese since a remote antiquity, have never been used by them extensively, and are not sold in dram-shops. The favorite narcotic of the Chinese is opium, which stupefies its consumer without taking him through a noisy or quarrelsome condition. It is the drug of a peaceful people.[3]

SEC. 201. *Matrimony.*—The Chinese are divided into about a hundred exogamous masculine clans, which average 4,000,000 members each, each clan having its distinctive name, which is part of the name of all its clansmen. Some of these clans extend through many provinces, and include persons who must go back at least thirty or forty generations to find a common ancestor. But no matter how remote the relationship, if they have the same clan name, which is known to all acquaintances, they cannot intermarry. There are large villages in which all the inhabitants are fellow-clansmen, and the men must go to other villages for wives. In the smaller villages the clan relationship is recognized as an intimate bond of social union and obligation, and it often influences the election of the local officials, the administration of justice, and the support of persons disabled by age or sickness.

Polygyny is permitted by law, without legal limit to the number of wives, but the first or main wife has a position much superior in social honor and legal rights to the others. The minor wives, by some writers called concubines, can be sold at any time; the main wife cannot be sold or divorced when she is in mourning for either parent, nor when she has no living parent to receive her, nor when her husband has grown rich after marrying her. Under other circumstances, and especially among the poor, whose wives are obtained by purchase, the husband can sell or divorce his wife at pleasure, and without the intervention of any court. It is discreditable to take many minor wives, or to take one while the first wife has a son living; but the rich men usually have several wives. The great majority of men have but one wife, and remain faithful to her through life. Public opinion demands that every man should marry. Common maxims say that "there are three great acts of disregard to parents, and of these the chief is to die without progeny," and that "without sons a man lives without satisfaction and dies without honor."[1] Parents, especially fathers, are treated with great deference by children, as is the rule in all countries where ancestral spirits are worshiped. Women are considered greatly inferior to men in social dignity and rights, but the mother is honored by her sons and daughters-in-law. Girls are bred in seclusion and ignorance, and must accept the husband selected for them by their father.

The country is overcrowded with people, and infanticide is frequent.[2] The victims are usually girls. The law does not interfere, partly because the authority of the father over his infants is considered supreme, and partly because the excess of population is within the observation of everybody. Every family must keep a book with a record of all marriages, births, deaths, wills, and judgments of family councils, which are called together on important occasions.[3] Each family occupies a separate house.

Sec. 202. *Music, etc.*—The music of China is a ludicrous combination of squall and racket. It is the harmony of bedlam. Dr. Johnson defines music as the least objectionable kind of noise, but he had never heard a Celestial orchestra. In the instrumentation of the Chinese, the predominant tones are those of a shrill trumpet, a gong, a cymbal, and a treble violin string. The effect of their song is almost equally strange; the women sing between squealing and screaming; the men without tenor or bass. Their airs are all in the minor key, and, save the cymbal and drum, all their musical instruments are, in pattern and tone, unlike those of Aryan countries. Although at their open ports the Chinese have been familiar with European music for centuries, they have made no attempt to learn its principles. And yet they consider themselves a musical people. They frequently hear semi-operatic pieces on their public stage, and their ears are trained from infancy in the different tones of their speech. They have a method of writing music, but, as compared with the European system, it is extremely defective on several important points.

There are no regular beats in Chinese airs; and many classes of European tunes which depend largely on their time, are unknown in China.

In their medicine, the Chinese are rude. They have no precise knowledge of zoölogy, anatomy, physiology, chemistry, or optics, and have contributed nothing of importance save inoculation to the art of healing disease.

One of their reputable medical treatises says: "If a man be restless and hysterical, when he wishes to sleep, and it is requisite to put him to rest, let the ashes of a skull be mingled with water and given to him, and let him have a skull for a pillow, and it will cure him."[2] Another sample of Chinese medical science is given thus: "To eat the flesh of a black horse and not drink wine with it will surely produce death. The heart of a white horse, or that of a hog, cow, or hen, when dried and rasped into spirit, and so taken, cures forgetfulness. If the patient hears one thing he knows ten."[3] Equally learned is the zoölogical information that the bat lives to a great age, because "it has the habit of swallowing its breath," and that "it flies with its head downwards because its brain is heavy."[4] The flying squirrel is described as "the only bird that suckles its young while it flies."[5]

In astronomy and mathematics the Chinese have never reached eminence. They do not yet use the Hindoo numerals in mercantile houses, but depend on the abacus, or counting-board, with which they add, subtract, multiply, and divide rapidly and accurately.[6] Their astronomical observations go back to a remote date. Their twenty-eight constellations of the zodiac commence with Spica in our own constellation of the Virgin, and if, as is supposed, their zodiac was adopted when the sun was in their first constellation in the spring, then they must have named their stars seventeen thousand years ago.[7]

SEC. 203. *Speech.*—In general character the Chinese tongue is the simplest and most primitive of languages. Every word is a single syllable, as if it had its origin before men learned the art of combining sounds in polysyllables. The words, unlike those of European languages, show no signs of having been formed from older elements. In English, "John's" is a consolidation of "John his," and "loved" of "love did," and "daisy" of "day's eye." Such consolidations abound in all the Aryan tongues. They furnished the materials for our conjugations and declensions. With their art we can trace the history of our modern English words through the medieval English, Saxon, French, and Latin to an intimate relationship with the Sanscrit and Zend tongues spoken three thousand years ago or more in Hindostan and Persia. But the Chinese words have no history. They show no signs of growth. Each is the same now as when it was first accepted as the representative of an idea.

On account of the brevity of the words, their number is very small, being about four hundred and fifty; and one word must have many meanings, which are distinguished by different tones or by the addition of explanatory words. Thus a word like pare, would be followed by the word cut, member, or fruit, to distinguish the kind of pare meant in the special case. Four notes of the gamut are used in common speech, and the same word may have four different meanings according to the key in which it is spoken. By different intonations the four hundred and fifty fundamental words are increased to about twelve hundred and fifty distinct sounds.[1] It is often easier for the Chinaman to distinguish the same word pronounced in two different keys than different words in the same key; easier to distinguish ming flat, from ming sharp, than ming from meng in the same key.[2]

SEC. 204. *Writing.*—The methods of writing and pronouncing have not varied materially in more than two thousand years. Poems composed as early as 500 B. C. are read now in the characters and rhymes with which they were originally written.[1]

The Chinese write with hieroglyphics, each of which means a word or the idea that would be expressed in English by several words. These hieroglyphics, 24,000 in number, were originally pictures, but in many centuries of rapid writing, have been so changed that most of them have lost all resemblance to the original designs.

The task of fixing such a multitude of arbitrary figures in the memory is an immense difficulty in the acquisition of Chinese scholarship; it is the work of half an average human life. On the other hand, a few hieroglyphics can be learned with comparatively little effort, and as a consequence, nearly all the poor men in China can read the hieroglyphics relating to their own occupations, and can write their names. As means of obtaining a high education and of recording general ideas for public and private purposes, two dozen alphabetic signs are vastly superior to two thousand dozen hieroglyphics. Only two thousand hieroglyphics are used in the penal code; and a knowledge of three thousand is considered sufficient for the purposes of persons not professional students.[2]

The Chinese hieroglyphics are divided by Williams into six classes.[3] The first class consists of imitative symbols or pictures showing the articles plainly. The second class is that of suggestive symbols, such as the sun above the horizon (indicated by a line) for morning; and something in the mouth (a dot in a square) for sweetness. The third class is one of combined ideas, as woman and broom for wife; dog and mouth for bark; and two trees for forest. The fourth class, including some that might come in the second, comprises inverted significations, as a hand turned to the right for right, and a hand turned to the left for left. The fifth class is that of uniting-sound symbols, using the character of one thing to mean something different in nature but the same in name. The sixth and last class is that of figurative symbols such as the hieroglyphic of home to mean mother, and of heart to mean mind or sentiment.

For conciseness and force of expression, hieroglyphics have some advantages over alphabet writing. Dr. Morrison tells us that the Chinese sentence often darts upon the mind with a vivid flash, a force, and a beauty of which alphabetic language is incapable.[4]

All schools are private institutions. The examiners are officials of the government, the teachers are not. There is no state fund for education, no state department of instruction, no compulsory attendance in any educational institution. In proportion to their means the people are very liberal in paying teachers for their boys; and there are schools and seminaries for girls, but the women generally are allowed to grow up in ignorance, perhaps as more consonant with woman's loveliness, and certainly as more conducive to her submissiveness. The less she knows, the more faith she has in her husband, and often she is the only person who has any faith in him, in China as well as elsewhere.

The Chinese "first teach children a few of the principal characters (as the names of the chief objects in nature or art) exactly as we do the letters, by rude pictures, having the characters attached. Then follows the Santse-king, or 'trimetrical classic,' being a summary of infant erudition, conveyed in chiming lines of three words or feet. They soon after proceed to the 'Four Books,' which contain the doctrines of Confucius, and which, with the five classics subsequently added, are in fact the Chinese Scriptures. The Four Books they learn by heart entirely, and the whole business of the literary class afterward is to comment on them or compose essays on their texts. Writing is taught by tracing the characters, with the hair pencil, on transparent paper placed over the copy, and they commence with very large characters."[5] On account of the multitude of phonograms to be learned, a Chinaman cannot read better at twenty-five than an English boy at ten or an Italian boy at eight.

Since ancient times every provincial capital has its circulating library, and its teachers for children and advanced scholars. In Euraryan countries one of the main purposes of the educational system is to make additions to the stock of knowledge, but not so in China, where the only object generally kept in view is to impart the knowledge already possessed to as large a portion as possible of the rising generation.[6]

Although the writing of the Chinese demands a vast amount of time for mastery, the system is one that must have required the labor of many men for many centuries to bring it into the completeness which it had reached as early as the VIIth century B. C. An eminent scholar has expressed the opinion that it "is one of the most extraordinary monuments of patient industry and refined analytic skill that record the labors of man."[7] Unfortunately for the Chinese, their language is one which will perhaps never be written otherwise than it is at present. Felton says: "The sounds of their words are indistinctly articulated; consonant, vowel, and nasal, run into the pronunciation so curiously that it is very difficult to represent them by alphabetic characters."[8] When it becomes clear to the Chinese people that they must use the alphabet, they may find that the easiest method of doing so will be to adopt the English tongue first.

The Chinese have their poetry, but without any metrical effect. "The verses contain a particular number of words and set pauses in each line, but there is nothing like an interchange of long and short sounds. Among the Greeks, the fall of the smith's hammer, the stroke of the oar, and the tread of the soldier in armor, suggested some poetic measure, and their music exhibits a world of curious meters. But nothing of the sort can be heard in China, amid all the sounds and noises that salute the ear in a noisy country."*

SEC. 205. *Imperial Power.*—The government is an aristocracy of scholars, under an unwritten constitution, which is understood and reverenced by the people, observed by the officials, and accepted submissively by the monarchs. Alone among nations with long careers, it has never had a large class of serfs or slaves. Alone among modern nations, it has preserved its constitution unchanged through many centuries. In the security of life and property no barbarous nation in the Old World has equaled China. Until within the last three centuries, it had the only permanent government without a large hereditary privileged class.

The authority of the emperor is limited by many constitutional provisions, among which the most important are, first, that the local affairs of the communes shall be managed exclusively by officers elected by the people; second, that all the higher provincial and imperial officers shall be taken from the scholars who have succeeded in passing the competitive examinations; and third, that no office save that of emperor shall be held by a hereditary title. His power is further limited by public opinion formed in the schools and communicated to him in his lessons as a boy. He is taught in the words of Confucius, that the ruler is responsible to the people for the proper performance of his duties; and in the words of Mencius, that the people are the most important element in the country, and the ruler the least important; and that the people have the right to depose and slay a tyrant.[1] The following maxims are found in the sacred books: "The emperor and the subject who break the law are alike to blame." "He who subdues by force is a tyrant; he who prevails by kindness is a king." "The hearts of the people speak the commands of Heaven." "An invader will find allies in a country oppressed." "The sovereign who gains his subjects' hearts strengthens his throne." "The bow may crack and the people may revolt."[2]

The chief executive officer of every commune, department and province, is responsible for the maintenance of order in his jurisdiction, and in like manner the emperor is responsible to the people and to Heaven for the prosperity of the empire. In 1832 a great drought afflicted China, and the emperor, considering the general misery a punishment for his sins, presented a written penitential memorial in the temple of heaven, and published it in the official gazette. He said: "The sole cause is the daily deeper atrocity of my sins; but little sincerity, and little devotion. Hence I have been unable to move Heaven's heart and bring down abundant blessings. . . I ask myself whether . . . in raising mausolea and laying out gardens, I have distressed the people and wasted property. Whether in the appointment of officers I have failed to obtain fit persons, and thereby the acts of government have been petty and vexatious to the people. Whether punishments have been unjustly inflicted or not. Whether the oppressed have found no means of appeal. . . . Whether or not the magistrates have insulted the people and refused to listen to their affairs. . . . Prostrate, I beg imperial Heaven to pardon my ignorance and stupidity and to grant me self-renovation; for myriads of innocent people are involved by me, a single man."[3]

The imperial power is exercised through a cabinet consisting of a collection of councils or boards, each having control of a department of the administration. The cabinet has supreme power over legislative, executive, and military affairs.

Once in three years a report is made upon the merits and demerits of all the prominent civil officials of the government, and upon the information there given, the emperor issues an edict, with commendations and condemnations, promotions, degradations, retirements, and expulsions.[4] In many respects the high officials are held to a strict responsibility, and he who provokes his subjects to open rebellion subjects himself to capital punishment.[5]

SEC. 206. *Examinations.*—Literary competition is the only road to political honor. All the high offices of the government, under the emperor, are given to men who pass with success through literary examinations under government inspectors. There are three successive examinations; first and lowest, that for the grade of bachelor, held every year in each of the one thousand five hundred and eighteen districts of the empire; second, that held every third year in each of the eighteen provincial capitals for the grade of master; and third, that held once in three years in Peking, for the grade of doctor. The competition for the master's diploma is open to bachelors only; that for the doctor's diploma, to masters only. Failure in an examination does not disqualify for another trial. Many of the applicants are middle-aged men who have failed repeatedly. In the list of ninety-nine graduates at a provincial examination, Dr. Martin found that sixteen of the new masters were more than forty years of age, one was sixty-two, and one eighty-three. Not unfrequently father and son are found competing for the same degree. The total number of bachelors for the empire may be 14,000 annually, selected from 100,000 competitors; of masters, twelve hundred, and of doctors three hundred at the triennial examinations; of masters four hundred, and of doctors one hundred for each year. Success in the district examination is considered a great triumph for the individual, and a great honor to his family. The bachelor's diploma puts the man on the road to power and wealth, and entitles him to wear a cap indicating his membership in the first social rank, that of scholars, and protecting him forever against corporal punishment or torture, which may be inflicted on all persons of inferior rank, even on the wealthiest merchants. It is estimated that the number of competitors for the grade of bachelor every year is 2,000,000 on the average, a much larger proportion of the population than undertake collegiate studies in Europe. "When the announcement of the successful candidates [for masters] is published," says Medhurst, "the multitude rush forward to gain the intelligence, and handbills are printed and circulated far and wide, not only for the information of the candidates themselves but their parents and kindred also, who receive titles and honors in common with their favored relations. Presents are then made to the triumphant scholars, and splendid apparel is prepared for them, so that they soon become rich and great. To-day they are dwelling in an humble cottage, and to-morrow they are introduced to the palaces of the great, riding in sedans or on horseback, and everywhere received with the greatest honors."[1]

The doctors, immediately after receiving their diplomas, are invited to another examination in the imperial palace, where a fourth degree, that of the Hanlin doctorate, is conferred on about twenty of their number. This diploma entitles its holder to membership in the Hanlin College, the members of which are attached to the imperial court in various honorable positions, including those of historian and poet, or they are sent to the provinces as managers of the examinations for the degree of master.

The branches in which the examinations are held are the jurisprudence, history, and statistics of China, and the writings of Confucius. This list of studies excludes all the science, European history, literature, and engineering taught in the higher educational institutions of Christendom. The scholarship of the Chinese has a scanty range of instruction and suggestion; like their speech and writing, it is a remnant of remote antiquity; it has been preserved several thousand years after it should have made room for something better. Mathematics, astronomy, and geology learned from Europe, are required in examinations for a few offices demanding scientific knowledge, but these studies have no place in the general scheme of education, and are of no service in attaining high political position.

Notwithstanding the serious defects in the course of instruction, the rule of making study the only road to high political power and social honor, has ever had an excellent influence on the people. On the one hand, it has inspired them with a fondness for books, and given them a preference for the kindly sentiments associated with literary tastes; on the other hand, it has made them averse to arbitrary power, class privilege, and war. A nation which selects its doctors of learning with so much care as does China, and then reserves for them all its high political positions, save that of emperor, must have some decided merits in its government.

The beneficent influence of making education the chief road to honor, power, and wealth, has attracted the attention and obtained the commendation of many European observers. Sir George Stanton says: "One of the most remarkable national peculiarities of the Chinese is their extraordinary addiction to letters, the general prevalence of literary habits among the middling and higher orders, and the very honorable preëminence which from the most remote period has been universally conceded to that class which is exclusively devoted to literary pursuits."[2]

Dr. Martin remarks that "in the genuine democracy of offering the inspiration of a fair opportunity, China stands unapproached among the nations of the earth;"[3] and Williams[4] says it is "the only pagan nation with democratic habits under a despotic theory of government." According to Davis,[5] the proportion of the community exclusively devoted to letters is much greater than in any other country, amounting from twenty to thirty per cent among the men.

SEC. 207. *Local Administration.*—The empire is divided into provinces under provincial governors; these into departments; these into communes; these into centuriate districts of one hundred families; and these into minor divisions of ten families. The least division is under a decurion, who must know the manner in which all his subjects live, and must expose and prosecute their crimes, or become responsible for them. The centurion is responsible for his subject decurions; and thus there is a continuous chain of responsibility, making a police system said to be unequaled in its efficiency.[1]

Each province has a governor clothed with extensive powers. The leading provinces are under the government of viceroys, each of whom levies his own taxes, maintains his own army and navy, and has a final court of appeal for suits arising under his jurisdiction.[2] He must not be a native of his province, nor marry or own land in it, nor have a son or brother holding office under him, nor must he continue to be governor in one province for more than three years. While he is in office an inspector from Peking examines his administration and makes a written report on his official conduct. At the close of his term, the governor must make a written report on the official conduct of his subordinates. These reports are always printed, and, being often very plain in their denunciations of misconduct and incapacity, have much influence on the careers of public men. The governor who acts oppressively exposes himself to popular petitions for his removal, and to denunciations in public meetings. To such expressions of popular indignation, he must offer no resistance. An attempt by him to break up such a meeting or to punish the leaders in it might prove more dangerous to him than to any other person. Popularity is a great aid, and the want of it a great obstacle, to promotion.

With the aid of "strict surveillance and mutual responsibility among all classes" the government succeeds in giving passable satisfaction to most of the people. The

poor stand in great fear of the government, and so indeed
do many of the rich."⁴ The inter-marriage of the Manchoos with the Chinese is forbidden, and the two nationalities are used to make a division of power, the former
holding the military and the latter the political offices;
and many judicious provisions serve to check the ambition
of those officials who might like to establish independent
governments.⁵

The salaries of office are in most cases insufficient, and
it is expected that the officer, if not wealthy before his
appointment, must exact unlawful tribute. The private
citizen involved in any governmental business usually
approaches the person in charge of it with a present;
and the men in the lower offices frequently receive messages from their superiors that on a certain day gifts
will be acceptable.⁶ In such cases there is an implied
promise that the superior will, if possible, protect his liberal subordinate against punishment for corruption.
Williams tells us that the officials and the people of China
are bad almost beyond belief; and yet he assures us that
the governmental business of the provinces is administered admirably. Common rumor says that the lawful
salary is not more than one-tenth of the average income
of the high offices.⁷

A censor speaking of the police says: " They no sooner
get a warrant to bring up witnesses than they assail both
plaintiff and defendant for money to pay their expenses,
from the amount of ten taels [dollars] to several scores.
Then the clerks must have double what the runners get;
if their demands be not satisfied they contrive every
species of annoyance."⁸ This statement becomes probable when our attention is called to the fact that the
numerous military, police and servants, connected with

many of the offices have no regular salary, and some of them are dependent for support on what they must receive as gifts or bribes.

Corrupt as the administration is unquestionably in many of its features, the mass of the people are safe in their person and property. Davis says the greatness and prosperity of the empire rests on the impartial distribution of the offices;[9] and he quotes a similar opinion from Milne. Staunton thinks that repeated acts of flagrant injustice do not escape with impunity, and on this point Williams seems to agree with him.[10]

Much care is taken to inform the people about their political rights and duties. Instructive discourses are read once a month in public to the inhabitants of every village and ward. The penal code is printed in cheap form for general circulation, and is composed in simple language, so that its meaning shall be clearly understood. Sir George Staunton, who translated it into English, said of it: "The most remarkable thing in this code is its great reasonableness, clearness, and consistency, the business-like brevity and directness of the various provisions, and the plainness and moderation of the language."[11]

The government has made a practice of selling admission into the rank of bachelor, with the right of wearing the cap indicative of the rank and all its privileges except that of competing for the diploma of master. Some inferior offices have also been sold, but these sales seem to amount to but little relatively.

SEC. 208. *Person and Property.*—There are no explicit legal guarantees of the rights of person or property. As already stated, the language has no word for liberty.[1] No habeas-corpus process or similar legal proceeding provides for the release of persons imprisoned illegally. No section in the code protects witnesses or persons accused of crime against torture, which they often suffer, though it is not among the punishments inflicted on criminals after conviction. The judicial proceedings are, in many cases, harsh and the penalties of crime cruel, but on the other hand the trials are prompt; the witnesses are not worried by frequent delays and new trials; and the accused and their friends are not plundered to their last dollar by criminal lawyers.

Chinese law permits a peculiar system of bondage to which the term slavery cannot be applied without the risk of conveying false impressions. This bondage has its origin in a sale by the parents, or in a judicial sentence for crime. The parents have power to sell their children, but very rarely do so, unless under the compulsion of deep poverty, and then the children sold are mostly girls under ten years of age. The most common motive for purchase is the desire to get domestic servants; a less common motive is the wish of a wealthy man to have a concubine or subordinate wife. If the bond-girl becomes a servant, the master must provide her, before she reaches the age of twenty-five, with a husband, who, from that time forward, has complete control of her. Bondage never passes by inheritance from the mother to her children. It is different with the bondmen. His sons and his grandsons, not his great grandsons, nor his daughters, nor his granddaughters, are in bondage. With her consent, the husband may sell his wife to be the wife of another man, but she does not enter into bondage. The male slave, when thirty years of age, is entitled to a wife, and it is the duty of the master to provide one for him. The male slaves are very few; female slaves are common in the families of the wealthy, ten or twenty being sometimes found in a house. There is no serfdom in China.

Taxes are light and uniform. The land outside of the towns and cities is held in fee-simple by the tiller of the soil, in small tracts. Most of the owners are individuals, some few are villages and clans. There is no very large estate, no entail, no primogeniture, no influence to make any notable change in the tenure or distribution of land. The law of inheritance gives a double portion to the eldest son, and the remainder is equally divided between the other sons; and the father often bequeaths his estate to the eldest son in trust for the equal benefit of all the sons.[2] The emperor can confiscate private property, but never does so unless under urgent and exceptional circumstances, and then he allows no compensation to the sufferers. Nominally he is the owner of all land, but the possessory title of the people is equivalent to fee-simple, subject to the sovereign's right to confiscate without indemnity.

Complaints and responses by litigants must be in writing; but there is no profession of the law, and the judge, in trying a case, listens only to the parties directly interested, and then to witnesses. Evidence is taken without oaths. Cases are never decided by ordeal, nor is official action ever determined by auguries or other appeals to supernatural power.

SEC. 209. *Confucius.*—Three forms of religion prevail extensively in China, Confucianism, Taoism, and Buddhism. The last is of Hindoo origin, and an account of it will be given in another chapter. Taoism has neither well-defined creed, nor a well-educated or well-organized clergy, nor any notable influence on the government or among the educated classes. Its priests devote themselves to ceremonial services demanded by the ignorant and superstitious, and thus what may be called the religion of Taoism is maintained as a mere matter of form. The Chinese Buddhists, Confucians, and Taoists have very little ecclesiastical animosity. They say, "Religions are many, reason is one; we are all brothers."

Confucianism, peculiarly Chinese in its character, was taught, not as an original doctrine but as a compilation of the wisdom of many antecedent centuries, by Confucius, who lived from 551 to 479 B. C. It is the faith of the scholars, and of the imperial government. Though not the religion of the majority of the Chinese people, it may be called the distinctive religion of China. Its main doctrines are that you must be virtuous; that you must worship the spirits of your ancestors; and that you must not bother yourself about any other divine existence or about a future life. Virtue, as understood by Confucius, includes every feeling that contributes to excellence as a relative, a friend, a neighbor, a citizen, or a fellow-man. He laid down the golden rule in a negative form by saying, "Do not to others what you do not wish done to yourself." He preferred virtue to life. He said, "I love life and I love justice, but if I cannot have both, I would give up life." He thus expressed his preference of virtue to popular applause: "I have the fidelity of a dog, and am sometimes treated like one. But what matters the ingratitude of men. They cannot hinder me from doing good. If my teaching be disregarded, I still have the consolation of knowing that I have done my duty." He asserted that the satisfaction of doing right, and the return which it generally obtains from men, are in themselves sufficient rewards for virtue. He advised his pupils to be virtuous for virtue's sake; and he defined universal virtue as comprising justice, benevolence, and constancy. In his opinion faithfulness and sincerity deserved to be considered as of primary importance for a well-regulated society. He taught that wealth and office are not requisite to the highest happiness, and that it was important that the people should not be blinded by their glitter. One of his sayings was that "to recognize that poverty comes by the ordinance of heaven . . . and in the face of difficulty not to fear, is the valor of the sage."[1]

To Confucius any kind of success obtained by the aid of injustice was detestable, and honesty was admirable, no matter what might be the fate of its devotee. He said, "The general of a large army may be defeated, but you cannot defeat the mind of a peasant determined to do right." In his opinion, death itself might become a triumph to a poor and friendless man if inflicted on him because he insisted on doing his duty. He would have us conduct this life as if it were certainly the only one, as if no late repentance could wipe out early wrong, as if mean selfishness would surely be punished by our contempt of ourselves, and by the contempt and neglect of our neighbors, and as if our constant regard for the welfare of others would entitle us to the esteem of the community, and would secure to us, from most of our acquaintances, responsive kindness. Confucius did not know how to enjoy life without contributing to the happiness of others, nor did he attach much value to mere official precept without example. He wanted virtue to begin at home, and in the highest circles. He said: "It is not possible for a man to teach others who cannot teach his own family. Therefore a ruler, without going beyond his family, completes the lessons for the state.

SEC. 210. NO SUPERNATURALISM.

. . . From the loving example of one family the whole state becomes loving; and from its courtesies, the whole state becomes courteous."[2]

He found within himself a predominant impulse toward the right, and he recognized it in others. According to him, "all men have compassionate souls; all have hearts ashamed of vice." He had a high idea of human dignity; he wanted his pupils to respect their own consciences; to constantly aspire to live as superior men; the character which he constantly held up before his pupils as the ideal which they should strive to approach even if they should despair of attainment.

SEC. 210. *No Supernaturalism.*—He rejected the idea that a belief in rewards and punishments hereafter is necessary as a sanction to social order here. Finding no satisfactory proof of the constitution or even of the existence of a supernatural world, he taught his followers to take no account in their actions of any considerations save those of a natural character. He protested against the acceptance of baseless fancies and hereditary superstitions unproved save by vulgar traditions. The essence of knowledge as he defines it, is to apply it when you have it, and when you have it not, to confess your ignorance. When he was asked about the immortality of the soul, he replied, "I do not know life, and how should I know death?" When asked where the souls of the ancestors are, he replied: "They have gone from the earth. Think of this and you will know what sorrow is." When asked whether ancestors should be worshiped, he said: "It is not proper for me to reply explicitly to this question. If I should say that the ancestors are grateful for the honors paid them; if I should say that they see and hear and know what passes among the living, then pious people, full of filial devotion, might neglect their own lives for the purpose of devoting themselves exclusively to the dead, and of serving them in the next world. If, on the other hand, I should say that the dead know nothing of what the living do, then children might neglect their duties to their parents, withdraw themselves into their own selfishness, and tear the holy bands which bind one generation to another. Continue, therefore, to pay the customary honors to your ancestors; act as if they were witnesses of all that you do; and seek not to know more of a future life." [1]

To a pupil who asked whether the human mind continues to have a conscious existence after death, he replied, "You need not know now whether it has or not; if it has, you will learn the fact at the proper time." He did not object explicitly to the worship of ancestors; perhaps his reasons for silence on that point were that his general teaching covered the ground, and that it was useless to waste his time in fighting a custom universally accepted in his time, merely because it had been universally accepted in previous times.

In China, as elsewhere, superstition is the associate of ignorance; and there, as in other barbarous countries, the telling of fortunes, interpretation of omens, and performance of exorcisms, are sources of profit to pretenders, who, in good or bad faith, claim to possess divine commissions. In reference to such persons Confucius said: "The wise man does not fear the omens, and while performing his duties, he knows how to protect himself against evil. To abstain from wrong-doing, and to live virtuously, are the best omens for the people and for the prince who should be as a father to them. . . .

Good or bad government is a surer sign of the happiness or misery of the people than the most wonderful natural phenomenon."

His influence checked such sacerdotal tendencies in ancestral worship as elsewhere reached high development. When he was sick, a suggestion that prayers should be offered for his recovery provoked the remark, " My prayer is constant." His conduct was such an unceasing devotion to virtue, that any formal solicitation on his behalf would be an imputation that the ruling spiritual powers, if such there be, lack intelligence or goodness.

In his time, no book purporting to be a divine revelation was known to the Chinese; and Confucius found no basis for faith save his perception and his reason, and no motive for virtue save his innate moral constitution and his personal interest. Guided by these, he taught a system of ethics that must ever command the respect of the good and the wise. Alone among the founders of religions, he neither claimed a divine character or commission, nor taught men to do anything to influence the fate of their souls after the death of their bodies. He made neither threat nor promise. He took no advantage of ignorance or credulity. He made no occupation for a professional priesthood. He left no pupils interested in misrepresenting his doctrines and building up a corrupt ecclesiastical system.

SEC. 211. *An Honored Sage.*—Though occasionally neglected and even insulted, Confucius was recognized during his life as one of the leading teachers of his country, and by many persons he was treated with respect and honor. He had distinguished pupils; he held high offices. Soon after his death, in 478 B. C., his greatness was extensively recognized, especially through the labors and influence of his eminent follower, Mencius, by whom he was exalted as the wisest and best of men. He is now called "the throneless king." Within two centuries and a half after his death—that is more than two thousand years ago—a title of hereditary nobility was conferred on his eldest male heir in the direct line, and this title, preserved to the present time, is the only hereditary nobility in China, and the oldest and most honorable title to nobility on the globe. After more than twenty generations there are now 40,000 descendants of Confucius possessing careful records of their pedigrees. Every provincial capital has a temple to Confucius where scholars and officials worship the spirit of the sage. "From the time of the emperor, Kaou-Ti (206-194 B. C.), to the present day, Confucius has been, outwardly at least, the object of the most supreme veneration and devout worship of every occupant of the throne. Temples have been erected to his honor in every city of the empire, and his worship, which was originally confined to his native state, has for the last twelve hundred years been as universal as the study of the literature which goes by his name. The most important and sacred temple is that adjoining his tomb in Shangtung, on which all the art of Chinese architecture has been lavished. . . . Second only to this temple is the Kiootszekeen at Peking, the main difference being that here there are no images. . . . To this temple the emperor goes in state twice a year, and having knelt and six times bowed his head to the ground, he invokes the presence of the sage in these words:—

"Great art thou, oh perfect sage. Thy virtue is perfect and thy doctrine complete. Among men there has not been thy equal. All kings honor thee. Thy statutes and thy precepts have been preserved faithfully. Thou art the pattern of this imperial school. Reverently have the sacrificial vessels been set out; reverently we sound our drums and bells."[1]

Brougham[2] observes that "for a long succession of ages there has been a veneration paid to the writings and memory of Confucius which is without any second example in the history of our race."

SEC. 212. *Chinese Ancestors.*—Ancestor worship occupies a more prominent place among the Chinese than in any other modern community. The common people among the Confucians worship nothing save the souls of their ancestors; the scholars and officials worship their ancestors and the spirit of Confucius; the emperor, besides worshiping his ancestors and Confucius, also pays his adorations to Shangti, a term which, according to the best authorities, means heaven. No word in the Chinese language distinctly conveys the idea of a divine creator and governor of the universe. The conception of such a being has no place in any religion widespread in China. There is no common recognition of a god; no mention of him in their ordinary devotions; no appeal to him in their courts; no oaths by him in their outbursts of anger.

Nearly every dwelling, even among the poorest people, has a room called "the hall of the ancestors," though it may be used mainly for ordinary occupation. It has a table with ancestral tablets, each a painted board perhaps a foot long and three inches wide, standing upright on a pedestal, with an inscription giving the name of a male ancestor, the time when he lived, and his private or public station. Before these tablets, on regular occasions, the male members of the family, especially the adults, bow, pray, and make offerings of food, flowers, incense, and paper images of money, clothes, tools, weapons, oxen, and men. It is supposed that the souls of the ancestors enjoy the spiritual substance of the offerings, the material portion of which can afterwards be taken away and eaten by mortals just as the priests and people have done and do in all other countries where sacrifice is or was a part of worship.

Besides the worship of ancestors at the funeral and in the home, it is celebrated at two annual festivals, one in April and the other in August. At the April festival, " the whole population, men, women, and children, repair to the family tombs, carrying trays containing the sacrifices, and libations for offering, and the candles, paper, and incense for burning, and there go through a variety of ceremonies and prayers. The grave is also carefully repaired and swept, and at the close of the services, three pieces of turf are placed at the back and front of the grave to retain long strips of red and white paper; this indicates that the accustomed rites have been performed, and these fugitive testimonials remain fluttering in the wind long enough to announce it to all the friends as well as enemies of the family; for when a grave has been neglected three years, it is sometimes dug over and the land resold." [1]

The August festival is called " burning clothes," for on this occasion "pieces of paper folded in the form of jackets, trousers, gowns, and other garments, are burned for the use of the suffering ghosts [during the approaching winter], besides a large quantity of paper money. Paper houses with proper furniture and puppets to represent household servants, are likewise made; and Medhurst adds that 'writings are drawn up and signed in presence of witnesses, to certify the conveyance of the property, stipulating that on its arrival in hades, it shall be duly made over to the individuals specified on the bond. The houses, servants, clothes, money, and all are then burned with the bond, the worshipers feeling confident that their friends obtain the benefit of what they have sent them.' . . . This festival like all others is attended with feasting and music. In order still further to provide for childless ghosts, their ancestral tablets are collected in temples, and placed together in a room set apart for the purpose, . . . and a man hired to attend and burn incense before them."[2]

The cleaning of the tombs for the annual festival to the dead is enforced by the penal code, as well as by public opinion, and is therefore rarely neglected. As an illustration of the spirit in which the ancestors are worshiped, a prayer made at the festival of the tombs is here copied:—

"I, Lin Kwang, the second son of the third generation, presume to come before the grave of my ancestor, Lin Kung. Revolving years have brought again the season of spring. Cherishing sentiments of veneration, I look up and sweep your tomb. Prostrate, I pray that you will come and be present, and that you will grant prosperity and honor to your descendants. At this season of genial showers, I desire to recompense the source of my existence, exerting myself sincerely. Always grant your protection to me. My trust is in your divine spirit. Reverently I present the fivefold sacrifice of a pig, a chicken, a duck, a goose, and a fish, also an offering of five plates of fruit, with libations of spirituous liquors, earnestly entreating that you will come and view them.

With the most attentive respect this announcement is presented on high."[3]

The dead are buried, not in large cemeteries but in separate lots, preferably on barren hills, on or near the land of the family. At the burial "crackers are fired, libations poured out, and prayers recited, and afterwards papers folded into the shape of clothes, houses, money, and everything which he can possibly want in the land of shadows (which Davis calls a wise economy) is burned for the use of the deceased."[4] If the family be too poor to buy a coffin, a son will sometimes sell himself into slavery to get one; and if the deceased died in debt his coffin may be seized by his creditor; and then relatives or friends make great efforts to pay.

SEC. 213. *China's Place.*—China has a small place in the culture of the present. Occupying a large space on the map of the world, and including more than a fourth of all the people on the globe, it does not take the lead in any branch of science, or of useful, ornamental, or literary art. Its language, its writing, its learning, and most of its industrial processes, are superannuated survivals of a remote past. They are so much inferior to the forms of culture in the same branches in other countries, that they cannot even serve as a good basis for future progress. The welfare and credit of the nation demand that they should be discarded as soon as possible, so that the people may enter into the race of progress without being impeded by an oppressive load of antiquated evils.

But while China is relatively insignificant to the culture of the present, she occupies a very important place in the culture of the past. She was the first country to invent or use the mariner's compass, the navigable canal, the artesian well, the petroleum lamp, natural gas fuel, coined money and paper money, distilled liquor, pisciculture, cast iron,[1] iron suspension bridges, the hand-roller cotton gin,[2] water-tight compartments in ships, distillation,[3] sugar,[4] porcelain, lacquer-ware, spectacles, paper, movable type, printed books, tea, and silk. This list of original contributions to industrial progress is one that entitles the Chinese to rank with the British and the Americans in advance of all other nations as inventors. The Chinese were possibly the first to cultivate rice, cotton, oranges, sweet-potatoes, and to invent the spinning-wheel and the water-wheel as a source of mechanical power.

China promises to hold an important place in the culture of the future. Her scholars do not know the vast superiority of Euraryan civilization in every department of thought; and their ignorance, prejudice, and national pride are fortified by selfish interests. The introduction of new ideas will bring with it new men and new institutions. The old system of instruction will have to be modified if not abandoned; and the change will be accompanied by an agitation for a new method of writing, and perhaps for a new official language. Hieroglyphical writing and a tongue which cannot be written with an alphabet are burdens too heavy for a nation to carry while keeping up with the foremost in the race of progress.

The Chinese of to-day have many of the qualities needed for the attainment and maintenance of national greatness. They are toilsome, sober, economical, faithful, peaceful yet not cowardly, teachable, observant, and skillful in the handling of tools and the management of men. They are competent merchants, bankers, and contractors. As merchants in San Francisco, Sydney, and Melbourne, their credit is better on the average than that of their white competitors. They have much capacity for organization and succeed in every branch of industry which is open to them on equal terms, and which promises a good profit. The existence of such qualities and capacities among the common Chinese in California implies the existence of similar qualities and capacities among their countrymen in their native land ; and they imply further that their nation will gain a prominent place in the industry and intellectual activity of some coming age.

SEC. 214. *Japanese Society, etc.*—The industry of Japan is similar to that of China, and so is the food and the architecture. Most of the dwellings are very cheap, those of well-to-do merchants not costing more than two hundred dollars, while that of a poor laborer who supports himself and family comfortably, as comfort is understood in their country, may cost fifty dollars. Every family has a separate house. Furniture is very simple. Among the common people, there are no tables, chairs, bedsteads, spring frames for beds, hair mattresses, feather pillows, costly rugs or carpets, large mirrors, or elegant bureaus. The dishes used at meals are usually of very cheap crockery, though the wealthy have costly porcelain. Food is conveyed to the mouth by chop-sticks, as in China. The dishes at meals rest on a mat on the floor, and while eating the people kneel, sit down, or rest on their haunches.

A long gown open in front, but worn so that one side laps over the other, is the principal garment of both sexes. Among the well-to-do, the material is cotton or silk; among the very poor, hemp. Laborers frequently wear nothing save a loin-cloth. Both sexes usually go bare-headed. A broad hat or an umbrella may give protection against rain; a parasol or fan against the sun. Straw sandals and clogs are worn on the feet.

Previous to the arrival of Europeans in their cities, nudity was not considered immodest; and now in the country, women are often bare to the waist in the presence of men. Until within a few years, the two sexes bathed together in public without clothes. Every person is supposed to take a warm bath every day, in most households all using the same tub and the same water.[1] After the bath, those who can afford it, frequently have their muscles kneaded.

In their social intercourse, the Japanese are, of all nations, the most punctiliously polite. The utmost care is taken to instruct children in the rules of saluting and addressing their elders and equals; and the adults make their practice conform to the precepts which they learned in their early years. The people are amiable, obliging, lively without being undignified, and generally happy. There is much domestic affection, and yet, like the Chinese, the kiss is not customary among them as an expression of either parental or connubial affection.

Until recently the husband did not eat with his wife and could divorce her at his pleasure; but now the wife has about the same social privileges and legal rights as in Europe. Under the laws as they were before 1850, the high nobles could each have eight concubines in addition to a wife; and the soldiers could each have two concubines in addition to a wife; but the serfs were each limited to one wife. Infanticide was a crime. The man who had no son was required to adopt one to keep up the family worship.

The nobles and soldiers had a strict code of honor,

and when one was seriously insulted, he must either kill the offender or commit suicide in such a manner as to throw the responsibility on the man who gave the insult and who must then commit suicide. If a noble was convicted of a crime, he was allowed to slay himself, and by so doing he washed out all stain from his memory and saved his estate to his children. The sentence of condemnation was read to him, and a knife ten inches long and very sharp was given to him. Thereupon, in the presence of several friends, he bared his body, and gave himself a mortal wound, cutting across his body below the navel. A friend, acting with previous instructions, cut off the head. If the victim, after gashing himself in the body, could thrust his knife into his throat, his memory was honored; and still more, if, after his throat wound, he could replace the knife in its sheath.[2] This mode of suicide is called harikiri or harikari; and the most remarkable application of it occurred early in the XVIIIth century, when a noble, having been insulted by a minister of state, wounded him and slew himself. Forty-five soldiers of the dead noble stormed the castle of the minister, slew him, and then sacrificed their own lives.[3] That is the Japanese Thermopylæ.

From the Chinese, the Japanese copied many of their useful arts, social customs, religious ideas and words, as well as signs used in writing. Their language being polysyllabic and agglutinative, however, they use fifty Chinese hieroglyphics to mean syllables, and have other hieroglyphics for words derived from China. Of these word signs, four thousand have been adopted in Japan,[4] but the tendency at present is to discard all save the syllabic signs.

The vocabulary of the Japanese is poor, and its agglutinative grammar is unfit for the full and precise expression of literary and philosophical ideas. The defects of their tongue and mode of writing have been keenly felt within recent years by many Japanese scholars; and by none more strongly than Arinori Mori, at one time Japanese embassador at Washington, who wrote a book advocating the adoption of a modified form of English as a second official language of his country. He proposed to change English by making all its inflections regular, and to modify its alphabet by making all the letters strictly phonetic.

SEC. 215. *Japanese Government.*—The government of Japan, until influenced in this century by contact with Euraryans, was an absolute monarchy under a hereditary sovereign called the Shogoon or Tycoon. Under him were eighteen daimios of the first class of nobles, each the lord of a province, and the smallest of the provinces paid to the daimios a revenue in rice worth $50,000. Two hundred and thirty daimios of the second class had an annual revenue of $25,000 or more. All the daimios are descendants of the Mikado or sacerdotal lord of the country. Every daimio is the owner of an estate in land, and under the Shogoonate, owed political allegiance to the Shogoon, with the obligation of spending part of every year with his family in the national capital, where he must attend frequently at the court of his sovereign. In times of war, he must take the field at the head of his soldiers, of whom he must maintain a number proportioned to the size of his estate.

The soldiers or samurais were a hereditary class who devoted themselves to arms, and when not in the house always carried arms. They did no agricultural or mechanical labor; but they superintended the labor of serfs.

Some of them lived at the tables of their lords; others had charge of part of the domain on which they dwelt. The serfs were compelled to obey them and give way to them. There were about a thousand samurais for every daimio, and a hundred serfs for every samurai, in a total population of more than 30,000,000.

SEC. 216. *Japanese Religion.*—The oldest and most extensive religion in Japan is Shintoism,[1] or the worship of ancestral spirits, to whom tablets similar to those used in China are dedicated in every house. Besides this domestic worship, there is a public worship of the gods in temples. The priests are few, and possess little influence. The Mikado, divine in his blood, is the hereditary high priest of the Shinto religion. Before 1868 he was the nominal head of the state but without political influence, and a prisoner in his palace where none save his wives and chief ministers under the control of the Shogoon, were permitted to see him. On rare occasions he gave audience to strangers, but then was hidden behind a curtain. His wife belonged to one of the five greatest noble families, and he had twelve concubines. If his wife had no son, his eldest son by a concubine inherited his office. Every son who did not become Mikado, and every descendant of a son in the male line, was a daimio. In 1868, the Mikado deposed the Shogoon, assumed the office of actual sovereign, abandoned the secluded mode of life, and made his sacerdotal subordinate to his political duties.

A form of Buddhism, not inconsistent with the Shintoism accepted by most of the Japanese, exacts from its adherents nothing save compliance with a few moral rules, and alms to the few bikshoos in the cities. One sect of Japanese Buddhists allows the bikshoos to marry.

CHAPTER XIV.
THE ANCIENT EGYPTIANS.

SECTION 217. *Egypt.*—Ancient Egypt from Syene, the modern Assouan, to the Mediterranean, is seven hundred and twenty-five miles long; and in the valley and delta of the Nile has an area of seven thousand one hundred square miles. The valley has an average width of about five miles, and for more than three hundred miles, this narrow strip contains all the tillable land of the country. According to Diodorus and Josephus, in their times, Egypt had 7,000,000 inhabitants, or nearly a thousand to the square mile, and almost three times as many as the country sustains in the XIXth century.

The tillable land includes the districts covered naturally by the river at its average annual rise, and those to which the water is supplied by artificial canals. A rise of twenty-four feet above low-water mark is necessary for a good crop; one of eighteen feet fails to reach the bulk of the tillable land and causes a famine; one of thirty feet drowns many of the cattle, and sweeps away many dwellings, tools, and stores of movable property. Rains being very rare and light, the country is dependent on the annual rise of the Nile for the moisture necessary for crops. There are no lateral streams, and no springs worthy of notice. Numerous canals lead the water out from the river, and dykes keep it standing on fields until the soil is thoroughly soaked, and until the fertilizing mud brought down by the flood has been deposited. The annual inundation comes in the midsummer, and in ancient times if the field needed water at other seasons, it was supplied by a shadoof (a pivoted pole with a bucket at one end), or by jugs carried on the shoulder. Irrigating wheels turned by oxen, and various forms of pumps, have been introduced in modern times, but these were unknown to the ancient Egyptians, if we can accept the designs on their monuments as conveying a correct idea of their industry.

SEC. 218. *Egyptian Agriculture.*—The only occupation of a very large proportion of the Egyptian people was agriculture. They cultivated wheat, doora, barley, beans, rice, cotton, flax, hemp, indigo, garlic, onion, leek, lotus, lettuce, melon, cucumber, palm, fig, vine, olive, almond, pomegranate, peach, and papyrus. The chief implements used to prepare the soil for seeding were the plough drawn by oxen, and the hoe; but it was not unusual to sow on the mud left by the inundation, and then drive herds of goats or other animals over the field, to tread in the seed. Wheat and barley were threshed by treading out, and the grain was separated from the straw and chaff by throwing it up into the wind. The only implement for reaping was the sickle, but sometimes the grain was pulled up by the roots. There was no flail, nor machine for threshing or winnowing.

Among the farm buildings were sheds for cattle and for chariots, which latter, shaped like war chariots, seem to have been the only wheeled vehicles used on farms, and were perhaps rarely employed save to carry the proprietor over his fields. They were kept rather for ostentation than for transportation. They had small wheels with spokes, felloes, and hubs, but they had neither metallic tires, nor metallic boxes on the hubs, nor metallic trimmings on the axles; and unless the axle and the rim and hub of the wheel have metallic protections, the vehicle soon runs with so much friction that its value for transportation is greatly diminished. The shape and size of the chariot, and the manner in which the horses were hitched to it, without collar, breast-band, or trace, rendered it unsuitable for heavy loads. The chariot was drawn by the pole fastened to a saddle, which being drawn sidewise constantly chafed the horse. The ancient Egyptians never learned to harness the horse to a wagon so that he could use his strength and speed advantageously. The ox did relatively better, for the ancient yoke is little inferior to the best of modern pattern; but the ancient ox-cart was so heavy, and its wheel rims and axles soon wore so unevenly, that the cheapest land transportation under ordinary circumstances was on the shoulders of slaves or the backs of horses, asses, or oxen. Four-wheeled wagons were known, but were used only on ceremonial occasions. Sleds drawn by oxen appear on the monuments in farm work. Asses were the most common riding animals, but the favorite conveyance was the boat, and where that was not available, the poor walked and the rich preferred the chariot. Several animals which were tamed by the early Egyptians for industrial purposes proved, after long trial, to be less valuable than kindred species kept for similar purposes, and were therefore allowed to disappear from the tame condition. Among these were several kinds of antelope and the hyena dog.

By its annual overflow, the Nile gave to its valley and delta a natural water supply more regular than that of any other large agricultural region; and the Egyptians appreciated their advantage, for they claimed that they "obtained the fruits of the soil with less labor than any other people,"[1] and they expressed their pity for the nations dependent on the uncertain rains, which are often scanty as well as irregular in those portions of Asia and Africa near Egypt.

SEC. 219. *Handicraft.*—Among the tools of the carpenter were the adze, chisel, plane, drill, bow for turning the drill, square, level, plumb-line, and a saw shaped somewhat like a carving-knife. Glue and metallic nails, and the processes of dovetailing and veneering, were common. Among the furniture of the wealthy were platforms which served as bedsteads, wooden head-rests or pillows, tables, and chairs. The last had seats of leather, wood, or plaited vegetable fiber. Springs were not used in chairs, beds, or wagons. Large boats were made with planks fastened to a wooden frame and were used extensively for carrying freight and passengers on the Nile. The common wine-press was a bag, which was stretched horizontally and then twisted,[1] and the wine-casks were either skins or earthen jars. The arts of the cooper and turner were unknown.

Although the Egyptians constructed public works of immense magnitude, they had very few of those complicated and large implements which we call machines. All the methods of increasing mechanical power by diminishing the speed of its application were unknown to them. They had no combination of pulleys, no screw and axle, no capstan. With such appliances, twenty modern Europeans will move an obelisk that required the united force of a thousand ancient Egyptians.

The spindle and the loom were found in nearly every house. The textile materials most used were flax, wool, and hemp. The loom was an upright frame, in which the warp was stretched vertically and the woof was pushed through with the fingers or with a stick.[2] Besides the material for clothing, weavers produced thick textures for rugs and carpets, strong cloth for sails, and nets for excluding gnats and mosquitoes.[3] The Egyptians also made nets for catching fish and birds; and they were expert in plaiting mats and baskets. Embroidery was practiced among them and one of their materials for it was gold thread. They had numerous bright dyes and they used mordants.[4]

As early as 4000 B. C. paper was made in large quantities by cutting the stem of the papyrus into thin slices and gluing them together in long strips from six to fifteen inches wide. Such paper was cheap, durable, and convenient for writing purposes. Leather was tanned with astringent substances, and used in shoes, sandals, shields, chairs, and chariots. At least as early as 400 B. C. artesian wells were bored to a depth of seven hundred feet.[5]

When the great pyramids were built, the potter's wheel was already known to the Egyptians. Pottery was made with and without glazing, into kitchen and tableware, lamps, ornamental vases, water jars, and jars large and small for holding wine, oil, fruit, grain, flax, and fresh and salted meat. It appeared also in idols, amulets, and toys. The pottery of Egypt never equaled that of Greece in beauty of shape, color, and decoration with human figures. Tiles were made with and without glazing, and bricks were used crude and burned. The crude brick, or adobe, was a common building material and appeared in some public edifices; but when the flood reached the adobes, they soon crumbled away. These structures could be erected with so little labor, and their contents usually had so little value, that their destruction was one of the smaller items in the loss by a flood. Roofs were usually of thatch, and floors of clay. The elegant buildings were paved with tiles or stone. There were no chimneys; windows were few, small, and without glass, but could be closed by shutters. The huts of the poor had only one story; the larger dwellings had two stories; and some of the dwellings in large cities had four or five.[6]

The arts of making glass, clarifying it with manganese, coloring it with pigments, blowing it into bottles, cutting it, and making it into imitations of various precious stones, were known before 2000 B. C. So also was the art of fusing together small rods of different colors into a large rod, which when cut across at right angles anywhere would show a flower, the name of a king, or some other interesting design. Emeralds, amethysts, turquoises, and various other gems were well known and were cut, polished, and set in metallic rings and other ornaments.

Painting was used extensively in decorating the walls and ceilings of temples and sepulchral chapels and vaults with scenes of public and private life, including battles, ecclesiastical processions, royal installations, funerals, agricultural labor, hunting with dogs, fishing, and fowling.

As Kenrick says, "The profusion with which the Egyptians employed sculpture and painting in their temples, palaces, and tombs, has no parallel in the history of art." But the art was rude. Each color was put on without shading. There was no attempt to obtain relief by the arrangement of light and shade. The drawing was equally rude. There was no foreshortening or linear perspective.

Any complicated scene showing a number of figures, was represented with the aid of ludicrous conventionalities, some portions of the design being exhibited in a bird's-eye view, and others from a portion on the same level. The drawing of a man represented his head and legs as seen from the side and his body as seen from the front. A king was represented as much larger than other people. The colors were mixed with water and glue and included three each of yellows and browns, and two each of reds, blues, and greens, besides black and white.

SEC. 220. *Egyptian Architecture.*—In much of their work, a high artistic taste was apparent. "The grace and delicacy of their floral designs [in architectural ornamentation] are still the models of our best patterns."[1] "No one," says Wilkinson, "can look upon the elegant forms of many of the Egyptian vases, the ornamental designs of their architecture, or the furniture of their rooms, without conceding to them due praise on this point of originality."[2] Some temples of Egypt are older by many centuries and perhaps by millenniums than any similar edifices in Asia or Europe, and are the earliest buildings known to us, in which men exhibited architectural skill on a grand scale and in durable material. In these structures we find what seems to be the beginning of pillars for the support of the roof in large halls. Some pillars are square without capital, pedestal, or ornament on the sides; others are octagonal, plainly polygonal, or polygonal and fluted. The capital and pedestal appear in plain, fantastic, and tasteful forms. In the valley of the Nile we find the remote antecedents of the Doric, the Ionic, and the Corinthian orders. The palm leaf and the blossoms of the lotus and papyrus are suggestions of local originality.

After seeing Luxor, Harriet Martineau wrote that

"instead of ugliness, I found beauty; instead of the grotesque, I found the solemn; and where I looked for rudeness from the primitive character of art, I found the sense of the soul more effectually reached than by works which are the results of centuries of experience and experiment."[3] Sayce tells us that "the city-like ruin of Karnak, with its obelisks and columns and carvings, the huge monuments of granite that watched over the plain of Thebes, the temple of Abusimbel, hewn out of a mountain and guarded by colossi, whose countenances betokened the divine calm of undisputed majesty, were all so many memorials of Titanic conceptions and more than human pride."[4] Although the columns are thicker in proportion to height, and nearer together, and in many respects the architectural proportion and ornamentation are less elegant than in Greece, grand effects are nevertheless obtained in many of the Egyptian buildings.

Among the numerous Egyptian statues and reliefs of men and of gods in human form, rarely do we see one that looks as if the face were a careful portrait of a model, and there is among them all not one that deserves for a moment to be classed with the great productions of statuary art. The vast majority of the Egyptian statues are works of stone-cutters or wood-carvers, not of sculptors. And yet much study was given to the human form, and plaster casts were made of the various parts of the body, to be put together in different postures.[5]

SEC. 221. *Pyramids.*—Some of the most remarkable of all stone-work was done by the Egyptains. Their notable structures preserved to our times are temples and tombs, the latter including pyramids. No royal palace, no fortification, no private dwelling, remains standing, and few of such structures are recognizable in their ruins. So far as we can learn, the country never had a large bridge of stone or an aqueduct. Of temple ruins, the number is large but uncertain, because in many places it is doubtful whether the remnants belong to one building or to several. Of the subterranean tombs there are thousands. The stone pyramids of Egypt are the oldest of buildings, the most solid, the most durable, and the most immense results of great skill combined with great labor. Their total number now standing is sixty-two,[1] and besides there are four pyramids made of adobe. The latest were erected about 2000 B. C.; the earliest, perhaps before 5000 B. C. More wonderful than the great pyramids, in the opinion of Herodotus, was the labyrinth, which is now a mass of ruins, far less imposing than those of Karnac.

The largest of the pyramids, known as that of Cheops, at Ghizeh, near Cairo, is seven hundred and fifty-six feet square on the ground, and, as Lenormant says, it is "the most prodigious of all human constructions." It covers thirteen acres, or twice as much ground as there is in the area of St. Peter's cathedral at Rome, the largest of modern buildings. The original height was four hundred and eighty-six feet, of which fifteen feet at the top have been tumbled down, and the total contents are 3,290,000 cubic yards of masonry. The body of the structure is of cut limestone, obtained from the hills on the eastern side of the valley; the casings of the outside and of the internal galleries are of granite from Syene, more than five hundred miles distant by the course of the river. The construction, including the necessary road-making, continued for more than thirty years, and the total number of days' work done on it was, according to tradition, 2,460,000,000. This is the sum calculated from the report that 100,000 men, relieved at intervals of three months, were employed on it for ten years; and that 360,000, relieved at intervals of a year, were employed on it for twenty years, allowing three hundred days in the year for each laborer. The stone is in layers from two to five feet thick, and the blocks generally are from five to ten feet long; but many are as much as thirty feet long, five wide, and four thick, with a weight of forty-five tons each. There are some chambers and passages, but the space which they occupy is insignificant as compared with the great mass of the masonry. The date of its construction has not been ascertained with certainty, but was not later than 2700 B. C., and was perhaps as early as 4500 B. C.

The continuous employment for thirty years of a force which averaged about 270,000 men, or nearly one-sixth of the adult males of the nation, on a work of royal vanity, indicates that the country must have been very populous; that its institutions were ancient and stable; that its accumulated wealth was considerable; that its government was powerful and despotic; and that a large proportion of the people spent much of their lives in severe and compulsory toil. Although this pyramid is the greatest structure that can be traced to the reign of any one king, there is no reason for assuming that in his time the people were subject to exceptional oppression. The multitude, the magnitude, and the elaborate finish of the other pyramids, and of the temples and subterranean tombs, imply that the ancient Egyptians did not lead an idle or an easy life. No European monarch of ancient or modern times could undertake or have undertaken such a work with prudence.

Southwest of the great pyramid, and less than six

hundred feet from it, is the second pyramid, known as that of Mycerinus, the son of Cheops. It has a base seven hundred and seven feet square, and a height of four hundred and fifty-four feet, and more than 2,500,000 cubic yards of masonry. The other pyramids are smaller than these, most of them less than one hundred feet, and many less than fifty feet high. These piles of stone are so vast, and seem so well qualified to defy all destructive influences, that an Arab writer has said that while "all other things dread time, time itself dreads the pyramids."

The subterranean tombs are cut into the rock of the hills bordering the Nile Valley. At the entrance there is a chapel, from which a passage usually vertical, or sloping downwards, leads to the burial vaults, the walls of which are in many cases covered with reliefs and paintings. There the mummies of the family were kept.

Each of the great pyramids was built to be the tomb of a king, and of no other person. His wives and children were buried elsewhere, in some cases in smaller pyramids.² The burial chamber was usually in the bed-rock under the pyramid, and was carefully concealed.

Much of the stone-work, in cutting, fitting, and decorating with reliefs and hieroglyphics, was done with remarkable nicety, and this at a time when, according to most Egyptologists, steel was as yet unknown. Under the fourth dynasty, as early as 4000 B. C., "architecture already shows an inconceivable perfection with regard to the working and building up blocks of great dimensions. The passages in the interior of the great pyramid remain a model of exact joiners' work which has never been surpassed."³

"No one can possibly examine the interior of the

Great Pyramid without being struck with astonishment at the wonderful mechanical skill displayed in its construction. The immense blocks of granite brought from Syene—a distance of five hundred miles—are polished like glass, and so fitted that the joints can hardly be detected. Nothing can be more wonderful than the extraordinary amount of knowledge displayed in the construction of the discharging chambers over the roof of the principal apartment, in the alignment of the sloping galleries, in the provision of ventilating shafts, and in all the wonderful contrivances of the structure. All these, too, are carried out with such precision that, notwithstanding the immense superincumbent weight, no settlement in any part can be detected to the extent of an appreciable fraction of an inch. Nothing more perfect, mechanically, has ever been erected since that time." [4]

SEC. 222. *Egyptian Temples.*—The temples of the Egyptians were, so far as we know, all built on the same general plan which was original with them, and has not been imitated by any modern nation. A large area was inclosed with a high stone wall, which was blank except at the entrance, where two towers about one hundred feet high, with simple architectural and sculptural decoration on their fronts, stood at either side of a wide gate-way fifty feet high. The general effect is one of much grandeur. After entering, the visitor found himself in a large court designed for the use of such laymen and processions as participated in the public ceremonies of the temple. Many of such courts were decorated with large monolithic obelisks and colossal statues of deceased kings. The obelisks varied in height from ten to one hundred and eight feet, and the diameter at the base was from one-eighth to one-eleventh of the height, while the diameter at the top was about one-fourth less than at the base. The largest was ten feet thick at the ground, and weighed two hundred and ninety-seven tons. The largest statues were seated, and though not so high as the tallest obelisks, were much heavier. One statue of Rameses measured twenty-two feet across the shoulders, and weighed eight hundred and eighty-seven tons.

On the farther side, or rear, the court is bounded by a portico, or covered hall, sustained by many columns; and beyond the portico are the adytum or holy of holies where the most sacred image or shrine is kept, and the apartments where the priests of the temple dwell.

The towers and pilasters of the gate-ways, the outer walls, and the interior columns of the temples usually had the lines of their sides converging towards the top, and conveying an impression of great solidity. In many cases, the shafts of the columns were covered with hieroglyphics, and their capitals were carved with flowers or buds of the lotus, or the leaves of the palm, for which in the kindred Corinthian capital, the Greeks substituted the leaves of the acanthus. The Egyptian column has a height five or six times greater than its diameter, which again is equal to the intercolumnar space, proportions ungraceful as compared with the slimmer columns and wider intercolumnar spaces of the Greek temples.

Referring to the Palace Temple of Karnac, which is, perhaps, the noblest effort of architectural magnificence ever produced by the hand of man, Fergusson[1] says: "Its principal dimensions are twelve hundred feet in length by about three hundred and sixty in width, and it covers therefore 430,000 square feet [about ten acres] or nearly twice the area of St. Peter's at Rome, and more than four times that of any medieval cathedral existing. This, however, is not a fair way of estimating its dimensions, for our churches are buildings entirely under one roof; but at Karnac a considerable portion of the area was uncovered by any buildings, so that no such comparison is just. The great hypostyle hall, however, is internally three hundred and forty by one hundred and seventy feet, and with its two pylons it covers more than 88,000 square feet, a greater area than the cathedral of Cologne, the largest of all our northern cathedrals; and when we consider that this is only a part of a great whole, we may fairly assert that the entire structure is among the largest, as it undoubtedly is one of the most beautiful buildings in the world. . . . St. Peter's with its colonnades, and the Vatican, make up an immense mass, but is insignificant in extent as in style when compared with this glory of ancient Thebes, and its surrounding temples.

"The culminating point and climax of all this group of buildings is the hypostyle hall of Manephthah. . . . No language can convey an idea of its beauty, and no artist has yet been able to reproduce its form so as to convey, to those who have not seen it, an idea of its grandeur. The mass of its central piers, illumined by a flood of light from the clerestory, and the smaller pillars of the wings gradually fading into obscurity, are so arranged and lighted as to convey an idea of infinite space; at the same time the beauty and massiveness of the forms, and the brilliancy of their colored decorations, all combine to stamp this as the greatest of man's architectural works, but such a one as it would be impossible to reproduce except in such a climate and in that individual style in which and for which it was created."

The approach to the temple from the landing-place on the bank of the Nile was by a grand avenue.

"The road from El-Uksur to El-Karnac," says Harriet Martineau, "once lay . . . between Sphinxes standing six feet apart, for a mile and a half. Those which remain, headless, encumbered, and extending only a quarter of a mile, are still very imposing. Then came pylons, propylæa, halls, obelisks, temples, groves of columns, and masses of ruins, oppressive to see and much more to remember. . . . Here are the largest buildings and the most extensive ruins in the known world; . . . the great hall is three hundred and twenty-nine by one hundred and seventy feet, and eighty-five feet high, containing one hundred and thirty-four columns, the twelve central ones of which are twelve feet in diameter and the others not much smaller; the whole of this forest of columns being gay with colors and studded with sculptures."[2]

The same author writes thus of the ruins of a building known as the Rameseum at Thebes: "It is melancholy to sit on the piled stones amidst the wreck of this wonderful edifice, where violence inconceivable to us has been used to destroy what art inconceivable to us had erected. What a rebuke to the vanity of succeeding ages is here! What have we been about, to imagine men in those early times childish or barbarous—to suppose science and civilization reserved for us of these later ages, when here are works in whose presence it is a task for the imagination to overtake the eye-sight."[3]

A remarkable production of Egyptian architectural industry is the rock temple of Abusimbel, cut into the solid rock of a mountain-side. On each side of the entrance are four sitting human figures each sixty-eight feet high as they sit, in the highest relief, attached to the bed-rock at the back. A vestibule twenty-five feet long leads into a hall eighty feet long, half as high, and sixty-five wide, the roof being supported by eight square columns, each with the figure of a priest thirty-three feet high in strong relief. Behind this is a chamber fifty feet square, and behind that a sanctuary thirty feet long and fifteen wide; and at the sides there are other chambers. After leaving the vestibule, artificial light must be used.

One of the notable curiosities of ancient Egypt preserved to our time, is the great Sphynx, which has been cut out of a rock which projects above the general level of the ground near the pyramids of Ghizeh. It is about seventy feet high, including twenty-eight feet in the head. The length of the body is one hundred and forty feet.

SEC. 223. *Metals in Egypt.*—Copper, tin, bronze, gold, silver, lead, and iron were known, and were produced in the country, and in adjacent regions to which Egyptian laborers were sent for the purpose of mining. Iron was less abundant and later in the date of its introduction than bronze, and some authors suppose that steel was unknown in the valley of the Nile until many centuries after the construction of the largest pyramids. As late as 1000 B. C., bronze was used extensively in weapons, tools, ornaments, and kitchen utensils, and was cast solid and hollow. Smiths had bellows without valves, anvils, pincers, tongs, punches, files, gravers, burnishers, solder and soldering irons, blow-pipes, crucibles, moulds, and earthern cores to be used in the center of castings. Vases, bowls, goblets, platters, mirrors, and the handles of swords, daggers, and falchions were of gold, silver, and bronze, elegantly shaped and ornamented with polished gems. Metallic boxes were made in many fanciful shapes, including those of mollusks, fishes, reptiles, birds, and quadrupeds. The two metals, now distinguished by the title precious, were prized as materials for ornaments of the person, of the table, of the palaces of the great, and of the temples of the gods. They were used in rings or ingots as mediums of exchange, according to their weight, and were not coined into money until after the valley of the Nile had become subject to the Assyrian kings.

SEC. 224. *Egyptian Homes.*—When we examine the social life of the early occupants of the Nile Valley we find that the men could have any number of wives and concubines. Priests, however, were excepted from the general rule and were limited each to a single wife. The first wife in point of time had a superiority of social dignity, if not of legal right, over all taken afterwards; and among the wealthy she was often protected by a marriage contract which stipulated that if the husband should take a second wife he must pay a certain sum to his first wife's family, or return her whole dowry. This contract, in other cases, transferred all the man's property to the wife, and bound her to support him in comfort and to bury him in a manner suitable to his rank,[1] or it provided that she should be the head of the house and that he must obey her.[2] Greeks in Egypt were often astonished by finding the man at work in the house while the wife was attending to business in the street. She had a social freedom and industrial privilege unequaled in any other oriental country of ancient or modern times.

Her life was spent in relative ease. It was not necessary that she should give to the loom all the hours otherwise unoccupied. She could give entertainments to the husbands and wives of friendly families, and the women like the men drank wine on such occasions, and once in awhile would drink too much, as is evident from the old pictures. In many cases the name of the mother, without that of the father, is given in the tomb; as if the maternal blood were the more important. There was no law prohibiting the marriage of brother with sister.

The domestic life of the ancient Egyptians seems to have been happy. In many places the husband and wife are depicted with their arms round each other's necks, and as speaking to each other in terms indicative of great regard. All children born to a man in his house, no matter whether the mother was a first wife, second wife, or concubine, inherited equal shares of the father's property. Children were numerous, and were highly prized, especially the sons, whose worship was necessary to the happiness of the paternal spirit after death. Whether it was permitted to expose infants to die we do not know; but there is no evidence of such a custom of infanticide as prevailed in many other ancient nations. Among the poor, the cost of rearing a child to adult life did not exceed $3.25; so that after making much allowance for the greater value of money as compared with our time and country, the expense of a large family of children in ancient Egypt was not great.

Under the influence of a hot climate and of the traditional idea that the exposure of the body above the waist and of the leg below the knee is not unbecoming, clothing was scanty. Till the age of ten, children were nude. The poor man while at work usually wore nothing but a loin-cloth or a short petticoat. On ceremonial occasions this under-garment was covered by a long robe. The poor woman wore a short petticoat, and over it a gown reaching from the waist or neck to the ankles, with or without sleeves. The material of the clothing in the warmest weather was linen, and in winter, wool.

The head of the man was shaved clean, and was usually

covered with a light, close-fitting cap; in full dress, the educated man wore a wig. Women wore their hair long and in braids. There was no hat or cap for the common man or bonnet for the woman. The people were ordinarily barefooted, though sandals of leather or vegetable fiber were worn by nobles, soldiers, and some artisans. Following the example of their savage ancestors, they anointed themselves every day with unguents, using for that purpose various vegetable oils, which, for the wealthy, were perfumed. At fashionable entertainments, servants poured perfumed oils on the hair of the ladies and on the wigs of the gentlemen. Among the common ornaments were rings for ears and fingers, bracelets, armlets, and necklaces of gold, silver, bronze, and other materials. The patterns were numerous and the designs of many tasteful. Some rings had flat faces for seals, with an inscription of the name of the owner or of the soveriegn.

The food of the poor consisted chiefly of doora and dates, with onions, leeks, and salt fish for variety and flavor. Besides these things, the tables of the rich had wheat, barley, beef, geese, game, grapes, and other fruits. The favorite drink of the rich was wine grown near Lake Moeris; that of the poor was doora beer, for the sale of which there were numerous shops, which were frequently visited by some patrons. The earliest lecture to a toper is preserved in the following Egyptian letter: "It has been told to me that thou hast forsaken books and devoted thyself to pleasure; that thou goest from tavern to tavern smelling of beer. . . . Thou art like an oar started from its place. . . . Thou art like a shrine without its god. . . . Thou knowest that wine is an abomination; that thou hast taken an oath that thou would'st not put liquor into thee." [3]

At meals, the common people sat on the floor, and men, women, and children ate together. Each helped himself from the common dish by thrusting in the fingers of his right hand. The left was considered unclean and was not used in eating.[1] There was no fork, plate, or spoon, but there was one knife for cutting the meat. The rich had chairs, tables, and spoons.

Grain was ground by hand, and the millstones were the same in pattern as those now used in many oriental countries. The miller was a woman, and she turned the upper millstone by taking hold of a peg. Bread was leavened, and men served as cooks in the kitchens of the wealthy.

The people were fond of natural and artificial flowers. At entertainments, the servants put chaplets on the heads of the guests, garlands round their necks, and nosegays in their hands.

There was a remarkable permanence in social stratifications and in family fortunes. Among serfs or free peasants, as among the nobles, there were occupations followed by all the males of a family through many generations. The poor nobles were provided with public office that would yield a comfortable support. There was no numerous and influential middle-class engaged in industrial occupations. Foreign commerce was not permitted until after the country became subject to alien domination; and all manual labor was servile and disgraceful.

The common amusements were mora, dice, checkers, and the chase for participants; and for spectators, music, dancing, wrestling, juggling, acrobatic exercises, and fighting with single-stick by hired performers. Ladies had embroidery as a pastime, and children had dolls and toys, among the latter, crocodiles with snapping mouths,

There was no theater, ballet, boxing match, quoit throwing, gladiatorial show, fights with wild beasts, or horse-race, nor did the men engage for pleasure in any game requiring great muscular effort, similar to cricket, baseball, or the Greek athletic exercises.

Although the life in the flesh, according to their religion, was merely a brief preparation for the future spiritual existence, the general tone of the social life, of the ecclesiastical teaching, and of the sacerdotal profession, was joyous. The exaltation of the gods did not require the humiliation of mankind. Heaven could be merited without making a hell of earth. Self-respect, a jovial disposition, matrimony, resistance to evil, and the possession of wealth, were not inconsistent with devotion. There was no sacerdotal monasticism or asceticism. Celibacy and mendicancy were not avenues to public veneration. Everybody was advised to get all possible enjoyment out of life, consistently with justice to his neighbors; and at feasts it was customary for servants to show a figure representing a mummy and remind the guests to make the best of life while they could.

A wife in her tomb thus addresses her husband: "Oh my brother, my husband, neglect not to eat and drink. Drain the cup of pleasure. Enjoy woman's love and the privilege of holiday. Follow your desire. Turn your back to worry so long as life lasts. The world of spirits is a region of darkness, of sorrow, and of deep sleep. Here we wake not; we see neither father nor mother; we care not for spouse or child. The living enjoy the refreshing water; the dead are thirsty forever."[5]

The song of King Antuf of the eleventh dynasty says: "Gratify thy desire while thou livest. Put perfumes on thy head, clothe thyself with fine linen, and adorn thyself with jewels. . . . Gratify thy desire with all good things, whilst thou art upon the earth, according to the dictation of thy heart. The day will come when thou wilt not hear the voices of the living; when the living will not hear thy voice. Feast in tranquillity; no one will carry his wealth with him to the next world." The song of the Harper says: "Enjoy perfumes and song and instrumental music, and turn thy back to care. Devote thy thoughts to enjoyment in anticipation of the pilgrimage to the region of eternal silence."[6]

SEC. 225. *Hieroglyphics.*—As far back as we can trace the life of the Egyptians, we find them in possession of the art of writing with hieroglyphics, which they used extensively for industrial, historical, and ecclesiastical records. Herodotus, speaking of their customs in his time, says: "When anything occurs, they put it down in writing, and pay particular attention to the circumstances which follow it, and if in process of time any similar occurence takes place, they conclude that it will be attended with the same results."[1]

The hieroglyphics of Egypt were original in the country, and are the oldest, most complex, and most highly developed of all hieroglyphical systems. They are written in three styles, first, the pictorial; second, the hieratic or easy hand; and third, the demotic or very easy; and they represent three classes of ideas, first, things; second, syllables; and third, letters.

Their hieroglyphics were at first only pictures of visible objects conveying literal ideas, as when the figure of a gazelle meant nothing but a gazelle. The next step was presumably to attach figurative as well as literal meanings to pictures, as when a gazelle might mean swift, swiftness, and to run. The third step was to combine several figures using one to qualify the other, as when the figure of a god with that of a house meant a temple. Another advance was taken when some part or feature of a thing was made to indicate the whole, as when a waved line or several parallel waved lines were made to mean water. An important addition to the art of writing was made by adopting certain arbitrary signs such as a dot above a line for over, and one under a line for below. These five classes may be said to include all the word signs, which must be very numerous, extremely difficult to learn and remember, and often uncertain in their meaning. It was a great improvement to use a picture to mean not the full name of a thing but only its first syllable, and by combining a number of syllabic signs any word could be spelled. Of syllabic signs there were three hundred and fifty-five, including duplicates, in the Egyptian mode of writing, the number being much less than that of the word signs. Another step in the same direction was to use the picture to represent only the first sound, whether vowel or consonant, of its name. Thus the pictures became alphabetic signs, of which the Egyptians had twenty-five. To advance from several thousand word signs to several hundred syllabic signs, and from them to a few more than a score of alphabetic signs, were the great achievements of the Egyptians in the world of letters, and the three steps were accomplished by them alone among nations. It is very doubtful indeed whether any other nations save the Chinese and Aztecs originated hieroglyphics; and both those nations showed much less original thought in this matter.

While the Egyptians were making improvements in the ideas which they attached to the pictures, they were also advancing the method of drawing their pictures, which, with frequent repetition, became more and more simple, until a mere conventional scratch was understood to stand for a house, which once showed its walls, door, and roof plainly. From the time when the Greeks conquered Egypt the native mode of writing fell into discredit, and before the time of Constantine, it had been entirely neglected and forgotten.

Although the Egyptians discovered the principles of alphabetic writing and had a sufficient number of alphabetic signs to dispense with ideographic and syllabic hieroglyphics, they continued to use the latter, partly because they were sacred, and partly because familiarity with them was necessary in reading and imitating the ancient records on monuments and in books. In the late days of the Egyptian monarchy, after its overthrow, so long as books were written in the old tongue, so long were ideographic, syllabic, and alphabetic signs retained in common use; and a knowledge of all was required for the purpose of reading public and private records. Not only was a knowledge of the three modes of writing required in an ordinary education, but the three were often mixed up in the same document or inscription. Thus "we find a word spelled out alphabetically, a needless syllabic sign is then added, and this is followed by an unnecessary ideogram. The plan is so cumbrous as to seem to us almost inconceivable. We have letters, syllabics, and ideograms piled up one on another in a perplexing confusion. So many crutches were thought necessary that walking became an art of the utmost difficulty."[2]

Even when an Egyptain undertook to write alphabetically, he found himself hampered, and his readers puzzled, by the multitude of signs at his command, for he could use any one of four hundred syllabic hieroglyphics for the letter representing its initial sound. The same mark might mean letter, syllable, or polysyllabic word; and as a consequence there was nothing equivalent to our simple alphabet, composed of several dozen signs, each with a value easily ascertainable. There was no Egyptian alphabet fit for adoption in Europe and Asia; on the basis of Egyptian signs, the Phœnicians devised one that was copied more or less closely in the writing of all the leading nations which use letters.

They had signs for each of the numerals, one, ten, a hundred, and a thousand. Thus, if they wished to write nine thousand nine hundred and ninety-nine, they used nine of each of their numerals, beginning with the largest and ending with the smallest. Unlike the Romans, the Egyptians had no single sign for five, or for fifty, or for five hundred.

SEC. 226. *Egyptian Books, etc.*—The ancient Egyptian books preserved to us are remarkable for the prominence given in them to ecclesiastical and ethical topics. Some of the hymns possess the merits of stately diction and highly devout spirit, but the literature generally, as compared with that of Greece, is lacking in vigor of thought and elegance of form.[1] It has no masterpiece in any class of composition, and in many classes it has no sample. Of course, we may suppose that among the books that have been lost there were some of much excellence in many different departments, but there is little satisfaction in such a supposition unsupported by the least evidence. We are told that the sacred scriptures of the Egyptians consisted of forty-two books, including two about the gods, as many of hymns, ten of liturgy, as many about the arts, eight on civil law, six on medicine, and four about astrology. The Funeral Ritual was probably part of the ten liturgical books; all the others are lost.

The remains of the literature of ancient Egypt, including duplicates, are sufficient to fill a thousand volumes. The knowledge of a few hieroglyphics was very common. Cattle were branded, and tools and clothes marked with the owner's names; but women were not taught to read, and the artisan and peasant classes could not read much.[2] Some of the temples had large collections of books, and one library was called a Health Institute of the Soul. The great library of Alexandria, collected under the Ptolemies and destroyed by the Christians, had 400,000 volumes.

In their astronomical observations and in their arithmetical calculations they were inferior to the Chaldeans. They did not divide the ecliptic into the signs of the zodiac, nor the circle into three hundred and sixty degrees, nor did they have such square and cubical multiplication tables as are found on the Assyrian bricks. They knew the true meridian and the length of the sidereal year, and laid off the fields accurately after the landmarks had been covered up by the mud from the annual flood of the Nile.

Of the medicine of the Egyptains we know little. They administered purges, emetics, and clysters, and used plasters and fumigations. The prescriptions of their physicians were "made out in precisely the same way" as in modern Europe.[3] The assertion that teeth plugged with gold have been found in the heads of the old mummies has been contradicted, and is not sustained by the best authorities. Notwithstanding their habit of embalming, there is no proof that they understood much of anatomy. No picture represents a surgical operation more difficult than that of setting a broken bone.

Their musical instruments included the harp with three, five, seven, eleven, or even as many as twenty-two strings, the guitar, the lyre, the tambourine, drum, sistrum, castanets, flute, pipe, and trumpet. One of the pipes was made to contain a straw, which emitted sounds like those of the bagpipe. In many of the monuments three musicians are represented playing together, as two with harps of different sizes and one with a flute; or a harp, guitar, and double pipe; or three pipes of different lengths, indicating that they must have played treble, tenor, and bass.

SEC. 227. *Political Condition.*—About the political condition of the country, our information is not complete. According to Herodotus, Diodorus, Strabo, and Plato, the Egyptians were divided into hereditary classes or castes, but these authors do not agree with one another, or with the monuments. The four agree in making a caste of priests, and another of soldiers; but from better authority we know that "the three great classes of society, priests, scribes, and warriors, were by no means castes in the sense of hereditary succession. . . . The priest of a god was often a military or naval commander, exercised the office of scribe, and invested with the supervision of local works or local government. Public employments were monopolized by a few great families, considered by some to be an advantageous arrangement of civil government; but the key-stone of caste, the limitation of marriage to women of the same order, is unknown to monumental Egypt."[1]

Though the Greek authors mentioned in the preceding paragraph do not speak of serfs or slaves, it is probable that the common soldiers belonged to the former class, and many of the laborers to the latter. Diodorus tells us that the land was divided into three parts, one belonging to the king, another to the priests, and the third to the army. In the absence of explanation we may assume that the share of the army was held by the high military officers, each of whom was required to maintain a certain number of serf soldiers in active service. There was also a class of free peasants. The abject submission of the many to the few is implied by the magnitude of the public monuments, the insignificance of the dwellings of the multitude, and the frequency with which the laborers were beaten by the overseers. A large part of the time of the people, not required in the production of the simplest necessaries of life, was spent in building temples and tombs for the wealthy; and work of this kind must have been done under compulsion. We look in vain through the monuments and books of ancient Egypt for the mention of institutions and movements that have elsewhere been associated with popular freedom.

In the king were centralized all the powers of the government. He was the head of the army and of the church; he controlled all the political and judicial officers. But custom and religion imposed restrictions on him; before his installation, he took an oath of office in which he made certain promises, one of which was that he would not change the official year which regulated the dates of the ecclesiastical festivals. He was regarded as divine. One of his titles was "Son of the Sun." In painting and sculpture he was frequently represented with the attributes of divinity.

Private individuals were not permitted, in any case, to use violence in obtaining redress for injustice. Retaliation was strictly prohibited. While the master was permitted to beat his slave, he was not allowed to inflict any serious injury. Judicial proceedings were conducted according to well-established rules and ancient customs. In important cases, the complaint, the answer, and the judgment were in writing; and written reports of cases were common. There were appellate tribunals, with fixed jurisdiction. After 812 B. C., no suit for debt could be maintained unless the obligation had been incurred in writing. The most remarkable security, and one that was regarded as certain of redemption if a debtor had the means, was the mummy of his father. The interest on a loan was not allowed to exceed double the amount of the principal. For police purposes, every person was required to report his name, abode, and occupation to the magistrate of his district.

It was the opinion of Diodorus that "this unparalleled country could never have continued throughout ages in such a flourishing condition if it had not enjoyed the best of laws and customs;" and Wilkinson[2] agrees with him. The evidences which the latter cites are that the people were extremely submissive to their government; that they hated and resisted alien domination; that the principles of morality were impressed upon every class with all the power of a mighty priesthood; that no merit was attached to noble birth before the gods; and that even the monarchs were subject to strict rules. The submission of the multitude was caused by their superstition and their ignorance of the use of arms. That the laws were well devised to keep many in subjection, is proved by the result; but that they were framed for the purpose of securing the happiness of the people, does not appear.

Although, in the long course of their national existence, the Egyptians sent many military expeditions to Syria and Mesopotamia, their general policy was peaceful. Their isolation made it as difficult for them to conquer as to be conquered. They always maintained, however, an army of about 400,000 men, many of whom in time of peace served as local police. The soldiers were divided into battalions, each of which had its standard of a sacred animal, which was perhaps that of a provincial god. Cities were inclosed with ditches, draw-bridges, and walls, which last had projecting angles, from which assaulting enemies could be bothered by a flanking fire.

Their military system is not mentioned with high commendation by any ancient author. They had no organization that competes in military history with the Spartan regiment, the Macedonian phalanx, or the Roman legion. Not one of their victories or generals has a great fame. They never gained a great victory or suffered a glorious defeat. The Assyrians, Persians, Greeks, and Romans conquered them without much difficulty; and in the later centuries their best troops were foreign hirelings. They never were a martial nation.

SEC. 228. *Egyptian Gods.*—The Egyptian religion was polytheistic and was distinguished from other religions of its class by the preservation of the mummy, by the teaching of formulas to be recited in the next world as aids to salvation, and by the great prominence given to the worship of living animals as representatives of the divinities. It had a worship of ancestors, an immortality at least for the good, future rewards and punishments, a comprehensive and precise moral code, and a popular devotion that was unsurpassed in the appearance and perhaps also in the sincerity of its zeal. The divinities were innumerable, including great gods similar in general character to those of Greece, as personifications of the powers and phenomena of nature, but they were not conceived so distinctly, nor were their attributes the same in all the provinces. There is much more confusion of names and jurisdictions in the Egyptian than in the Greek pantheon. Most of the greater gods of the Nile Valley seem to have been at one time provincial divinities. The worship of the sun was very prominent; Ra, Amon-Ra, Ptah, Tum and Mentu, and even Osiris, were represented and worshiped in certain districts as the sun.

The gods were conceived as similar to men in mind and body, and were represented in sculpture and painting in the forms of men or beasts, or in figures with the head of the symbolic beast on a human body. Thus the statue of Osiris might have the shape of a man or a bull, or the body of a man with a bull's head. The entire beast is seldom used to represent a divinity; its head on a human body conveyed the idea with equal distinctness and greater dignity. In the pictures of the final judgment of the soul in the world of spirits, Horus has the head of a hawk, Anubis that of a jackal, and Thoth that of an ibis.

A prominent feature of the ecclesiastical system was the custom of worshiping three gods in conjunction, and in many cases the first was the father, the second the mother, and the third their son or daughter.[1] Each province had its own triad, which at Phile consisted of Osiris, Isis, and their son Horus; at Mermonthis of Mentu, Rata, and their son Harpara; at Esneh of Kneph, Neith, and Hakt; at Thebes of Amon-Ra, Mut, and Khonsu; at Syene of Kneph, Satis, or Juno, and Anoukis or Vesta; and at Silsiles of Ra, Ptah, and Nilus.

All classes of the people, nobles, commoners, serfs, and

slaves, were intensely devout. They were strict in observing the ceremonial laws of their faith, in paying devotion to their ancestors, and in reverently treating the sacred animals. He who killed one of the latter in its own province, even unintentionally, must die. Cities, provinces, kings, and nobles were named after the gods and the sacred animals; and thus ideas of piety were kept constantly before the public mind. Busiris, Bubastis, and Pitum were the cities of Osiris, Bast, and Tum, and the cities called by the Greeks Heliopolis, Lycopolis, Crocodilopolis, and Oxyrinchus were those of the sun, of the wolf, of the crocodile, and of a fish. The names of the great gods Amon, Ra, and Ptah appear in the titles of many kings. The ceremony of circumcision dedicated the priests and probably all the nobles to their divinities, and was one of the marks of their separation from the unclean aliens.

SEC. 229. *Osiris the Mediator.*—In some hymns the sun is represented as the omnipotent creator who appoints Osiris to mediate between him and mankind.[1] In the Book of the Dead, Osiris presides at the final judgment, and his son Horus appears as the guide and advocate of the soul on trial. Ra, Amon, and Ptah were higher in dignity than Osiris but were not so extensively or fervently worshiped. In some provinces, however, Kneph, called also Knumis, was considered the greatest of the gods.

The most popular and poetical myth of the Egyptians related the life of Osiris. It told how he came to save mankind; how he struggled against the evil spirit Typho; how he was slain by the latter; how his wife Isis obtained the corpse for the purpose of burial; how Typho stole it from her, and cut it into fourteen pieces, each of which he hid in a different province; how Isis with great labor found them all and buried them in Phile; and how Horus, son of Osiris and Isis, conquered and punished Typho. A common but very solemn oath among the people was, "By him who sleeps in Phile." Osiris was the judge of the dead, and to a certain extent at least the equivalent of Pluto in the mythology of the Romans and Greeks. Thoth was the inventor of writing and the author of the sacred books. Neith, in her attributes, resembled the Grecian Athena, whose name if reversed with an initial and a final a has a similar spelling. Bast was the Egyptian Diana. Her temple at Bubastis had a prominence like that of the Ephesian Diana among the Greeks, and according to Herodotus attracted 700,000 pilgrims to its annual festival.

The name of a god was often assumed by a man. A favorite name for a human soul on its trial was Osiris; and the living king sometimes styled himself Horus. Thus in an inscription at Luxor, King Amenhotep speaking of himself says: " The mighty and wise Horus, who rules by justice, who has established order in his country, who holds the world in peace, who is great by his power, who has conquered the barbarous nations, the king, the Lord of righteousness, Amenhotep, the much-beloved son of the sun, the sovereign of the pure country, has had this building erected in the southern district of Thebes, and has consecrated it to Amon, the divine master of the three regions of the world."[2]

SEC. 230. *Sacred Beasts.*—Every god had a favorite or sacred beast. Thus the bull was the animal of Osiris, the cow of Isis, the lion of Ra, the ibis of Thoth, the hawk of Horus, the jackal of Anubis, the asp of Knumis, the scarabæus of Ptah, the vulture of Neith, the mouse of Buto, the viper of Amon, the goat of Mendes, and the crocodile of Sebak. One god might have several sacred animals, as the bull and the antelope of Osiris; or the jackal, wolf, fox, and dog of Anubis; and one animal might be sacred to several gods, as the cow to Isis and Hathor.

Each province had its local divinity and its sacred animal, which latter must never be eaten, purposely injured, or killed in the province. The provincial temple, in some cases at least, had a divine living specimen of this animal, which was housed, fed, bathed, caressed, gratified, worshiped, and after its death embalmed. Among the beasts of which mummies have been found in modern times are the bull, cow, ram, dog, cat, fox, vulture, hawk, goose, ibis, crocodile, asp, viper, frog, fishes of several kinds, and the scarabæus beetle.

The most remarkable exhibition of animal worship in Egypt was that of the bull of Osiris at Memphis. This beast was an object of affection and of at least indirect adoration to all Egyptians. His title, in all his generations, was Apis, and the people said that the cow which gave him birth was impregnated by a god, and was always a virgin. When Apis died, the priests of his temple gave great attention to the selection of a successor, which must be a young bull, and must possess a multitude of marks indicative of his divine character.

The new Apis, having been chosen or perhaps revealed, was taken to the temple as the incarnate god, and treated with the utmost veneration and indulgence. He usually lived about a quarter of a century, and his funeral was celebrated with extraordinary pomp, the expenses of his obsequies sometimes amounting to as much as $50,000, which sum had ten times as much relative value in Egypt then as it has in the United States now.

At Heliopolis, another bull called Mnevis was selected in a similar manner and worshiped with similar rites; at Hermonthis another bull named Pacis held a like position; and at Momemphis there was a sacred cow; but these animals had a mere local sanctity, whereas Apis was adored throughout Egypt. Alone of the sacred bulls and cows, his death was regarded as a subject for mourning along the Nile from Syene to the Mediterranean.[1]

SEC. 231. *Kings and Gods.*—Religion was part of the government. By virtue of his royal office, the king was at the head of the priesthood, and on many occasions the leader in public worship. The gods did not permit the fidelity of devout monarchs to go without reward. When one of the Egyptian kings was in great danger on the battle-field, he prayed for help to Amon, who immediately responded—so we are told: "I am with thee, Ramses Meriamon. I succor thee. I, thy father, am at thy side. My hand is with thee, and is better than hundreds of thousands of soldiers."[1]

On a granite tablet now in the museum of Boolak, the god Amon thus addresses Thutmes III. at his coronation: "Come to me; rejoice thyself and admire my glory. Thou art my son who honorest me. . . . I shine in the light of the morning sun through thy love; and my heart is enraptured if thou directest thy noble steps to my temple. . . . I will distinguish thee marvelously. I give thee power and victory over all lands. All people shall feel a terror before thy soul. . . . I make thy enemies fall under thy feet. Smite the hosts of thine enemies. Thus I commit to thee the earth in its length and breadth. The inhabitants of the East and the West shall be subject to thee."[2]

A priest says to the king: "Amon gives to thee his kingdom, with the crown and the throne of Hor. The remembrance of thee as king in Egypt shall endure forever. To thee Amon has given the whole world in peace. All nations shall bow before thee." The king responds: "Amon is more enraptured with me than with all the kings who have existed in this country since it was founded. I am his son who loves his holiness. . . . All nations bow themselves before my spirit. The fear of me is in the heart of the nine foreign nations."[3]

Shashank I. thus addresses Amon-Ra: " My gracious god! grant that my words may live for hundreds of thousands of years. It is a high privilege to work for Amon. In recompense for what I have done, grant me a long reign. Grant me welfare, health, long life, power, strength, and a prosperous old age."[4]

The gods, the religion, and the revelation of the Egyptians were national. They were exclusively for the benefit of the people of the country. All aliens were impure, hateful to the gods, and detestable to the people. Their cooking pots and the food cooked in them, their knives and the beasts slain with them, their drinking-cups, and their clothes, were unclean. An Egyptian was contaminated by marrying one or eating with one. The business of the salt-water sailor was disreputable, because it brought the Egyptian into contact with foreigners, and the sea was impure, because it was a channel of communication with the aliens.

SEC. 232. *Monotheistic Expressions.*—Although everywhere in Egypt we find proofs of polytheistic belief, there are many inscriptions suggestive of monotheism. Thus, one of the hymns says: " Hail to thee, Ra-Tum-Horus, of the two worlds, the one god, living by truth, who makest all things, who createst all beasts and men by the glance of thine eyes. Lord of heaven, lord of earth, maker of everything above and of everything below. . . . King of heaven, lord of all gods! O supreme king among the gods; almighty god, self-existent, two-fold substance, existent from the beginning."[1]

A hymn, supposed to have been written about the XIVth century B. C., says: "Glory to thee, who hast begotten all that exists; who hast made man; who hast made the gods, and all the beasts of the field; who makest man to live; who hast no being second to thee. Lord of generation, thou that givest the breath of life, that makest the world to move in its seasons, and orderest the course of the Nile, whose ways are secret. . . . He is the light of the world; he shooteth in the green herb, and maketh the corn, the grass, and the trees of the field."[2]

In all polytheistic countries such language is common, and is meant henotheistically. It does not signify that the worshiper repudiates the popular mythology, or denies the existence of all the divinities save one, or acts the hypocrite whenever he conforms to the rites of the established superstition. It is merely a compliance with the rules of ecclesiastical politeness; it abases the man who speaks and solicits a favor, and exalts the deity who is spoken to and solicited to grant a favor. For that occasion, to the devotee his divine patron is everything that is good and wise and powerful; and an hour later, in a new emergency, he will apply similar titles to another divinity, without any thought that he has been impious or insincere. He uses the customary language of compliment, which neither gods nor men understand literally.

Although we may reasonably presume that some of

the Egyptian priests had outgrown the popular superstition, yet no one said so in unmistakable language. The ancient literature of the country may be searched through in vain for a complete renunciation of polytheism, for the unquestionable recognition of an omnipotent Creator who looks with equal favor on all nations. The idea may have existed in Egyptian thought, but never found its way into Egyptian expression. One Egyptian sovereign, Khunaten, did partially repudiate the national polytheism. He ordered that the only great god worshiped in Egypt should be Aten, a national divinity who loved Egypt and hated other countries. Khunaten failed, but if he had succeeded his success would not have led to the establishment of monotheism. The worship of a national god is essentially polytheistic; it implies that every nation must have its own divinity, and that each national divinity shall be considered as the rival and enemy of all other national divinities.

SEC. 233. *Adoration of Ancestors.*—The highest duty of the Egyptian was to worship his ancestors, and especially those in the direct male line. The temple for this worship was the tomb constructed with special regard for this purpose, and visited by devout descendants of the dead for century after century. It was on the hill-side, with an outer chapel for worship and offerings, a sepulchral chamber excavated in the rock for the mummy, and a shaft, incline, or hall connecting this chamber with the chapel. The latter was decorated on its walls with paintings or sculptures or both; and if the deceased was a person of wealth, his tomb contained his statue. The tomb was far more costly and durable than the dwelling. The former was regarded as an eternal home, the latter as a place of brief sojourn. A common maxim said: "Give the water of the funeral oblation to thy father and thy mother who repose in the tomb. Renew the water of the divine oblation. . . . Thy son will do it for thee in like manner."[1] One of the most malignant curses was to wish that a man should die without a son to make offerings at his tomb.

Ramses II., about 1300 B. C., thus addressed the soul of his deceased father, Mineptah I.: "Awake, raise thy face to heaven, behold the sun, my father, Mineptah, who art like god. Here am I who make thy name to live. I am thy guardian, and my care is directed to thy temple and to thy altars, which are raised up again. . . . Thou enterest on a second existence. . . . I built the house which thou didst love, in which thy image stands, in the necropolis of Abydos forever. I set apart revenues for thee for thy worship daily. . . . If anything which seems wanting to thee can be done by me, I do it for thee. Thy heart shall be satisfied that the best shall be done for thy name. I appoint for thee the priests of the vessel of holy water, provided with everything for sprinkling the water on the ground, besides meat and drink. I myself have come here to behold thy temple near that of Unnofer, the eternal king. I urged on the building of it; I clothed the walls; I did that which thou didst wish, that it may be done for thy whole house. I established thy name therein to all eternity. . . . I dedicated to thee the lands of the South for the service of thy temple, and the lands of the North. . . . I gathered together the people of thy service, one and all, and assigned them to the chief priest of thy temple. All thy property is granted in perpetuity, to keep up thy temple for all time. . . . Thou hast entered into the realm of heaven. Thou accompaniest the sun-god Ra. Thou art in the company of the stars and the moon. . . . Come, intercede for me with Ra, that he may grant long years of life to his son, . . . that he may grant years upon years . . . to King Ramses. Well will it be for thee that I should be king for a long time, for thou wilt be honored by a good son, who remembers his father. I will be the guardian of thy temple every day of my life. . . . Thou shalt be treated as if thou wert still alive. So long as I reign, my attention shall be directed continually to thy temple. My heart beats for thee. . . . The very best shall be thy portion so long as I live, I, King Ramses."[1]

In some cases the offerings were made, not directly to the ancestor, but to a god for the ancestor's benefit. Thus an inscription says: "This is an offering to the lord, Osiris, of Amenti, the great god, who dwells in Abydos. Let him grant offerings for the dead, thousands of oxen, of geese, of incense lumps, of clothes, of wine jars, of milk jars, and of all pure and sweet foods for the soul of Chalun, the priest of Amon." Here Osiris was besought to take good care of Chalun forever and was paid for this service.[3]

SEC. 234. *The Mummy.*—In the opinion of the ancient Egyptians, it was a matter of vast importance to future happiness that the soul should be enabled to re-occupy its earthly body, which was therefore preserved by mummification against decomposition, and protected against destruction by being placed in a tomb designed to last as long as the earth itself. Soul and body were however not considered the only constituent parts of humanity. Sayce[1] says the Egyptians divided man into the body, the soul, and the spirit; but Birch[2] tells us they distinguished the shade, the existence, and the intelligence from the soul, and the mummy from the body, so that there were five, if not six, main parts in the deceased person. The soul or spirit was represented in sculpture and painting by a figure with the body and wings of a hawk, and the head and arms of a man, this combination being designed to personify "its volatile and solar character, and its human intelligence." The spirit, under certain circumstances, could assume the forms of different beasts; but transmigration was not a dogma of the Egyptian religion.[3]

The proper worship of the ancestor required the preservation of the body by embalming; the construction of a tomb with a chapel; the decoration of the chapel or its hall with a record of the good deeds of the deceased; the deposition of the mummy in the sepulchral chamber with jars of food, drink, and perfumes, though these jars might be very small, and intended merely to suggest the good-will of the worshiper; and visits, prayers, and offerings of food, flowers, and perfumes at certain festivals.

The corpses of all persons whose families could bear the expense, including probably most of the freemen, were embalmed, the motive being to have the body ready to receive its soul after the lapse of a long period, which, according to one authority, was three thousand years.[4] The process, in the hands of the most skillful operators, was so successful that the mummies have lasted four thousand years in good condition. At the funeral, which sometimes did not occur until a year after death, there was a great display of mourning, as if the loss was recent. Wailing women mourners threw dust on their heads while walking in front of the sled bearing the mummy drawn by oxen, and priests followed singing a dirge.⁵ A picture shows us the funeral of a distinguished warrior. The mummy sled is followed by a multitude of servants with fruit, wine, ointments, flowers, cooked food, idols of various gods, the arms of the deceased, his chariot and horses, gold vases, and his decorations and symbols of office. After these came the priests with the shrine of a god, presumably that of the provincial divinity, a terra-cotta image of the deceased, and bottles of sacred liquor for libation or purification, and last of all the mourners.

All burials, at least for people dying above the delta, were in the hills west of the Nile, and not unfrequently the mummy was taken to some distant cemetery. The transportation was by boat as far as possible, and then by sled from the river bank across the valley land. The deposition of the mummy in the tomb could be prevented by an accusation of serious crime supported by proofs; but the accuser made himself responsible for his objection, and if his evidence, which must be ready at the moment, was unsatisfactory, he became subject to severe punishment and the burial proceeded. The officiating priest pronounced a eulogy on the deceased, commending him for his good qualities, and besought the gods to admit him to the abode of the blessed in the world of spirits.⁶ In some cases the priests declared that the deceased was born again, and had entered the new life, cleansed from all the impurities of the flesh.⁷

People looked forward to the future life with serious apprehension. The tombs contain many brief prayers for the dead, such as that his soul "may rest in peace," and that the "gates of heaven may open to admit his spirit." A common inscription says: "May a favorable inscription be granted in the other world, the land of the ancient, the good and the great spirits, to the deceased who is faithful to the great god. May he advance in the blissful paths of those who are faithful to the great god. May the funeral oblation be paid to him at all the chief festivals and at the feasts of the month, the half month, and every day."[8]

At Abydos is the tomb of Schotepabra, who, in an inscription, thus solicits the prayers of the pious: "Ye priests of Osiris in the West, in the city of Abydos, ye temple servants of the same god, ye priests of King Amonemhat III., the eternal and ever-living, and of King Usurtasen III., the deceased, and ye temple servants of the same kings, ye inhabitants of this city and every one in the province of Thinis, who shall visit this grave traveling this way or that way, be sure you love your king, be sure you glorify the gods of your country, and then will your children sit in your seat. Ye who enjoy life and do not yet know death, repeat the prayer . . . for the dead."[9]

A prayer in the tomb of a woman says: "May she be counted as one of the elect that serve Osiris. May her soul be restored to youth with their souls, and may her body endure in the depths."[10]

The future existence, as conceived by the Egyptians, was to be similar to the present, in its occupations and emotions, but its happiness as the reward of virtue or misery as the punishment of vice, were to be far more intense. The eternity and the greater acuteness of the pleasures and pains beyond the grave reduced mortality to relative insignificance. All possible terrestrial enjoyments were mere trifles as compared with the celestial. The actual was sacrificed to the imaginary. The people impoverished and enslaved their bodies to secure the wealth and freedom of their souls. They sacrificed this life to the next.

Sec. 235. *Egyptian Morality.*—No other religion teaching a future life of rewards and punishments, and claiming control of the path of salvation, gives so much relative prominence to morality as does the faith of ancient Egypt. The trial before Osiris required such explicit declarations of innocence on all the main points of conduct, without possibility of deception, that people familiar with their mode of examination, and believing in its necessity for future happiness, must have been more impressed with it than by the sacerdotal teaching of ethics in any other religion. The virtues of the ancient Egyptians were very similar to those of Europe in the XVIIth century, before political equality and religious freedom were established principles. They recognized the duties of gentleness and politeness, of mercy and justice, of truthfulness and conjugal fidelity. Renouf[1] remarks that "the triumph of right over wrong, of right in speech and action (for the same word signifies both truth and justice) is the burden of nine-tenths of the Egyptian texts which have come down to us. Right is represented as a goddess ruling as mistress over heaven and earth and the world beyond the grave." There is no suggestion anywhere in the Egyptian books of the demoralizing ideas of sacerdotal indulgences or absolutions for crime. No wrong to mankind can be compensated by conciliating the priest. The sinner is never told that the record of a long life spent in evil shall be wiped out by an hour of credulous and terrified repentance on the death-bed. There is no hope of salvation for any save the just. The Song of the Harper who tells man to enjoy his life, tells him also to enjoy it in a manner consistent with justice:

"Think ever of the day when thou shalt start for the land whence none return. Good for thee there, will have been a virtuous life here. Therefore be just and hate iniquity. He who has loved what is right will triumph there."[2]

"It was usual under the old empire [before 3900 B. C.] for the deceased to speak in his own person and commemorate all his virtues and his public services" in inscriptions on his sepulchral monument. Of such inscriptions the following is a sample: "I honored my father and my mother. I succored the afflicted. I gave bread to the hungry, drink to the thirsty, and clothes to the naked. I sheltered the outcast. I offered to the gods their dues, and funeral oblations to my ancestors. I gave the same treatment to the rich and to the poor. My doors were open to the stranger. I was a wise man and my heart ever loved the Lord. . . . Never did I sow hatred among men. In my day the district which I governed suffered no want, even though there was a famine in the land."[3]

At Beni Hassan, the tomb of Ameni, governor of the province of Antinoë, has an inscription recording the chief incidents in his life, and the chief points in his moral conduct, all told in the first person. The last paragraph in this brief autobiography says: "I was a kind master of a gentle character, a governor who loved his city. I passed many a year as governor in the province of Antinoë. All the works for the palace of the king were placed in my hands. Also the chiefs of . . . the temples of the province of Antinoë gave me thousands of cows with their calves. I received thanks for this on the part of the royal palace, because of the yearly supply of milch cows. I gave up all the produce to the palace, and I kept back nothing for myself out of all the magazines.

The whole province of Antinoë worked for me with activity. No child of the poor did I afflict; no widow did I oppress; no land owner did I displace; no herdsman did I drive away; from no small farmer did I take away his men for my own works. No one was unhappy in my time; no one was hungry in my days, not even in years of famine. For I had tilled all the fields in the province of Antinoë, up to its southern and northern frontiers. Thus I prolonged the life of its inhabitants and preserved the food which it produced. . . . I distributed equally to the widow as to the married woman. I did not prefer the great to the humble in all that I gave away; and when the inundations of the Nile were great, then the owner of the seed was master of his property; nothing of the produce of the land was withdrawn from him by my hand."[4]

SEC. 236. *Egyptian Gospels.*—The Egyptians had their sacred books written by the god Thoth with his own hand. Of these scriptures many portions have been lost, the most important preserved to our time being the Book of the Dead. Its divine origin did not protect it from alterations and additions, especially comments and explanations, which were inserted in the text by copyists, as if they had been portions of the original work.[1]

A hymn says: "Come, O Thoth, writer of the books of the gods, . . . be my protector. Make me skilled in thy works, for they exceed all other works. He that gives himself up to them is found fit for high places. Many have wrought, and it is thou that hast wrought for them. They stand before the king; they are rich and great through thee. . . . Come then to me and be my guide."[2]

The Book of the Dead or Funeral Ritual, already mentioned as the longest and most important relic of Egyptian revelation, is a guide-book for the soul through the dangers that beset it between the death of the body and the final judgment before Osiris. Much of it consists of talismanic formulas which the soul must repeat at certain places and addresses which it must deliver to certain divinities. These formulas and addresses were deposited in the wrappings of the mummy, where the soul should see them at the critical moments and read them off readily and effectively, that is if it did not remember them from having committed them to memory while in the flesh. The heading of one chapter says, "If this chapter is known on earth or inclosed in the sarcophagus, its possessor can enter his eternal home on any day that he may choose."[3]

"The ritual is, according to Egyptian notions, essentially an inspired work; and the term 'Hermetic,' so often applied by profane writers to these books, in reality means inspired. It is Thoth himself who speaks and reveals the will of the gods, and the mysterious nature of divine things to man. This Hermetic character is claimed for the book in several places, where the hieroglyphs or theological writings and the sacred books of Thoth, the divine scribe, are personified. Portions of them are expressly stated to have been written by the very finger of Thoth himself."[4]

While a virtuous life was indispensable for justification before Osiris, it was not sufficient to secure happiness in the future life. Before reaching the judgment-hall, the soul was exposed to great danger from flames, torrents, lions, crocodiles, serpents, and demons; but from all these, the pure spirit would escape with the help of amulets and the sacred texts. One chapter of the Book of the Dead says: "If this chapter be recited over him he will go forth over the earth, pass through every kind of fire, and be safe from injury by any demon."[5]

SEC. 237. *Last Judgment.*—The Egyptians did not accept the hypothesis of one judgment-day for all mankind, after the final destruction of the world, with an omniscient and instant perception, by the divine judge, of the guilt or innocence of every human being, and with an immediate and infallible separation of the two classes to their respective destinations. Instead of this summary decision upon a concourse of countless millions at once, each Egyptian had a separate trial, and if he knew the formulas and could prove his innocence, he had a long and deliberate hearing, being allowed to plead his own case, and to show his right to admission among the blessed. The most important step in this trial was before the great judge of the dead, Osiris, who sat with forty-two prosecutors, each the representative and avenger of a special vice, and perhaps each originally the local deity of an Egyptian province.

We have an ancient Egyptian picture of this celestial court. Osiris the judge sits on his throne. Behind him are the provincial deities, as small squatting figures, many of them with the heads of the locally-sacred beasts. Before Osiris is a table or altar with offerings, and in front of that the kneeling soul, escorted by its advocate Horus, who is accompanied by Anubis, the jackal-headed god. The ibis-headed god, Thoth, the recorder of the tribunal, stands with his tablet and pencil, ready to write down the merits and demerits of the soul and the final judgment. Another figure appears, a monster ready to eat up the guilty soul after condemnation. A large scale stands ready to be used in weighing the soul, which is represented as inclosed in a vase, and on the other side of the scale is a figure of the goddess Mat or Righteousness, with a scepter and the Egyptian cross, as an emblem of eternal life.

Having been brought into the presence of the great judge, the soul said: "Oh ye Lords of Truth! Oh thou great God, Lord of Truth! I have come to thee, my Lord. I have brought myself to see thy blessings. I have known thee. I have known thy name. I have known the names of the forty-two gods who are with thee in the Hall of Two Truths, living by catching the wicked, fed on their blood. . . . Placer of Spirits is thy name.

"Oh ye Lords of Truth, let me know ye! I have brought ye truth. Rub ye away my faults. I have not privily done evil to mankind. I have not afflicted men. I have not told falsehoods in the tribunal of Truth. I have had no acquaintance with evil. I have not done any wicked thing. I have not made the laboring man do more than his task daily. . . . I have not been idle. . . . I have not been weak. I have not done what is hateful to the gods. I have not calumniated the slave to his master. . . . I have not caused weeping. I have not murdered. I have not given orders to smite a person privily. I have not defrauded my neighbor. I have not used false measures. I have not injured the images of the gods. I have not taken scraps from the bandages of the dead. I have not committed adultery. . . . I have not withheld milk from sucklings. I have not hunted animals in prohibited places. I have not netted sacred birds. I have not caught sacred fish. I have not stopped running water. I have not diverted water from its channel unlawfully.

I have not put out a light which should have been left burning. I have not stolen the offerings of the gods. . . . I am pure! I am pure! I am pure! . . . Let no evil be done to me in the land of Truth. I know the names of the gods who are with thee in the hall of Truth. Save me from them."

Having thus addressed the presiding judge, the soul on trial addresses by name each of the forty-two prosecutors, mentions the province or city which he represents, and declares himself innocent of the special sin under his jurisdiction. Many of these sins are among those of which he had previously asserted his innocence. Among the speeches to the associate judges are the following:—

"Oh Gaper [mouth?] of Kar, I have not waylaid!

"Oh Nostril of Hermopolis, I have not boasted!

"Oh Lion-gods of Heaven [?], I have not counterfeited rings!

"Oh Eyes of Flames of Khemmo, I have not been a hypocrite!

"Oh White Tooth of the Frontier, I have not plundered!

"Oh Eater of Hearts of —— [?], I have not conspired!

"Oh Follower of Heliopolis, I have not let my mouth wander!

"Oh Beholder of Khem, I have not polluted myself!

"Oh child of Hekh, I have not been inattentive to the words of truth!

"Oh Swallower of Khenem, I have not blasphemed!

"Oh Palace Overthrower of Uten, I have not clipped the skins of the sacred beasts!

"Oh Lord of Purity of Sais, I have not multiplied words in speaking!

"Oh Tum Sap of Tattu, I have not reviled the face of the king or of my father!

"Oh Eye in his Heart of Salu, I have not defiled the river!

"Oh Yoker of Good, of Heliopolis, I have not injured the gods or calumniated a slave to his master!

"Oh Arm-leader of Ankar, I have not despised a god secretly or openly!"

Having completed his separate addresses to the associate judges, the soul on trial thus continues:—

"Hail ye gods in the Hall of Truth, without deceit. . . . Save ye me from the god Aa, who eats vitals on the day of judgment. Let the Osiris [the soul] pass on. Ye know he is without . . . sin. . . . Do not torture . . . him. He lives off the truth. . . . He has made his delight in doing what men prescribe and what the gods wish. . . . He has given food to the hungry, drink to the thirsty, clothes to the naked. . . . He has given the sacred food to the gods and to the spirits. Therefore do not accuse him before the Lord of the Mummies; . . . his mouth is pure, his hands are pure. Oh . . . Lord of the Crown . . . save Osiris from the waylayers and the delusions which lead the uninstructed to defilement or annihilation. The Osiris has been faithful to the Lord of Truth. He is pure, his heart is pure."

The judges tell him to pass on, and when he does so different parts of the building, including the sill, the left jamb, the right jamb, the key, the key-hole, and the lock of the door, arrest him, and each asks him to tell its name, which he must do.

The soul thus addresses Thoth: "Place me before thee, O Lord of Eternity! I have no sins, no perversion. I do no evil. I have done what men prescribed, what the gods wished. Hail, Lord of the West! Let me pass the roads of darkness."[1] Thoth replies: "Go forth, thou hast been introduced. Thy food is from the eye, thy drink is from the eye. . . . The Osiris has been justified forever."[2]

The soul, passing on to purgatory, where four gods in the shape of apes sit as judges, thus addresses them: "Oh great Four Apes, seated in front of the boat of the sun, sending truth to the universal lord, judging my deficiencies and my abundance, welcoming gods with the fire, . . . giving divine offerings to the gods, . . . living in truth, fed with truth, . . . abominating wickedness, extract ye all the evil out of me, obliterate my faults, annihilate my sins, and let me pass the gate of the West."

The gods of purgatory reply: "Thou mayest go. We pardon all thy faults; we wash out all thy sins. Thou hast been cleansed of everything earthy. . . . Thou mayest pass the secret doors of the West. Thou canst come forth and go in as thou wishest, like one of the spirits hailed daily within the horizon."

Having passed through purgatory, the soul thus addresses the gate-keepers of the gate of the highest heaven in the West: "Hail, ye gods dwelling in the West! Hail, ye lords, keepers of the gate! . . . Let me pass. . . . My soul enters your domain. I am one of ye."

They reply to him: "Thou hast spoken truth against thy enemies, O great god. . . . He who dwells in the West serves the Osiris. He is justified in the gate like the stars." And then, as if addressing one another, they say: "Open ye the gates; . . . prepare ye his hall. . . . Let him have the food of the gods of the gate. Let him have the head-dress which belongs to his rank. . . . The Osiris has been crowned as the living soul of the sun in the heaven. He has made all the appointed transformations. He has been justified before the chiefs. He has passed through the gates on earth and in heaven, like the soul of the sun."

The soul says: "I have opened the gate of heaven and earth. The soul of the Osiris rests here. . . . I go in and come out as I choose." The soul appears in adoration before the throne of Osiris, Isis, and Horus, and in response to his address, Osiris says: "Welcome. . . . Thou hast come, thy genius with thee. Thou art at peace in the name of Ka and Hetp. Thy genius is spiritualized under the name of Akher; he is adored under the name of Kfa. . . . I place all thy enemies under thee, everywhere. Thou art justified before the associate gods. . . . Thou hast been made a great god."

SEC. 238. *Egyptian Priests.*—The Egyptian priests were abundantly endowed by the government, and they were organized thoroughly in a number of ranks and occupations under the king, who was the chief priest. The sacerdotal office was reserved for persons of noble blood, and usually the sons of a priest followed the profession of their father; but they might also hold political and military offices. The priests were required to follow strict rules of diet, clothing, and personal cleanliness, but were not forbidden to marry. They became judges, scribes, sacrificers, temple custodians, and soothsayers. Some of the temples had augurs who predicted the future according to omens; others had oracular revelations which they delivered to applicants, and in some instances, through the mouth of a hollow statue, in which the concealed priest spoke in the name of the pretended god.[1]

The higher priests and no others were admitted to a

secret society called "The Mysteries." Their rites, though carefully concealed from outsiders, were spoken of as of great importance for the life to come. It is supposed that these Egyptian mysteries were similar to the Greek Eleusinian mysteries—the latter, however, were open to respectable freemen generally—and that their main purpose was to teach the initiated the movements, words, and tones with which the spirits and god should be approached and addressed in the next world, before the soul was finally justified in the great judgment before Osiris.

The ecclesiastical ceremonies included prayer, vocal and instrumental music, dancing, processions, incense burning, decoration of the idols with jewels, fine cloth, and garlands, and of the temples with banners, sacrifices of beasts, and offerings of vegetable food, and of fermented liquors. In their public worship the high priests wore a sacerdotal costume, including miter-like caps. When praying, they raised their hands and turned their palms outward.[2] In their processions, they carried the shrines of their gods, sometimes as many as sixteen priests combining to support one of these burdens. The shrine, the portable home of the god, and the shelter of his small idol, was a square wooden box bearing the decoration of the scarabæus[3] or the goddess Ma, either of which there had outstretched wings. As a support, the shrine rested on a boat or sled, suggesting the boat or sled used for moving the heavy mummy of the dead man to his final resting-place.[4]

The chief feature of worship was the feeding of the gods with meat by sacrificing brutes, for which every temple had its altar. The legs were usually taken off, to be eaten by the priests and the worshiper; the body, after having been disemboweled, was filled with bread, figs, honey, etc., and burned. Human sacrifice is not mentioned on the monuments or in the books of the Egyptians, nor did the Greeks find any evidence that it was ever practiced in the valley of the Nile; but an unmistakable trace of its existence there is found in the seal on an ox designated for sacrifice. This is the figure of a man with his hands bound behind him, and a knife pointed at his throat.[5]

There was no sacred day, save as an annual festival, no preaching or reading from sacred books to the people at brief intervals, no sacred building suitable for congregational worship, and no parish priest supervising the intellectual, moral, social, and charitable affairs of his district. When the layman needed supernatural aid or advice, he took a beast to the temple, where the priest sacrificed it, and made a prayer for the aid needed, inspected or interpreted the omens or lots, or announced the divine oracles; and such offerings three or four times in the year might be the man's only participation in the worship of the great gods.

The laying of the corner-stone of a great temple and the final dedication of the completed building were occasions of much ecclesiastical display. An inscription commemorating the consecration of a temple says, "The king makes a gift of the house to thee his god;" and the divinity responds by promising long life and dominion over all countries to the monarch.[6]

SEC. 239. *Egyptian Antiquity.*—Ancient Egypt enjoyed a long period of peaceful prosperity, unequaled in its length by any other country save perhaps China. In more than forty centuries, it suffered no serious revolution in blood, language, religion, or system of government.

Several times it became subject to foreign rulers, but these adopted the manners, customs, tongue, and faith of their subjects, so that the only notable change was one of dynasty.

Until after the rise of Christianity, there was no ecclesiastical persecution or war in Egypt. Dislike of alien religions stimulated the people to resist alien dominion, but it was not the primary motive of any important military movement. When they invaded Western Asia, they did not attempt to establish the Egyptian religion there; nor did the Arabian, Assyrian, or Persian conquerors attempt to suppress the ancient forms of Egyptian worship, or to introduce any new priesthood or erect temples of a different faith in the valley of the Nile.

The only notable project of religious change or reform was undertaken in the XVth century B. C. by Amenhotep IV. (Khunaten), who seems to have been a thorough Egyptian in blood, education, and sentiment. He limited his adoration to Aten, the god of light, and undoubtedly wished to establish a monotheistic faith and worship; but he did not persecute those who thought differently, and his projected reform died with him.[1]

The Egyptians claimed to be the oldest of nations. Their traditions, extending back more than 10,000 years, receive at least partial confirmation from the settled condition of the political and ecclesiastical institutions at the date of their oldest monuments, from the great change in the height of the inundation of the Nile after they began to keep their records, and by the rise of the Nile Valley, as evinced by the finding of pottery deep below the surface, and by the deposit of many feet of sediment around the bases of many monuments. Herodotus says:

"When Hecateus, the historian, was at Thebes [about

480 B. C.] and, discoursing of his genealogy, traced his descent to a god in the sixteenth ancestor, the priests of Jupiter [Amon] did to him exactly as they afterwards did to me, though I made no boast of my family. They led me into the inner sanctuary, which is a spacious chamber, and showed me a multitude of colossal statues in wood, which they counted up and found to amount to the exact number which they had said, the custom being for every high priest, during his life-time, to set up his statue in the temple. As they showed me the figures and reckoned them up, they assured me that each was the son of the one preceding him. . . . Their colossal figures were each, they said, a piromis [man] born of a piromis."[2]

"They [the Egyptians] told me that the first man who ruled over Egypt was Men [Menes] and that in his time all Egypt except the Thebaic canton [the valley north of the southern point of the Delta] was a marsh, none of the land below Lake Mœris then showing itself above the water. This is a distance of seven days' sail from the sea up the river."[3]

"They [the Egyptian priests] declare that from their first king to this last-mentioned monarch, the priest of Vulcan [Sethos, about 690 B. C.], was a period of three hundred and forty-one generations; such, at least, they say was the number both of their kings and of their high priests during this interval. Now three hundred generations of men make 10,000 years, three generations filling up the century; and the remaining forty generations make thirteen hundred and forty years. Thus the whole number of years is 11,340 [it should be 11,366⅔], in which entire space, they said, no god had ever appeared in a human form; nothing of this kind had happened under the former or under the later Egyptian kings. The sun, however, had within this period of time on four several occasions moved from his wonted course, twice rising where he now sets, and twice setting where he now rises." [4]

This last sentence has been a puzzle to scholars. Their most probable explanation of it is that it had its origin in a misunderstanding of a statement that the heliacal rising of Sothis or Sirius on the 28th of July had been observed four times by astronomers, and as the interval from one such rising to another is fourteen hundred and sixty years, these observations would carry back the records of the Nile Valley four thousand three hundred and eighty years beyond the beginning of the Sothic cycle in which Herodotus lived, that is, to 5700 B. C. In the works of that author there are several passages suggestive of the antiquity of Egypt. He says, "Almost all the names of the gods came into Greece from Egypt."[5] "The Egyptians were also the first to introduce solemn assemblies, processions, and litanies to the gods, of all which the Greeks were taught the use by them."[6]

Diodorus reported that four hundred and seventy-nine kings had reigned in Egypt before Cambyses, and this number, with an average of four reigns to a century, would carry the foundation of the monarchy back to 11,700 B. C. Plato wrote of Egyptian works of art 10,-000 years old still existing in his time, and he said that the Egyptian priests had told Solon, "You Greeks are always children."

One of the evidences of the great antiquity and of the indigenous origin of Egyptian culture, is found in the fact that the language, like that of China, has no grammatical inflection, and that the same word may be noun, adjective, or verb, according to its position in the sentence. The early adoption of a mode of writing seems to have acted as a check on the growth of the art of speaking.[7]

All Egyptologists admit that before 1000 B. C. no Egyptian date can be fixed with entire accuracy, and they differ much in their approximate estimates of the dates before 2000 B. C., the differences between high authorities amounting in some instances to more than a dozen centuries. Mahaffy, who is one of the latest scholars, and whose opinions are usually based on careful research and judicious estimation of evidence, places the Old Empire from Menes to Ptahhotep, and, including the first five dynasties, between 5000 and 3900 B. C.; the Middle Empire, including four dynasties, from the eleventh to the fourteenth, between 3050 and 2400 B. C.; and the New Empire, including fourteen dynasties, from the eighteenth to the thirty-first, between 1700 and 340 B. C. At the end of the Middle Empire, Egypt became subject to the Hyksos, or Shepherd Kings, who seem to have been Arabs, and who held possession of the throne for five centuries or more. The monuments and books tell very little about these rulers; indeed, if it were not for information from foreign sources, we should not understand the references made to them by the inscriptions in the valley of the Nile. They seem to have adopted the religion, customs, and ideas of the Egyptians. Perhaps it was while they were in power, and perhaps not until afterwards, that the Egyptians began to invade Syria and Mesopotamia, which they ravaged repeatedly, their most successful expeditions being in the XVth and XIVth centuries B. C. In the Xth century there were several sovereigns with Assyrian names, Shashank, Tiglath, Sargon, and Nimrod (though the Egyptian spellings were different from these), who were sons of an Egyptian king by an Assyrian wife. Having been born and bred in the valley of the Nile, they were true Egyptians. Not long after the time of these Egyptians with foreign names, the Assyrians conquered the country, but their rule was disturbed by revolts, and they were soon expelled. The land, however, never regained perfect peace and prosperity under its old institutions. Cambyses with his Persians became master in 527 B. C., and Alexander with his Greeks in 332 B. C., after which no ruler of the ancient blood sat on the throne.

SEC. 240. *Egypt's Place.*—The situation of Egypt was favorable to the rise of an indigenous culture. In early antiquity, before armies and fleets had been organized and well prepared for distant expeditions, the valley of the Nile was not easily reached by any large military force from abroad. There was a desert on the east and another on the west. To the north lay the sea, and to the south lay a torrid region not favorable to the growth of a formidable military power. Protected by her isolated position, Egypt grew through many centuries with little interference by foreign invasion.

Although it is probable that the Egyptians made many inventions, yet we have no conclusive evidence that any important useful art originated among them. They may have learned from other nations to smelt copper, tin, and iron from their ores, to quarry and cut stone, to erect buildings with lime mortar, to use the square, level, and plumb-line, to irrigate fields, and to manage large herds of domestic animals. The only feature of Egyptian industry not found in very early times in Western Asia was the artesian well.

The most notable original contribution of Egypt to culture was a comprehensive system of hieroglyphics or word signs, which were afterwards developed into syllabic signs, and then into primary sound signs. The Chinese also invented word signs, as did the Aztecs, with perhaps the suggestion from some person who had seen or heard of the hieroglyphs in the old world; but the people in the Nile Valley are entitled to the credit of having first devised an alphabet, though they did not reduce it to the simplest form and use it exclusively. For that reduction and exclusive use we are indebted to the Phœnicians.

In their sculpture and architecture the Egyptians were original, and in the latter they developed an impressive national style. The Egyptian religion has many original features, including the ritual of the future life, the elaborate system of animal worship, and the importance to a future life of a mummy. But these novel religious conceptions have not been adopted in other countries, and have been of no value to general culture.

Coming next, in this respect, to the Menu Hindoos, the ancient Egyptians had a powerful priesthood and an oppressive religion. The common people were held in the most complete subjection, with the aid of the national superstition, which consumed a large part of their energies, and gave them little in return. Their government was despotic, their army weak, their literature and art without high merit.

CHAPTER XV.

THE HINDOOS, ETC.

SECTION 241. *Primitive Aryans.*—Before considering the Hindoos, the main subject of this chapter, let us take a glance at the primitive Aryans, the ancestors of the Hindoos, Persians, Medes, Armenians, Afghans, Belooches, Phrygians, and Circassians in Asia, and of the Greeks, Latins, Celts, Teutons, and Slavonians in Europe. We cannot be indifferent to the blood from which are descended the nations that in the past have played the greatest parts in the history of the world; that in the present century occupy or dominate over most of the temperate regions of the globe; and that, for many centuries to come, will continue to lead all other branches of the human family in industry, social refinement, wise government, enlightened religion, and polished literature.

"The Aryan nations who pursued a northwesterly direction, stand before us in history as the principal nations of northwestern Asia and Europe. They have been the most prominent actors in the great drama of history, and have carried to their fullest growth all the elements of active life with which our nature is endowed. They have perfected society and morals; and we learn from their literature and works of art, the elements of science, the laws of art, and the principles of philosophy. In continual struggle with each other and with Semitic and Turanian races, these Aryan nations have become the rulers of history, and it seems to be their mission to link all parts of the world together by the chains of civilization, commerce, and religion."[1]

Our knowledge of the primitive Aryans is derived almost exclusively from the study of the languages of their descendants. These tongues form a distinct linguistic family differing from all others in their modes of inflecting words and combining them in sentences, and also in their fitness for giving expression to the leading classes of human thought and emotion with precision, fullness, force, brevity, elegance, and dignity.

When we compare the words used by the Hindoos, Persians, Greeks, Latins, Teutons, Celts, and Slavonians, to express some of the most common ideas, we find that notwithstanding some difference in spelling, they are substantially the same and must have come from a common source. This identity in speech implies that all those ideas were familiar to the primitive Aryans. By similar evidence we know that they had horses, sheep, goats, and pigs; that they burned pottery, wove cloth of wool and hemp, built boats, worked in gold, silver, copper, and bronze; they had lamps, and windows in their houses, they tilled the ground with hoes and ploughs, had ox-yokes and ox-carts, milked their cows, drank mead, ornamented themselves with rings, bracelets, and necklaces, made music with the flute, trumpet, and drum, and that they fought with sword, bow, spear, and shield.

"Many words still live in India and in England that have witnessed the first separation of the Northern and Southern Aryans, and these are witnesses not to be shaken by any cross-examination. The terms for god, for house, for father, mother, son, daughter, for dog and cow, for heart and tears, for axe and tree, identical in all the Indo-European idioms, are like the watchwords of soldiers. We challenge the seeming stranger; and whether he answers with the lips of a Greek, a German, or an Indian, we recognize him as one of ourselves. Though the historian may shake his head, though the physiologist may doubt, and the poet scorn the idea, all must yield before the facts furnished by language."[2]

That they were an intellectual people is proved by the possession of many terms for abstract ideas, including thought, will, memory, and soul. They established and framed the essential forms of the original grammar of inflected speech, which has reached its highest development in the literature of the Aryan nations.[3]

As to the time when the primitive Aryans began to divide, and as to the region which they occupied before they separated, there is no conclusive proof. Perhaps the preponderance of authority as to the date is in favor of 4000 to 3500 B. C., and as to the place, in favor of Bactria, but the latter point is very doubtful. Much can be said in favor of the supposition that the original home of the primitive Aryans was in Southern Russia. Wherever that home was, it was a center from which a dozen conquering migrations to different regions led to the establishment of as many Aryan nations and tongues.

Some authors have described the society of the primitive Aryans as divided into patriarchal families, each including a number of adult males with their wives and children, under a patriarch who might be the chief or a sub-chief in a masculine clan. In this system, which prevailed in various Aryan nations, including the Celts, and still exists among the Slavonians and Hindoos, the individual owns no property in land, houses, or herds. These belong to the family, clan, or village. In several Aryan nations, however, we find traces of the feminine clan, which could not have existed with or after the patriarchal family. As we are unable to prove that the feminine clan disappeared among the primitive Aryans before they began to separate, so we cannot safely assert that the patriarchal family was part of their common social system.

SEC. 242. *Hindostan.*—Hindostan, or India, reaches from the eighth to the thirty-fifth degree of north latitude, and has an area of 1,300,000 square miles. Its soil generally is fertile, and well situated for cultivation and irrigation. The streams are numerous and large, and rains are abundant. The supply of snow in the Himalayas is unsurpassed in extent and depth. Except in those mountains, the climate is tropical or subtropical, and not conducive to either mental or physical energy. The total population is about 200,000,000, of whom 160,000,000 are believers in the Brahminical religion, and perhaps an equal number are predominantly of Aryan blood.

The earliest inhabitants of Hindostan known to history were the Dravidians, a dark-skinned people, apparently of the black race, whose descendants are now numerous in the southern part of the peninsula, and are also found in Ceylon. At some remote time, probably as early as 3500 B. C., Aryans coming from the northwest invaded and conquered the basin of the Indus, established there their laws, customs, language, and religion, and enslaved the surviving Dravidians. At a later time the descendants of these Aryans conquered the remainder of the peninsula.

Since a remote time, the population has been so dense that their food has been almost exclusively vegetable. The most productive cereal in many of the valleys is rice, which contains a small proportion of nitrogen, and gives relatively little nourishment to the muscles. Climate and diet contributed to diminish the energy which other Aryans have shown in colder countries, and which these doubtless had when they first invaded the basin of the Indus.

SEC. 243. *Vedic Hindoos.*—The Aryan conquerors of the Indus basin composed a series of hymns, of which about a thousand of unknown authorship and date, preserved for centuries without the aid of writing, and still in existence, make up the Rig Veda, the oldest sacred book of the Brahmins. Many of the hymns of the Rig Veda may have had their origin as late as 1500 B. C., and perhaps none were reduced to writing before 800 or 600 B. C.; but these dates are suggested only as the results of surmise. The Vedic hymns are the only sources of information about the condition of those Aryans who conquered the non-Aryan occupants of the Punjab. Rice and the Ganges are not mentioned, and therefore we are led to infer that when the hymns were written the Aryans had not yet left the basin of the Indus.[1]

Like all other branches of the early Aryan stock, they were a martial, aggressive, and conquering people. Their position as invaders and conquerors improved their drill and increased their military efficiency. The activity and energy of their Northern blood may have adhered to them for many generations, and was perhaps strengthened by successive migrations. Before reaching Hindostan, they had presumably been familiar with the hereditary classes of nobles, freemen, and slaves, but whether the two latter classes were included among the invaders is uncertain. The first expeditions, undertaken when the country which they hoped to conquer was not well known, and when the result of their venture was considered doubtful, would be made by none save the nobles or professional warriors. There must also have been a class of men who devoted themselves to ecclesiastical business and composed and preserved the hymns, prayers, and formulas for controlling the divinities. There is nothing to indicate that the priesthood had become a separate hereditary class.

The wealth of the people was mostly in cows, from which they derived the names of many plants, birds, and other things, and also those of the principal divisions of the day. They undertook many plundering expeditions to capture the herds of their enemies. " The gift of a cow was a mark of honor reserved for notable occasions, such as the entertainment of an honored guest, the marriage of a daughter, or the death of one of the family, when a cow was slaughtered on the funeral pile. Finally, the simple fancies of the people found suggestions of their precious domestic animal in the grand phenomena of nature. For them the clouds were celestial cows which nourished the earth with their milk; and the stars were a luminous herd led across the firmament by the solar bull."[1]

SEC. 244. *Vedic Religion.*—The Vedic Hindoos had a distinct idea of a continued life after death; a life in which ancestors and relatives would be recognized; a life with joy and sorrow; a life with rewards for the good and punishment for the bad. Yama was the god who ruled over the realm of spirits, where the good soul appeared in a purified and glorified body. Wolves and dogs beset the path of the new-comer, but if he had lived a devout life, Yama would drive them off. There were regions of brightness and delight for the blest, and pits of darkness for the evil-doers and contemners of the gods.

The gods were numerous, most prominent among them being personifications of fire or Agni, the sky or Varuna, the earth, the sun, the moon, the dawn or Ushas, and the storm winds or Maruts. Besides these great gods, worshiped publicly, were the ancestral divinities adored in every household. Fire, being used in most of the ceremonials of worship, was considered one of the chief emblems of divine power, and was the divinity nearest and dearest to the people. Next to fire were Varuna the sky and Mitra the sun. Worship was paid by the sacrifice of animals, by offerings of vegetable food, by libations, prayers, hymns, and processions. There was no temple; no altar save the family hearth; no system of public worship. The most precious sacrifice was that of a horse; the most precious libation, the fermented juice of the soma, and when offering it to the gods, the worshiper partook of it and enjoyed its exhilaration.

The corpse was sometimes buried,[1] and sometimes burned; and the widow might die on the funeral pyre of her husband if she wished; but the Veda did not demand that she should sacrifice herself in this manner.

The general tone of the Rig Veda is joyous. The people are prosperous. They are not yet overcrowded. The fears of a future of miserable transmigration have not settled down on them. They have not lost their skill in arms. They look forward with confidence to new conquests, and they expect as much from their gods in war as in peace.

In the Rig Veda we find a number of highly poetical myths, which, in the delicacy of their conception, and the beauty of their phraseology, have no equals save in Greece; and indeed it is evident from a comparison of the myths of the two countries, that many must have come from a common source, and that source the spirit of a people endowed with a very fertile imagination and a refined taste. The following hymn to Aurora is from the Rig Veda:—

"The fair and bright Ushas [Eos, Dawn] with her bright child [the sun] has arrived. To her the dark night has relinquished her abodes; kindred to one another, immortal, alternating Day and Night go on changing color. The same is the never-ending path of the two sisters, which they travel, commanded by the gods. They strive not, they rest not, the prolific Night and Dawn, concordant though unlike. The shining Ushas, leader of joyful hymns, has been perceived. She has opened for us the doors of the sky; setting in motion all moving things, she has revealed to us riches. Ushas has awakened all creatures, . . . arousing one to seek royal power, another to follow after fame, another for grand efforts, and another to pursue as it were his particular object. Ushas awakes all creatures to consider their different modes of life. She, the daughter of the sky, has been beheld breaking forth, youthful, clad in shining attire, mistress of all earthly treasures. Auspicious Ushas, shine here to-day."[2]

In one of the hymns the worshiper prays for "strength, glorious, invincible in battle, brilliant, wealth-conferring, praiseworthy, known to all men." The prayers solicited rapid increase of herds, abundant crops of grain, and all forms of riches, "wealth durable, rich in men, defying all onslaught, wealth a hundred and a thousand-fold always increasing." It was clearly understood that the benefits of the adoration were to be reciprocal. The devotee and the god had made a compact for their mutual advantage.

Each owed a duty to the other, and the priest did not neglect to remind the divinity of his obligation, and even to suggest that he was shirking his task. Thus he says: "If you, sons of Prisni, were mortals and your worshiper an immortal, then never should your praises be unwelcome, like a deer in a pasture-field, nor should he go on the path of destruction."[3] Another Vedic poet says:[4] "Were I Indra, like thee, the sole lord of wealth, the singer of my praises should be rich in wealth."

SEC. 245. *Vedic Hymns.*—Here are copies of Vedic hymns:—

"Giver of life and immortality,
 One in thy essence, but to mortals, three;
 Displaying thine eternal triple form
 As fire on earth, as lightning in the air,
 As sun in heaven. Thou art the cherished guest
 In every household—father, brother, son,
 Friend, benefactor, guardian, all in one.
 Deliver, mighty lord, thy worshipers,
 Purge us from taint of sin; and when we die,
 Deal mercifully with us on the pyre,
 Burning our bodies with their load of guilt,
 But bearing our eternal part on high
 To luminous abodes and realms of bliss,
 Forever there to dwell with righteous men.

"Behold, the rays of Dawn, like heralds, lead on high
 The Sun, that men may see the great, all-knowing God.
 The stars slink off like thieves in company with Night,
 Before the all-seeing eye, whose beams reveal his presence,
 Gleaming like brilliant flames to nation after nation.
 Surya, with flaming locks, clear-sighted god of day,
 Thy seven ruddy mares bear on thy rushing car.
 With these thy self-yoked steeds, seven daughters of thy chariot,
 Onward thou dost advance. To thy refulgent orb
 Beyond this lower gloom, and upward to the light
 Would we ascend, O Sun, thou god among the gods."[1]

"What god shall we adore with sacrifice?
Him let us praise, the golden child that rose
In the beginning, who was born the Lord—
The one sole Lord of all that is—who made
The earth and formed the sky, who giveth life,
Who giveth strength, whose bidding gods revere,
Whose hiding-place is immortality,
Whose shadow, death; who by his weight is King
Of all the breathing, sleeping, waking world.
Where'er let loose in space, the mighty waters
Have gone, depositing a fruitful seed,
And generating fire; there He arose
Who is the breath and life of all the gods,
Whose mighty glance looks round the vast expanse
Of watery vapor—source of energy,
Cause of the sacrifice—the only God
Above all gods."[2]

Creation is thus described:—

"In the beginning there was neither naught nor aught;
. . . .
There was neither death nor immortality;
There was neither day nor night, nor light nor darkness,
Only the existent One breathed calmly, self-contained.
Naught else but he there was—naught else above, beyond.
Then first came darkness hid in darkness, gloom in gloom;
Next all was water, all a chaos indiscrete,
In which the One lay void, shrouded in nothingness.
Then turning inwards, he by self-developed force
Of inner fervor and intense abstraction, grew.
First in his mind was formed Desire, the primal germ
Productive, which the Wise, profoundly searching, say
Is the first subtle bond, connecting Entity
With Nullity."[3]

A great first cause is recognized henotheistically:—

"I see thee, mighty Lord of all, revealed
In forms of infinite diversity.
I see thee like a mass of purest light,
Flashing thy luster everywhere around.
I see thee crowned with splendor like the sun,
Pervading earth and sky, immeasurable,

Boundless, without beginning, middle, end;
Preserver of imperishable law,
Spirit everlasting; the triple world
Is awe-struck at this vision of thy form,
Stupendous, indescribable in glory.
Have mercy, God of gods; the universe
Is fitly dazzled by thy majesty,
Fitly to thee alone devotes its homage." [4]

"The mighty Varuna, who rules above, looks down
Upon these worlds, his kingdoms, as if close at hand.
When men imagine they do aught by stealth, he knows it.
No one can stand, or walk, or softly glide along,
Or hide in dark recess, or lurk in secret cell,
But Varuna detects him, and his movements spies.
Two persons may devise some plot, together sitting,
And think themselves alone; but he, the King, is there—
A third—and sees it all. His messengers descend
Countless from his abode, forever traversing
This world, and scanning with a thousand eyes its inmates.
Whate'er exists within this earth, and all within the sky,
Yea, all that is beyond, King Varuna perceives.
The winkings of men's eyes are numbered all by him;
He wields the universe as gamesters handle dice." [5]

One of the hymns has this prayer for a happy future life: "Where there is eternal light, in the world where the sun is placed, in that immortal, imperishable world, place me, O Soma! Where King Varvasvata reigns, where the secret place of heaven is, where the mighty waters are, there make me immortal! Where life is free, in the third heaven of heavens, where the worlds are radiant, there make me immortal! Where wishes and desires are, where the bowl of the bright Soma is, where there is food and rejoicing, there make me immortal! Where there is happiness and delight, where joy and pleasure reside, where the desires of our desire are attained, there make me immortal!"

The hymns here quoted are decidedly superior in

merit to the bulk of the Rig Veda. Max Müller tells us that much of it is artificial, and that if we expect to find in all its parts high poetical diction, striking comparisons, and bold combinations, we shall be disappointed.[6] Many of the hymns are "childish in the extreme, tedious, low, and commonplace."[7]

SEC. 246. *Hindoo Literature, etc.*—The greatest achievements of the Hindoos have been of a literary character, perhaps because all other classes of people were made slavishly subservient to the students or priests. The ancient language was one that was well adapted for the expression of the widest range of ideas with force, elegance, and precision.

"The Sanscrit is not only more copious in grammatical forms than the Greek or any other tongue, but more regularly derived throughout, from roots within the language itself; and the reason of this is that the people speaking it were earlier settled in their preappointed habitations, passed through a less interrupted development, and were exposed to fewer invasions from abroad than their westward-marching brethren. Besides this, when they first moulded their social and political organizations, they introduced into their fundamental institutions certain principles of permanence which gave such durability to their legislative and religious system, that it has undergone few and slight changes, except a single great religious schism, for more than four thousand years."[1]

Much progress was made at a very remote age in the science of language, and of the art of literary composition. "The Sanscrit system of accentuation is identical with that of the Greek, . . . and its principles were discussed and settled by Sanscrit grammarians two centuries before the time of Aristophanes, the Greek grammarian to whom the first systematic treatment of the subject has been attributed."[2]

The Hindoos deserve credit for making the first grammars and dictionaries, for thinking out the first systems of metaphysical philosophy, and for originating many religious ideas, which afterwards found extensive acceptance in other countries. They anticipated the Christians in accepting the doctrine of an incarnate divinity, who assumed the human form for the purpose of saving sinners; and they elaborated the most comprehensive and precise theory of revelation.[3]

In grammars and dictionaries the Hindoos were far in advance of the Greeks and of all other nations, with the exception perhaps of those in the basin of the Euphrates. Their sacred poetry is unequaled in excellence, and the revelations surpass all others in quantity. The Rig Veda is about as long as the Iliad; the Ramayana is nearly twice as long; the Mahabarata, more than ten times as long; and the Puranas, in the aggregate, a hundred times as long. Besides these, there are many others, so that to read all the sacred scriptures of the Brahmins is no light task even for a person familiar with the tongues and dialects in which the oldest copies are written.

All these works have the tone of poetry rather than of prose, of fiction rather than fact, of extravagance and metaphysical subtlety rather than of simplicity and direct statement.[4]

Much of the Hindoo poetry possesses high literary merit, and among its greatest works are the Ramayana and the Mahabarata, from which latter several quotations will appear in later sections of this work. Among the great national epics, the Iliad, Shahnameh, Nibelungen Lied, and Kalavala, the Mahabarata deserves the second place in literary merit, and in popular interest and influence in modern times the first place.[5]

As for historical composition, there is none among the older books of Hindostan, or at least none that deserves to be compared for a moment with the writings of the Greek and Roman historians. The favorite subject of study seems to have been the human mind, in various phases, many of which led the authors into abstract speculation. The "Arabian Nights" and "Æsop's Fables" are copied from the ancient books of the Hindoo.

Two very important inventions in arithmetic are the abacus and the Hindoo numerals. The abacus, or counting-board, has separate columns for units, tens, hundreds, thousands, tens of thousands, and hundreds of thousands, and sliding balls on rods to indicate the number of each class. The value of the ball depends on the column to which it belongs. The same principle of positional value is the main idea in the Hindoo, or, as they are often called, the Arabic numerals. The abacus was probably Chinese, but possibly Hindoo in its origin;[6] the numerals of positional value were almost certainly Hindoo.

Several centuries before the Christian era, the Hindoos had a system of musical notation, and the word "gamut" is supposed to come from the Hindoo word "gama," a musical scale.[7] But their music was no better than that of many nations which had no method of recording tones.

Before 600 B. C. the Hindoos had no architecture worthy of note. They erected no splendid temples, tombs, palaces, castles, or fortifications. The Buddhists seem to have founded a national architecture, in which the most peculiar structures are rock temples, Hindoo pagodas, and topes. The rock temples are excavated in the bed-rock of hill-sides, and are wonderful productions of toil, but there is neither elegant exterior nor comfortable interior. To make the temple of Ellora, more than 50,000 tons of rock were excavated, and dumped down the hill.[8] The Hindoo pagodas approach the pyramid in shape, being much larger at the base than at the top, and gradually decreasing in length and breadth, which are nearly equal with elevation. The most splendid Hindoo pagoda—that at Tanjore—has a base eighty feet square and a height of two hundred feet, divided into seventeen stories.[9] The topes are mounds or buildings, shaped like cones or cupolas, and are designed to hold relics of sacred personages. The later Hindoos have erected numerous elegant pagodas and pagoda-like temples, and the Mohammedans have built some of the most beautiful structures in India.

SEC. 247. *Brahminism.*—After they had established themselves in the Ganges Valley, the Aryan conquerors modified their religious, social, and political institutions under a hereditary priesthood styled the Brahmins, and a law-book called the code of Menu. After ceasing to be Vedic Hindoos, probably before 1500 B. C. but possibly as late as 800 B. C., they became Brahminical or Menu Hindoos.

The change from the Vedic to the Menu faith seems to have been gradual and slow. Many of the later priests did not know that there had been a revolution. They read the Rig Veda as the most sacred of books, and did not perceive that it was inconsistent with their faith and practice. The book of Menu[1] says, "The source of the law is the whole Veda and the traditions and customs of those who know the Veda." These traditions and customs, however, are as inconsistent with the Veda as the medieval Christian church was with the Mosaic law.

The new features introduced in the Vedic religion of the Hindoos by the Brahmins were the establishment of caste; the organization of a hereditary class occupied exclusively with sacerdotal business; the acceptance of the code of Menu regulating social, political, civil, criminal, and ecclesiastical relations as of divine authority; and the adoption of the dogmas that individual existence is an evil, that impure souls transmigrate, that the purified souls are absorbed into the soul of the universe, and that the best method of purifying the human soul from sin is to spend the closing years of life in ascetic practices.

This later religion, imposed on the Hindoos as a reform developing and perpetuating the Vedic faith, was really a series of hostile and destructive changes, which were introduced gradually as the priests obtained a clearer conception of their class interests, and as they found the road to success open to them. They did not wish, and, if they had wished, they would not have dared, to repudiate the Vedic hymns. These were deeply rooted in the traditions and affections of the people. The sacerdotal modifications of the old faith and practice seem to have been small at any one time, and little understood by the multitude, or by most of the priests. There was no violent break with the past. No religion, at least none above the lowest stage of savagism, has started as an entirely original growth. Every new faith has been a sprout from an old root, or, as in this case, a graft on an old stock. In other nations we shall find similar sacerdotal grafts which were given to the people as improvements in full harmony with the tendency of the original stock, whereas in fact they were destructive substitutes.

SEC. 248. *Menu.*—The code of Menu is about as large as the Koran and half as large as the Hebrew Bible. If we can trust the preponderance of internal evidence, it was written before the rise of Buddhism or the publication of the Atharva Veda, before the appearance of Siva and Vishnu as prominent gods in the Brahmin worship, or the Aryan conquest of Ceylon and of the region south of the Vindya Mountains, and probably before 800 B. C.[1] But we cannot confidently fix the century of its composition. Nor do we know by whom it was composed. It purports to have been inspired by Brahma to Menu, who was divine or semi-divine; and by Menu it was delivered to Bhrigu with instructions to make it known among men. When and where Bhrigu lived, and how he published his law-book and obtained recognition for it, we do not know.

This code contains twelve chapters, of which the first, relates mainly to the creation of the world and the division of men into castes; the second to education; the third to marriage; the fourth to the Brahmin's mode of life; the fifth to diet and to woman; the sixth to domestic worship; the seventh to the duties of the king; the eighth to the administration of justice; the ninth and tenth to Vaisyas, Sudras, and other subject classes; the eleventh to the expiation of sin; and the twelfth to a future life. It was designed to be a comprehensive book of the main principles of civil, political, and ecclesiastical law, and it has been so accepted by the Brahmin Hindoos for more than two thousand years. It is still regarded as sacred in its origin and supreme in its authority, as to matters of polity and ecclesiastical discipline.

It does not purport to comprise all the law of the Hindoos; on the contrary, in the beginning of chapter VIII, relating to litigation, it expressly provides that the courts shall be governed by the written codes and local usages which define private rights and prescribe the rules of judicial procedure. Lawsuits are there divided into eighteen classes, each under its appropriate title. "Of those titles the first is debt on loans for consumption; the second, deposits and loans for use; the third, sale without ownership; the fourth, concerns among partners; the fifth, subtraction of what has been given; the sixth, non-payment of wages or hire; the seventh, non-performance of agreements; the eighth, recision of sale and purchase; the ninth, disputes between master and servant; the tenth, contests on boundaries; the eleventh and twelfth, assault and slander; the thirteenth, larceny; the fourteenth, robbery and other violence; the fifteenth, adultery; the sixteenth, altercation between man and wife and their several duties; the seventeenth, the law of inheritance; the eighteenth, gaming with dice and with living creatures. These eighteen titles of law are settled as the groundwork of all judicial procedure in this world."[2]

This classification of lawsuits implies in words copied from Menu that it was the result of experience accumulated through many centuries, until judges and lawyers had learned to systematize the business of courts, and to define the rights of person and property in logical order.

This code purports to be compiled from old compilations. It declares that it comprises the "immemorial customs."[3] In the comprehensiveness of its principles, the perspicuousness of its language, the lucidity of its arrangement, its freedom from repetitions, from serious omissions, and from matter either incongruous, trivial, or of merely brief temporary interest, it is far superior to the laws of Moses and Mohammed, and to all the codes produced anywhere before the day of Justinian, and preserved to our time.[4] Its acceptance of the system of caste is a great blot upon it as a record of human rights; but for this the compiler was not responsible. If he wished his book to possess any authority he must recognize the ecclesiastical, social, and political institutions of his country.

SEC. 249. *Caste.*—The code of Menu is preëminently the law-book of caste. It is the chief legislative authority for the division of the Hindoos into strictly hereditary classes. It separates them into Brahmins or priests, Shattriyas or warriors and rulers, Vaisyas or tillers of the soil, and Sudras or servants and mechanics. It declares that the Brahmins issued from the mouth of Brahma, the creator of the world; the Shattriyas from his arm; the Vaisyas from his leg; and the Sudras from his foot.[1] One of the names of every Brahmin should suggest holiness; of every Shattriya, power; of every Vaisya, wealth; and of every Sudra, contempt.[2]

The Sudras were descendants of the aboriginal or earlier inhabitants of Hindostan, conquered by the Aryans, who reserved for themselves the three higher castes, with superior political, ecclesiastical, and industrial privileges. The Sudras were not permitted to study the Vedas or to have them read, to learn the methods of expiating sin, to be witnesses against men of the higher castes, or to accumulate much wealth. In reference to the latter point, Menu says:[3] " No superfluous collection of wealth must be made by a Sudra, even though he has the power to make it, since a servile man, who has amassed riches, becomes proud, and by his insolence or neglect gives pain even to the Brahmins." The three higher castes are called twice-born, that is, regenerated by the gods, and worthy to share their communion,

The Brahmin is high above men of the other twice-born castes in privilege, dignity, and divine favor. He is the chief of the whole creation;[4] his birth is an incarnation of the god of justice;[5] his benevolence enables other mortals to enjoy life.[6] He is an object of veneration to the gods.[7] The Sudra is made for the purpose of serving him.[8] The slaying of a Brahmin is the greatest of crimes. When the purpose is to preserve one, perjury is justifiable.[9] "Though convicted of all possible crimes," a Brahmin must never be executed, maimed, whipped, or even deprived of his property. The severest punishment that may be applied to him legally is banishment.[10] He has exclusive authority to give instruction in the sacred scriptures, and in the modes of expiating sin. He explains the ecclesiastical tradition; he interprets the law; and he declares how it applies to new cases. He has charge of the sacrifices on all sacramental occasions; and when officiating for others, he is entitled to "liberal gifts."[11] It is made the duty of the other castes to give wealth to the Brahmin,[12] and of the king to provide abundantly for him and his household.[13] All the wealth of the world is declared to belong to the Brahmin.[14] And finally the king is ordered to perform all his royal duties under the advice of some learned Brahmin. If Hindostan had been governed in accordance with the requirements of the code of Menu, it would have been far more priest-ridden than it has been; and it has been the most miserably priest-ridden of all countries, ancient and modern.

Besides the four original or main castes, there is a lowest rank of Pariahs, who have violated the rules of their respective orders, and have become outcasts. Never since the Hindoos have been well known to European observers have political office and the use of arms been limited to Shattriyas or the cultivation of the soil to Vaisyas; on the contrary, the occupations of those castes have fallen, to a large degree, into the hands of Sudras, and many Brahmins, notwithstanding the orders that they should be liberally supported, finding scanty means of subsistence in sacerdotal business, have become officials, soldiers, domestic servants, and gardeners. Some distinguished authors have doubted whether the Shattriya and Vaisya castes ever had any extensive existence save on paper; in some districts, their descendants in modern times are very rare.

Although the long-continued existence of caste in Hindostan suggests the possibility that it may have rendered some valuable service to humanity, I am not able to see that much can be said in its favor. Its blessings, if it ever conferred any on the Hindoos, have not been distinctly stated and clearly proved by any of the learned and able authors who have studied the country, its institutions, and its history. A hereditary priesthood had a beneficial influence in many savage tribes; but it does not follow that every sacerdotal caste must be a blessing. Extremes are usually pernicious, and Brahminism is the most excessive development of priestly arrogance and oppression in history. At least the later stages of culture, the division of the people into numerous hereditary classes, with strict rules of descent, and with different political, industrial, and ecclesiastical privileges for each class, such as we find in Hindostan, is one of the greatest obstructions that can be placed in the way of the general prosperity and intellectual activity. It discourages enterprise, checks the accumulation of wealth, corrupts the ruling class, prevents a harmonious co-operation of the national forces, and obstructs the growth of a healthy and powerful public opinion.

Caste found its highest development and most extensive dominion among the Hindoos, and is probably largely responsible for the fact that, in proportion to their numbers, they, of all the Aryans, have done the least for culture. For several thousand years, they seem to have been nearly as numerous as all the Europeans, and yet they have played a relatively insignificant part on the stage of human development. Among them, we find no strong political unity, no contribution to constitutional liberty, no formidable military. Every department of their government save the legislative and judicial seems to have been weak. They had no monarch noted for administrative and organizing talents; no general eminent as a conqueror or disciplinarian; no famous historian, no political orator. Neither in physical science, nor in plastic or pictorial art, nor industrial invention, did they become distinguished.[15]

SEC. 250. *The Brahmins.*—The chief duties of the Brahmin are to adore the gods, to study the sacred scriptures, to marry and leave a son or sons to maintain the family worship, to observe the ceremonial rules laid down in the law and traditions of his caste, and after he has became an old man, to spend the closing years of his life as an ascetic. Every day brings numerous formalities, which may contribute to his future salvation but must interfere greatly with present comfort.[1] In many cases, it is impossible for him to comply fully with these requirements; and only a small minority of the Brahmins now live as Menu and the traditions say all of them should live.

The Brahmin boy when about ten years of age should

be placed in the house of a master, where he should remain not less than nine years,[2] and study the written and unwritten law. While a student, he should get his food by begging from door to door; and he or his friends should pay his preceptor. However, the instruction now obtainable from individual Brahmins is so inferior to that given in public institutions of learning in Hindostan, and the ambitious young men generally are so unwilling to get their food as mendicants, and the more learned of the Brahmins are so averse to the ill-recompensed toil of teaching the inferior scholars who offer themselves, that this fundamental rule of Brahmin life is falling into general neglect. In fact, many parts of the Brahminical system have ceased to control the conduct of the people who still claim the privileges of the Brahminical caste.

When a twice-born man, "the father of a family perceives his muscles become flaccid, and his hair gray, and sees the child of his child," he should become an ascetic, leave his house, take up his residence in the solitude of a forest, abstain from all productive labor, eat nothing save herbs, fruit, and roots gathered by himself or obtained by begging, and spend his time in study and contemplation, without desire for life or death, and without interest in the welfare of his relatives or in any worldly affairs. But no one is permitted to become an ascetic until he has prepared himself by an active life in accordance with the law which demands that he shall be the head of a family, shall leave a son to maintain the domestic worship, shall study the Vedas, and shall worship the gods with sacrifices for year after year. The adoption of an ascetic mode of life is sinful in a person who has not reached the border of old age.[3]

SEC. 250. THE BRAHMINS.

Under the code of Menu, as under the Veda, there was no temple or public worship. All the ecclesiastical ceremonies were conducted in the family circle, by Brahmins, on such sacramental occasions as the birth of a son, giving him a name, taking him out to see the sun, feeding him with rice, and cutting his hair for the first time, investing him with the sacred cord, attending him at his final return from school, his wedding, and his funeral. Of all the sacraments, the most solemn is that of the investment of the young man of the three higher, twice-born castes, with the sacred cord, which is a symbol of his admission into the communion of the gods. The frequency of the ecclesiastical ceremonies, their complexity, and the number of priests invited to participate, are proportioned to the wealth and social dignity of the family. The priests are always entitled to pay for such services.

The Brahmins succeeded in gaining exclusive control of the sacerdotal business of their country, and holding possession of it for centuries; but they did not perceive the importance of organizing themselves into a compact body, with different ranks under a central head, and rules for effective discipline. They are a sacerdotal rabble, not an army.

If any man could not support himself in the occupation proper to his caste, he might be excused for engaging in that of a lower, but never in that of a higher rank; as he might take a wife, a concubine, or a temporary feminine companion, from a lower, but never from a higher class. There was always a degrading contamination in thus crossing the bounds of caste, and the wider the interval crossed, the greater the contamination. One of the vilest of all sins was committed by the intimacy of a woman of the highest with a man of the lowest class.

To the Vedic Hindoo, life was joyful, the gods were propitious here and hereafter, and the future existence was one of pleasant personal experience somewhat like that on earth. To the Menu Hindoo, on the contrary, life is a burden, and the gods are cruel.[1] A demoniac curse weighs heavily on humanity. After death the souls of a large proportion of mankind, in punishment for their sins, must pass into brutes, to be reborn thousands of times, before they become fit for absorption into the divine soul of the universe.

SEC. 251. *Suttee, etc.*—Although not ordered or authorized in the Rig Veda or in the book of Menu, human sacrifices were made occasionally under the Brahminical governments. The victim was always a Vaisya or Sudra, that is, a person of low caste, a man between twenty-five and forty-five years of age, in excellent health, without serious physical defect, or the stain of crime; and by his mode of death he became one of the gods, and was made secure of great happiness in the future life.

An offering highly acceptable to several of the Hindoo gods, was a small teaspoonful of the worshiper's blood, drawn from a cut in the forehead, the cheek, the breast, or the arm, and laid upon the altar in a lotus flower. That the idea of human sacrifice was once widespread among the people, is shown by the phrase common among them when a child dies, that "the gods have eaten it."[1]

Many practices and opinions of an ecclesiastical character accepted by the Brahmins are not expressly authorized by their principal sacred books. In the class of traditional but unscriptural usages is that of suttee, or the sacrifice of the widow on the funeral pile of her husband.[2] This was always voluntary; that is, there was no physical compulsion. A moral pressure was, however, used to induce the widow to immolate herself. She was told that if she survived her husband she would disgrace herself and her relatives; she would be despised and neglected; she would have no happiness here nor hereafter. Public opinion demanded her sacrifice; and the wealthier her family, and the more distinguished her relatives, the more influence this demand had upon her. The majority of the widows preferred to live; and even those who expressed a willingness to die were not allowed to go to the funeral pile, at least after the middle of the last century, unless they convinced the managers of the ceremony that they had the fortitude to persevere.[3] After the announcement of a suttee, and the collection of relatives to witness and celebrate it, the refusal of the widow, at the critical moment, to do her part, was regarded as highly disgraceful. To prevent such a result, the widow was sometimes required to hold her hand in the fire till it was severely burned, as a proof that she would do her part with credit; and not until she had done this was the suttee announced.

Before the British conquest of Hindostan, that is, under the dominion of Brahminical influence, executions for witchcraft were frequent. This imaginary crime was supposed to be the cause of drought, destructive conflagration, sudden death, and any disastrous epidemic among men or beasts. The commission of the offense having been proved to the satisfaction of the superstitious mob, measures were taken to detect the criminal, with a wisdom equal to that shown in discovering the crime. It was asserted by traditional superstition that witchcraft was always the work of women; and this assertion being accepted as proof, it followed that the offender must be a woman; and then it was inferred that she lived in the village where the misfortune occurred. To find the sorceress, the name of every woman in the village was tied to a collection of green twigs cut from a certain tree, and the name on the twig which withered first, indicated the criminal, who was then slain. Another method of finding the witch was to give the name of every woman in the village to a little bag of rice; and when the bags representing all the women were placed near a nest of ants, the first bag torn open by these insects pointed out the criminal. By such judicial proceedings thousands of women were condemned to death.

The Brahminical courts, acting under the ancient customs, accepted proof by ordeals, of which nine kinds are mentioned, including those with lot, fire, red-hot iron, boiling oil, and water in which an idol has been washed.

SEC. 252. *Brahmin Women.*—In Brahminical society, woman has a low position. Under the code of Menu, there is for her, except as associated with her husband, no worship, no sacrament, no participation in any religious rite. For her there is no instruction in the sacred books. She must never read them or teach them to her children. She must not recite any prayer or know how to expiate any sin. Her nature is declared to be corrupt and her appetites impure.[1] She is as foul as falsehood itself.[2] Her affections are fickle.[3] She should never be trusted, nor ever permitted to be independent, or to act according to her pleasure.[4] She should always be watched.[5] She should be married while a child,[6] after she is six and before she is thirteen years old, and always kept in subjection. Her husband must never eat with her,[7] or look at her while she is eating. She must not speak his name while he lives; he is too far above her for such familiarity; and after his death she must not mention the name of any other man, nor may she marry again, though she should be left a widow while yet a child.[8] Her husband can divorce her without delay, expense, or reason;[9] she cannot obtain a divorce from him under any circumstances. He can have numerous spouses, he may marry into a caste below his own, and she cannot. She may be the nominal owner of property, but her husband has the exclusive legal right of collecting and spending its income. She should worship him as he worships God.[10] She must not imagine that she is man's equal in a religious, or even in a zoölogical sense. She contributes no blood to her son; his relation to her is like that of the grain to the field on which it grows.[11] There is a fundamental difference in the natures of the two sexes. The woman is not allowed to be a witness against a man. The right of wife-beating is recognized, but it is limited to blows with the hand, a rope, or a small bamboo—the last perhaps as thick as the thumb—and the place of the blows is limited to the back part of the body.[12] An idol which has been touched by a dog, a sudra, or a woman, is desecrated, and immediately abandoned by the divinity who previously occupied it, and he will not return to it until the defilement has been washed out by Brahminical purifications.[13] In short, woman is regarded rather as a thing than as a person. And yet the mother is entitled to much show of respect from her children, and the same book of Menu which abounds with assertions of her depravity, and with limitations of her equal rights, declares that "where women are honored, there the gods are pleased."[14]

In modern Hindostan, woman is considered incapable of a literary education, and unfit to be trusted with it if she were capable. She is kept secluded, and the seclusion has perhaps been more severe since the Mohammedan conquest than it was before. She does not sew, nor knit, nor teach her child to read.[15] She marries very young, often before she becomes a young woman; and she is wrinkled before reaching her thirtieth birthday. She does not expect her husband to treat her as an equal, and when, under British influence, he does so, she complains that he degrades her and himself. She is usually an ardent adherent of the old religion, "an insurmountable obstacle to reforms" which would simplify the ritual of the Brahminical religion, or lead to the abolition of objectionable ancient rules, ceremonies, and festivals.[16]

SEC. 253. *Brahmin Morality.*—Morality occupies a small space in the code of Menu, and has a subordinate position among the requisites of Brahminical salvation; but some of the ethical maxims are good, and are expressed clearly. The following is the decalogue of Menu: "By Brahmins . . . a tenfold system of duties must ever be sedulously practiced: [1] content, [2] returning good for evil, [3] resistance to sensual appetites, [4] abstinence from illicit gain, [5] purification, [6] coercion of the organs, [7] knowledge of scripture, [8] knowledge of the supreme spirit, [9] veracity, and [10] freedom from wrath."[1]

The following is the most comprehensive passage: "Even here below an unjust man attains no felicity, nor he whose wealth proceeds from giving false evidence, nor he who constantly takes delight in mischief. Though oppressed by penury in consequence of his righteous dealings, let him never give his mind to unrighteousness; for he may observe the speedy overthrow of iniquitous and sinful men. Iniquity committed in this world produces not fruit immediately, but, like the earth, in due season, and advancing by little and little, it eradicates the man who committed it. Yes; iniquity once committed fails not of producing fruit to him who wrought it; if not in his own person, yet in his sons; or if not in his sons, yet in his grandsons. He grows rich for a while through unrighteousness; then he beholds good things; then it is that he vanquishes his foes; but he perishes at length from his whole root upwards. Let a man continually take pleasure in truth, in justice, in laudable practices, and in purity; let him chastise those whom he may chastise, in a legal mode; let him keep in subjection his speech, his arm, and his appetite. Wealth and pleasures, repugnant to law, let him shun; and even lawful acts which may cause future pain, or be offensive to mankind."[2]

The general drift of the book, however, is to make morality subordinate to ceremony and to hereditary privilege. We are told that the "inclination of death," and the dangers of misery in future life for twice-born men, come "through a neglect of reading the Veda, through a desertion of approved usages, and through various offenses in diet."[3] All meats not previously offered in sacrifice, the flesh of carnivorous quadrupeds, many kinds of bird and fish, and many vegetables, including garlic, onion, leek, and mushroom, are unclean, and cannot be eaten without sin. Nominally, the Hindoos are vegetarians, and many of them are so poor that they can rarely afford to buy meat; but the wealthy classes use much cow's milk, and not unfrequently can have meat from animals which have been offered in sacrifice to the gods.

A multitude of ecclesiastical formalities are imposed on the Brahmin every day, and for every neglect there must be an expiatory ceremony, which is requisite for the recovery of divine favor. Worship and its formalities are the chief business of the Brahmin's life.

Menu tells us that "perfect health or unfailing medicines, and the various mansions of the deities, are acquired by devotion alone,"[4] and that "whatever sin has been conceived in the hearts of men, uttered in their speech, or committed in their bodily acts, they speedily burn it all away by devotion."[5] "Devotion is equal to the performance of all duties."[6] "By open confession, by repentance, by devotion, and by reading the scripture, a sinner may be released from his guilt."[7] "A priest who should retain in his memory the whole Rig Veda would be absolved from guilt, even if he had slain the inhabitants of the three worlds."[8] "The sacrifice of a horse, the king of sacrifices, removes all sin."[9] "The gods themselves . . . have proclaimed aloud the transcendent excellence of pious austerity."[10] "Sixteen suppressions of the breath, while the holiest of the texts [the gayatri] is repeated with the three mighty words [earth, sky, and heaven[11]], and the triliteral monosyllable continued each day for a month, absolve even the slayer of a Brahmin from his hidden faults."[12] Penances imposed by the Brahmins are potent in washing out sin. A penitent must continually repeat the gayatri,[13] or common prayer, which says: "Let us meditate on the adorable light of the divine ruler; may it guide our intellects." "By the sole repetition of the gayatri, a priest may indubitably attain beatitude, let him perform or not perform any other religious act."[14] "All rites ordained in the Veda, oblations to fire, and solemn sacrifices, pass away, but that which passes not away is declared to be the syllable om [or aum] . . . since it is a symbol of god, the lord of created beings."[15] "Brahma milked out, as it were, from the three Vedas, the letter a, the letter u, and the letter m, which form by their coalition the triliteral monosyllable."[16]

SEC. 254. *Brahmin Henotheism.*—Many passages in the code of Menu, as well as in other sacred writings of the Brahmins, are strongly monotheistical. Thus we are told that "in the knowledge and adoration of one God, which the Veda teaches, all the rules of good conduct . . . are fully comprised."[1] In the account of the creation of the universe we read that "the sole, self-existing power, . . . he whom the mind alone can perceive, . . . who exists from eternity, even he, the soul of all beings, . . . willed to produce various beings from his own divine substance."[2] Again it tells us that of all duties "the principal is to acquire . . . a true knowledge of one supreme god; that is the most exalted of all sciences, because it insures immortality."[3] It mentions various divinities, but adds that "the divine spirit alone is the whole assemblage of gods; all worlds are sealed in the divine spirit."[4] Elsewhere we are told that this soul of the universe, this creator of all conscious beings, is named Brahm; that having created material forms and spiritual persons, and having designated their duties, he has withdrawn into quiescence, gives no attention to men, and wishes no worship by them. There is one Brahm and no second; but he has withdrawn from the business of governing either mundane or celestial affairs.

But while there are many monotheistic passages in the Brahminical scripture, there is no monotheistic book, temple, or orthodox sect. Priests and people all worship their ancestors as divine, and they recognize a multitude of superhuman divinities. Every Brahmin is required to make a daily oblation to Agni, the god of fire; to Dhanwantari, the god of medicine; to Cuhu, the goddess of the day; to Prajapati, the goddess of animated beings; to Prithivi, goddess of the sky; to Indra, Yama, Varuna, and Soma; to Sri, the goddess of abundance; to Bhadracali, the goddess of fortune; to Brahma and to his household gods and ancestors.[5]

Hindoo authors who speak of the soul of the universe as the one spiritual being who includes all other existence, not only prescribe rules for the worship of ancestors, and of many different gods, but assert that the devout Brahmin is superior in dignity to all the gods, and is able, by severe penances, to compel them to obey him.

SEC. 255. *Transmigration.*—The heaven of the Brahminical religion is absorption in Brahm; and hell is a repetition of separate or personal existences in the forms of men and brutes. In one verse of Menu,[1] the sinner is threatened with "unconquerable death," but the general belief is that the miseries of renewed birth must be suffered until at last the soul becomes pure enough to rejoin its original source; and these renewed births may continue through 84,000,000 years, including intervals spent in hells or heavens.

Physical defects and ailments are declared to be punishments for sins committed in a preceding state, as dumbness for reading the sacred scriptures without authority, dyspepsia for stealing winnowed grain, leprosy for stealing clothes, lameness for stealing a horse, and blindness for stealing a lamp.[2]

SEC. 255. TRANSMIGRATION.

According to their moral qualities, men are divided into the vile, the passionate, and the good. The vilest are born again as worms, insects, reptiles, fish, or jackals; the moderately vile as lions, tigers, boars, horses, elephants, savages, or sudras; the least vile as birds, giants, ruffians, dancers, or singers; the most passionate as athletes, actors, gamblers, or sots; the moderately passionate as soldiers, or kings; the least passionate as nymphs, genii, and musicians; the least good as hermits, religious mendicants, Brahmins, or demigods; the moderately good as sacrificers, holy sages, or deities of the lower heaven; and the best men are absorbed in the divine soul of the universe.[3] Some offenses are punished by new birth in special brute forms; thus a theft of grain in a rat; a theft of milk in a crow; a theft of meat in a vulture; a theft of oil in a beetle; a theft of salt in a cricket; a theft of a cow in a lizard; and a theft of fruit in an ape.

After stating in much detail the various grades of sins and of their penalties in a future life, the code of Menu continues thus: "As far as vital souls addicted to sensuality, indulge themselves in forbidden pleasures, even to the same degree shall the acuteness of their senses be raised in their future bodies, that they may endure analogous pains; and in consequence of their folly, they shall be doomed as often as they repeat their criminal acts, to pains more and more intense in despicable forms on this earth. They shall first have a sensation of agony in Tamisra, or utter darkness, and in other seats of horror; in Asipatravana, or the sword-leaved forest; and in different places of binding fast and of rending. Multifarious tortures await them. They shall be mangled by ravens and owls, shall swallow cakes boiling hot, shall walk over inflamed sands, and shall feel the pangs of being baked like the vessels of a potter. They shall assume the forms of beasts continually miserable, and suffer alternate afflictions from extremities of cold and heat, surrounded with terrors of various kinds. More than once shall they lie in different wombs, and, after agonizing births, be condemned to severe captivity, and to servile attendance on creatures like themselves. Then shall follow separations from kindred and friends, forced residence with the wicked, painful gains and ruinous losses of wealth, friendships hardly acquired, and at length changed into enmities, old age without resource, diseases attended with anguish, pangs of innumerable sorts, and, lastly, unconquerable death. With whatever disposition of mind a man shall perform in this life any act, religious or moral, in the future body, endowed with the same quality, shall he receive his retribution. Thus has been revealed to you the system of punishments for evil deeds."[4]

SEC. 256. *Krishna.*—It was probably after the rise and under the influence of Buddhism, about 400 B. C., that Brahminism adopted or gave greater prominence to various points, including temple worship, ecclesiastical festivals, ecclesiastical pilgrimages, the worship of three gods conjointly, the preeminence of the Brahma triad (with Brahma as the creator, Vishnu the preserver, and Siva the destroyer), and the belief in Krishna, the divine saviour who became incarnate in human form, once in a thousand years, more or less, when his services were needed to teach mankind and redeem them from sin. According to the Hindoo tradition, he was of royal lineage; immediately after his birth, his divine character was recognized by peasants and distinguished strangers;

he narrowly escaped by flight from a massacre of the innocents, ordered by a tryant who knew by prophecy of the distinct place and time of his birth; and he was tempted by the evil spirit. His story is so similar in many of its incidents to that of Jesus of Nazareth that the two must have been drawn from a common source. It is impossible to prove which is the older.

The chief record of the teachings of Krishna is in the Bhagavad-Gita, one of the most interesting of all the books that claim to be divinely revealed. It has been worthily translated into English, under the title of "The Song Celestial," by Sir Edwin Arnold, from whose version the following passages are selected:—

> "And whoso loveth Me cometh to Me.
> Whoso shall offer Me in faith and love
> A leaf, a flower, a fruit, water poured forth,
> That offering I accept, lovingly made
> With pious will.
>
> . . . .
> I am alike for all! I know not hate,
> I know not favor! What is made is Mine!
> But them that worship Me with love, I love;
> They are in Me, and I in them!"
>
> "I am the Sacrifice ! I am the Prayer!
> I am the Funeral Cake set for the dead!
> I am the Healing Herb! I am the Ghee,
> The Mantra, and the Flame, and that which burns.
> I am—of all this boundless universe—
> The Father, Mother, Ancestor and Guard!
> The end of learning! That which purifies
> In lustral water! I am Om! I am
> Rig Veda, Sama Veda, Yajur Ved;
> The Way, the Fosterer, the Lord, the Judge,
> The Witness; the Abode, the Refuge House,
> The Friend, the Fountain and the Sea of Life
> Which sends and swallows up; Treasure of Worlds
> And Treasure Chamber! Seed and Seed-sower,

Whence endless harvests spring ! Sun's heat is mine;
Heaven's rain is mine to grant or to withhold;
Death am I and immortal Life I am,
Arjuna!"

"The wise in heart
Mourn not for those that live, nor those that die,
Nor I, nor thou, nor any one of these,
Ever was not, nor ever will not be,
Forever and forever afterwards.
All that doth live, lives always! To man's fame
As there come infancy and youth and age,
As there come raisings up and layings down
Of other and of other life abodes,
Which the wise know and fear not. This that irks
Thy sense-life, thrilling the elements,
Bringing the heat and cold, sorrows and joys,
'Tis brief and mutable! Bear with it, Prince!
As the wise bear. The soul which is not moved,
The soul that with a strong and constant calm
Takes sorrow and takes joy indifferently,
Lives in the life undying! That which is
Can never cease to be; that which is not
Will not exist. To see this truth of both
Is theirs who part essence from accident,
Substance from shadow. Indestructible,
Learn thou! the life is, spreading life through all;
It cannot anywhere, by any means,
Be anywise diminished, stayed, or changed.
But for these fleeting frames which it informs
With spirit deathless, endless, infinite,
They perish. Let them perish, Prince! and fight!
He who shall say, ' Lo ! I have slain a man!'
He who shall think, ' Lo! I am slain,' those both
Know naught! Life cannot slay. Life is not slain!"[1]

The later Brahmins have temples, with numerous idols, priests, servant-women, annual festivals attended by many thousands of pilgrims, and public sacrifices. At the temple of Kali, near Calcutta, more than a thousand ruminant animals, mostly goats, were sacrificed annually about the beginning of this century. Besides the offerings of slaughtered brutes, numerous ascetics made sacrifices by torturing themselves in various ways as proofs of their devotion to the goddess. Some thrust long knives through their tongues, arms, or legs, and others allowed iron hooks to be thrust through the skin and muscles of their sides, and, supported only by these hooks, they were swung round at the end of a long pole, revolving on a pivot.[2] The temple of Jagannath has or had in this century an average attendance of 300,000 pilgrims, mostly poor women, at its annual festival; and before the establishment of the British authority, at every festival some devotee or devotees voluntarily sought death under the wheels of the great car containing the idol, as it was dragged through the streets. About 30,000 pilgrims go annually to Benares, which has two thousand public sanctuaries and a half a million idols. In a pilgrimage which may last for a month, about five out of a hundred participants die on an average.

In the modern Hindoo temple, "the main daily business is the sweeping of sanctuary, the keeping up of the lamps which shed on it a mysterious twilight, the ringing of the bell at every new act of homage, placing of flowers before the god, waking him up, dressing him, washing him, giving him his food, putting him to bed, [and] watching over him during his slumber."[3] The temple women sell themselves to obtain a revenue for the public worship; and the wives of the highest Brahmins there mark themselves with obscene symbols and worship obscene images.

SEC. 257. *Buddha.*—In the sixth century B. C., Buddhism, the earliest in its origin and extensive acceptance of the three universal religions, was founded in Hindostan as a reform of Brahminism, by Siddhartha, of the Gautama family, Sakya tribe, and Shattriya caste.[1] He assumed the title of Buddha, "the enlightened," and Tathagata, "the traditional teacher," or "the saviour." By others he was sometimes styled Sakya Muni, or "the teacher of the Sakyas." He was born in the town of Kapilavastu, about a hundred miles north of Benares. According to the Buddhistic legend, he was the eldest son and heir apparent of the king of the petty kingdom of Magadha, and spent his childhood, youth, and early manhood in his father's court. All his circumstances were propitious. He was healthy and active; he was surrounded by kindness, respect, and prosperity in every relation of life. When a young man he married a noble maiden worthy of a throne, and he lived in perfect harmony with her. He was a favorite with the people, who expected that after his father's death he should reign over them.

But suddenly, when he was twenty-seven years of age, he began to brood over the miseries of humanity, and then, without explaining his plans to anyone, he secretly fled from his wife, his son, his parents, his palace, and his station, and became a hermit for the purposes of saving his soul, and of aiding others to save theirs. He hid himself in a forest, clothed himself in rags, and obtained his food by begging. Thus he lived in solitude and privation, until he convinced himself that he had found the true method by which the whole human race could be saved. He then devoted the remainder of his life— forty-four years—to the preaching of his doctrines, and the organization and government of his church. After visiting many countries, though never going more than a hundred and fifty miles from Benares, making many converts, and finding a kind reception nearly everywhere, he died peacefully in the midst of his disciples.

He was a historical personage about whose life, character, language, and associates, we have much trustworthy information. He started out with the purpose of establishing a universal religion, that is, a religion designed to include all men, and he succeeded in establishing it on a permanent basis. He saw it accepted by monarchs, and by multitudes of people. He gave it full and precise codes of dogma and discipline. For more than forty years he was its revered head. He was followed, believed, and obeyed, almost as if he had been divine. Although the art of writing was practiced in his time by the Hindoos, yet he neither wrote out his doctrines and disciplinary rules, nor requested any of his disciples to do so; but this neglect finds its parallel in Christianity.

Having been educated in the religion of Brahminism, having never visited a country where any other faith prevailed, and perhaps having never met or conversed with a believer in any other creed, he accepted many of the leading doctrines of Menu, including those that life is not worth living; that human nature is depraved; that sin is punished by transmigration; that the average soul is condemned to suffer through a great multitude of successive lives; that besides its transmigrations, the soul may pass long periods in heavens and hells; that ultimate salvation is a cessation of human consciousness; and that an ascetic mode of life is a very important aid in obtaining salvation.

These ideas, borrowed from the older faith, are a large part of the Buddhistic religion. On the other hand, Siddhartha rejected the Brahminical dogmas that there is a deity; or that there are deities superior in dignity and power to humanity; that true religion has been divinely revealed to man in the Vedas and the book of Menu; that man's highest duty is to worship divinity with hymns, sacrifice, ceremonial observances, and self-torture; that the Hindoos are the favorites of heaven above all other nations, and the Brahmins above all other Hindoos; and that final salvation is an absorption of the human into the divine soul.

In his system, Siddhartha did not adopt either deity, immortality, or ceremonial worship. These three points which are prominent and fundamental features of most religions, were familiar to him only in the Brahminical faith, where they appear in a disadvantageous light. The ceremony of the Brahmins is a vexatious ritual intimately associated with the oppression of the multitude by the sacerdotal class; their conception of a future life is a metempsychosis of misery until humanity shall be swallowed up in the pantheistic soul of the universe; and their deities are a confused mob with almost as much of demoniac as of divine attributes.

If Siddhartha had been a learned man and had visited many foreign countries; if he had studied the institutions of Persepolis, Babylon, Tyre, Memphis, and Athens; if he had become familiar with creeds that were not pessimistic, with priesthoods that were not hereditary and oppressive, with the conception of a future life that was not miserable, with ecclesiastical ceremonies that were not slavishly burdensome, and with governments that taught men to assert the dignity of human nature;—if Siddhartha had been so prepared for his work, he would probably have taught an entirely different religion. But the only basis on which he could build was Brahminism, and to the gross defects of the foundation we must attribute much of the weakness of the superstructure.

He offered his ultimate salvation of Nirvana or annihilation on equal terms to all men of every caste and nationality, the chief aid to success being entrance into the order of bikshoos, or mendicant monks. He made it a duty of his followers to preach his doctrines to all men; he was the first religious teacher known to have depended on public preaching for the introduction and establishment of a new religion, and he is the only founder of a universal religion whose doctrines owe nothing of their spread or maintenance to persecution or war. The influence of Buddhism has contributed much to the tolerant spirit of all the nations in which it has been extensively accepted. The bikshoos feel none of that religious animosity which prevails among the Catholic, Protestant, and Greek clergy against other Christian sects. The Christians have been persecuted in China and Japan, but not by Buddhist officials, and not without excuses that were rather political than religious. Hiouen Thsang, a Chinese Buddhist whose pilgrimage to Hindostan in the VIIth century A. D. for sacred books was the most fruitful enterprise of its kind on record, wrote: "The schools of philosophy are always in conflict, and the noise of their passionate discussions rises like the waves of the sea. Heretics of different sects attach themselves to particular teachers, and by different routes walk to the same goal."

Siddhartha has missionaries and monks but no priests. After man has been taught how to be saved, he must work out his salvation by himself, without mediation, expiation, or absolution. No prayer, no penance, no death-bed repentance, no baptism, no faith will suffice to wash out sin. His religion has been much corrupted in most of the countries where it now prevails. Many of the Buddhist communities have gods, priests, temples, idols, prayers, exorcisms, worship of spirits, sacrifices to the dead, and belief in and interpretation of omens, all of which are unauthorized by the founder of the faith.

Siddhartha did not claim to be divine or divinely inspired. While he admitted the existence of spirits, to which the title of gods might be given, he did not believe in a creator and governor of the universe. The idea of deity has no prominence in his religion. He said: "I have no teacher; there is no one who resembles me. In the world of gods, I have no equal. I am the most noble in the world, being the irrefutable teacher, the sole all-perfect Buddha."[2] On another occasion he used these words: "I do not see anyone in the heavenly worlds, nor in that of Mara, nor among the inhabitants of the Brahma worlds, nor among the gods or men, whom it would be proper for me to honor, or in whose presence I ought to rise up, or whom I ought to request to be seated." Again he said: "Trouble not yourself about the gods. Disturb yourself not by curiosities or desires about any future existence. Seek only after the fruit of the noble path of self-culture and of self-control."

SEC. 258. *Nirvana.*—The future salvation which Siddhartha teaches is called Nirvana, a state of perfect rest. Many persons who have written about Buddhism, have asserted that Siddhartha did not teach the entire extinction of the saved soul; and that he did not throw away "so powerful a weapon in the hands of a religious teacher," as the belief in immortality.[1] But the doctrine of Siddhartha is not to be found in the inner consciousness of modern enthusiasm. He said that he was "weary of consciousness;" that freedom from pain is "incompatible with existence as a distinct individual;"[2] that "the source of sorrow is in self; get rid of self and sorrow ends;" and that when he died he would "return to nothingness." After his death, Anuruddha, his nephew and disciple, said to the mourners, "He has entered that state in which both sensations and ideas have ceased to be."[3] According to a phrase common among the Buddhists, life is "the shimmer of death;" and one of their maxims is that the desire to be born again in heaven is contrary to the plain teaching of Siddhartha.[4] Their conception of Nirvana is a state of absolute quiescence, which is inconceivable except as one of absolute unconsciousness. Having rejected the Brahminical doctrines of a divine soul pervading all nature, and of the absorption of the purified human soul in the deity, it would have been wise, if not necessary, that Siddhartha, if he had wished to teach the soul's immortality, should state and explain it in clear and full language. But he did not explain it. He saw no delights in immortality. He never spoke of Nirvana as a sphere of enjoyment, as a heaven of congenial association, of intellectual pleasure or triumphant piety. In the Buddhist faith, Siddhartha as a person has ceased to live. A Buddhist maxim says that "worldly happiness and happiness in the region of the gods is not worth one-sixteenth of the happiness resulting from the destruction of desires."[5]

According to the more intelligent Buddhists, the desire for a continuation of life after death is a "spiritual bondage," a "taint," a "delusion," a weakness of an egotistic mind, a discreditable hankering after what cannot be and should not be, a blindness to the analogies of nature, a "lust for prolonged existence." In many Buddhist books Nirvana is compared to a lamp that has been blown out, never to be lighted again. The Brahmins apply the title of Annihilationists to the [6] Buddhists, who make no objection to the designation.

As Siddhartha did not deny the existence of gods and demons, or good and evil spirits, who, however, have no control over the fate of the pious, and are inferior to them in dignity and power, so he did not deny the existence of places or conditions to which the name of heaven or hell could be given properly. Some of his followers corrupting his doctrine or expanding it without explicit authority from him, undertook to describe different celestial and infernal departments.

The relation between the different forms of the same soul as it appears in successive births, was not distinctly explained by Siddhartha or his followers, and was perhaps not distinctly conceived. There is no assertion of a continued consciousness and a clear recollection connecting the various forms. We are told that man should not worry about his previous states of existence; all such worry is a delusion. He should never ask himself, " What was I during the ages that are past."[7]

SEC. 259. *Bikshoos.*—The teaching of Siddhartha is mainly ethical. Having no deity, no immortality, no sacrifices, no worship, and no priestly mediation, he had no field for religious zeal save morality, but into that he went with a fervor which carried him to an unreasonable extreme. He demanded from the candidates for Nirvana the most complete renunciation of self, the most absolute humility, the most severe abstinence from everything that could gratify the senses or artistic tastes, the most self-sacrificing regard for the welfare of everything that lives. He not only taught his followers that they must love their neighbors, but that they must submit without resistance to all the evils which their neighbors might inflict on them. A Buddhist bikshoo must not only consent to be robbed, but he must aid the robbers to find and carry away his property. He must not defend his political rights, for he has no rights. He must disclaim all pretenses made on his behalf that he is entitled to protection against tyranny of any kind. He must accept without resistance, and without complaint, every form of injustice and oppression, even if it be slavery, torture, or death. He must submit not only to man but even to brutes and insects. He must not kill the poisonous serpent that has bitten him, or is about to bite him. He must not flee from the tiger. He must not brush away mosquitoes lest he kill them. He must not dig the ground, for in doing so he might hurt earth-worms. He must not take pride in himself, nor demand respectful treatment for himself, nor assert himself in any manner. He must make his own immediate comfort subordinate to that not only of other men but even of brutes. According to a Buddhistic legend, in a previous existence Siddhartha saw a tigress famishing with her cubs, and he placed himself within her reach so that she and her cubs could have a good meal. That is the spirit of Buddhistic ethics.[1]

Siddhartha divided his followers into two main classes,— first the bikshoos or ascetics, who hope to reach Nirvana when they die; and, second, the laity or common people, whose highest hope is, in their next life, to become bikshoos. For these two classes there are separate codes of morality. The commandments for the bikshoos are: (1) Do not kill any animated being; (2) live in the most continent celibacy; (3) never be unkind or unjust; (4) offer no resistance to evil; (5) do not toil for wages; (6) do not till the ground; (7) do not receive gold or silver; (8) do not accumulate property of any kind; (9) do not possess more than three garments, and those of the coarsest material; (10) if you have any property [besides clothing and a bowl for food], give it to the poor; (11) use no bedding save a piece of carpet; (12) abstain from ornaments, perfumes, music, dancing, jovial entertainments, and idle talk; (13) eat only one meal a day, and that in the forenoon; (14) eat no food save that obtained by begging; (15) spend much of your time in bodily quiet, while your mind is fixed on your salvation; (16) keep your mind and body in a condition as near as possible to absolute repose; and (17) teach others how to be saved. Besides these main rules for the bikshoos, there are two hundred and fifty others, regulating their conduct in and out of their monasteries, or viharas. The regulations, in regard to the method of collecting food and eating it, are strict. The mendicant must not tell in words, or by gestures, what he wants, nor must he make a noise, nor stand long before a house, nor go to a place where he has been repeatedly refused, nor be importunate in any manner. He may hold out his bowl, but must not indicate that he wants a particular kind of food, nor must he reject any that is offered, or select the best from his bowl, but must eat it as it comes.

The privilege of accepting a present of a garment is limited to a certain season, and if the garment be new, it must be soiled with dust or mud before it can be worn. If money be offered to the bikshoo to enable him to buy a new garment, he must refuse; but he may accept the garment from a friend who has taken the money and used it for the bikshoo's benefit. When walking in places where people may probably be met, the bikshoo must keep his eyes fixed on the ground about six feet ahead of him; and when he meets a woman, he must hold up a fan so as to hide his face.

If a bikshoo should find fruit on the ground under a tree that is individual property, he must die rather than eat the fruit without explicit permission from the owner. He must never solicit anything. A bikshoo when ill refused to take some medicine which had been prepared under his directions, while he was well, for another person sick with the same disease. If he had used it, the circumstances might lead to the suspicion that he had solicited it for himself. Alms-giving is one of the chief virtues of Buddhism, and the Buddhist layman must anticipate the wants of the bikshoos. Dhoutlagamini, who became a great king, when a child made a promise that he would never eat a meal without setting apart a share of his food for the ascetics. A Ceylonese king spent some days every year working in the rice-fields, so that the food which he gave to the bikshoos should be the product of his own labor.[2]

SEC. 260. *Laymen.*—The commandments for the laymen are: Do not kill any sentient being, do not steal, do not lie, do not commit adultery, do not drink intoxicating liquors, do not commit any injustice, and give alms to the bikshoos. The more strictly the layman obeys these commandments, and the more nearly he can approach the moral standard of the bikshoos, the higher will be his moral position in his next life. There is a broad line of demarkation between the laymen and the bikshoos. The former may marry, accumulate property, defend rights, live luxuriously, take part in jovial entertainments and frivolous conversation, and enjoy life in an innocent way. Thus Siddhartha made his yoke relatively easy for the multitude, and fitted it for acceptance by millions of Asiatics who were not sufficiently enlightened to perceive its doctrinal defects. If, on the other hand, he had required all laymen to obey the same rules as the bikshoos, in regard to defending rights and enjoying entertainments, he would have been unable to secure a basis for a widespread and long-enduring religion.

No Buddhist teacher lays down the doctrine, found in many Christian books, that the only sufficient motive for virtue is the fear of punishment in a future life. Vice is always foolish in the church of Siddhartha. According to his words: "All that we are is the result of what we have thought. . . . If a man speaks or acts with evil purpose, pain follows him as the wheel follows the foot of the ox that draws the cart."[1] Again he tells us, "If a man speaks or acts with a pure thought, happiness follows him like a shadow that never leaves him."[2] A Buddhist maxim says: "Perform carefully the precepts of the law, and abstain from all evil deeds; he who keeps the law, finds happiness in this world and the next."[3]

SEC. 261. *Viharas.*—The bikshoos are organized into communities, each of which has its convent or vihara, where its members must reside during the rainy season, from June to September inclusive, in Hindostan, though they may spend the remainder of the year in the forest. While in the convent, they hold congregational meetings at every change of the moon; and at the new-moon and full-moon meetings the main rules of the order are read through, and after each rule those present are called upon to confess whether they have violated it.

While the bikshoo, as an individual, is a pauper, his convent may own valuable lands and buildings, the income from which is not expended in providing luxurious food, clothing, or furniture for its inmates, but is applied to religious purposes. Admission to the community is obtained after examination, by ordination, and is not granted to a slave or to any person under twenty years of age. The vows taken do not bind the bikshoo for any definite period; and he can withdraw and become a layman again whenever he sees fit. The bikshoo is never a prisoner nor an unwilling ascetic. In Siam it is fashionable for wealthy laymen to become bikshoos for a month every year, as Christians and Mohammedans keep their annual period of fasting.

Besides the main classes of bikshoos and laymen, there are the minor classes of bikshoonis and novices. The bikshoonis are female ascetics, who have convents and rigid rules similar to those of the bikshoos. The novices are boys or young men between the ages of eight and twenty, who take the main vows of the bikshoos, and become the pupils and adherents of a convent, to which they have then a preferred claim for admittance when they reach a sufficient age. The bikshoonis and novices are relatively few, and in some Buddhist countries are entirely unknown.

Siddhartha established only one monastic order for men and one for women. No learning is required for either, nor is study made a duty after admission. Indeed, the intellectual quietude recommended is inconsistent with much activity, either mental or physical. No bikshoo has been eminent as a student or author in any field save religion; nor has any bikshoo convent become famous for the learning or eloquence of its inmates. The division of labor among the monastic orders of the Roman Catholic Church has no parallel in Buddhism,

Siddhartha organized the order of the bikshoos upon a plan which he intended should never be modified or amplified in any manner.

Although the viharas are not seats of learning or places of systematic study, and although the bikshoos generally have no credit for erudition, nevertheless, as a class, they do contribute a little to the cause of education. Siddhartha was the first to found a religion by preaching to the multitude, and the first to send out missionaries to convert all men without regard to their blood. The spirit in which he labored has always been maintained by his followers in every country where his faith has found a foot-hold. All bikshoos recognize the duty of performing missionary labor. A passage in a liturgical book of the Chinese Buddhists says: " Never will I seek salvation for myself alone, . . . but forever and everywhere will I strive for the redemption of all other living creatures." [1]

Every vihara has its weekly gathering to hear some passage of the sacred scriptures read, and in many cases there are sermons. When away from the viharas, the bikshoos are always ready to deliver little sermons to any gathering disposed to listen to them. The viharas usually have collections of the sacred books, and in many cases they have schools for the children in their vicinity.

Siddhartha provided for no ecclesiastical buildings save viharas. He had no house designed exclusively for congregational worship. Neither had he any saint, or relic, or image, or sacred tree; but in the course of time all these made their appearance among his followers. Several centuries after his death, his relics became precious, and then buildings called topes or stoopas and chaityas were erected to shelter them. The tope is a mound or mound-like structure, intended to represent a tomb. A chaitya is a house containing a relic shrine. The mound or shrine is a place of worship, where the worshipers sing hymns, recite prayers (regarded by some as a mere exercise of inward devotion), march round in procession, keeping the right side nearest to the shrine, read their sacred books, and sometimes deliver sermons.

Chang Wen, a Chinese Buddhist who went to Hindostan for books and relics in 671 A. D., says: "In India the chaityas [holy buildings] are reverenced by all the passers-by. Every evening the bikshoos come from the convents they occupy and walk three times round these stoopas. They pass round them in procession, scattering flowers and burning incense; then, sitting down, some skillful brother with clear voice chants the praises of the great Master. For this purpose they have hymns consisting of ten or even of twenty verses. They then return to the temple, and, having taken their seats in the preaching-hall, a preacher mounts the pulpit and then reads a short sermon. The pulpit is not far from the president's throne, but it is not so high nor so large. Whilst reading the sermon, they often chant from the collection of hymns compiled by Asvaghosha; and they also frequently recite the hymn of praise to the three honored names. After singing, they march in procession round the apse three times. They then say, 'It is well,' and the preacher descends from his pulpit."[2]

SEC. 262. *Discourses.*—Here is one of Siddhartha's discourses: "He who conquers himself is the greatest conqueror. His victory cannot be changed into defeat by any god or devil. No fire rages like passion, no imprisonment is like hate, no net binds like passion, and no torrent carries one away like desire; therefore dig up the roots of passion, so that the tempter shall not again bend you as the stream bends the bulrush. As the tree, when it is clipped, throws out new sprouts so long as the roots are uncut, so pain returns again if the hankering for pleasure is not eradicated. Let man lay aside his anger and his pride; let him break every bond. He who checks the rising wrath, as he stops a rolling cart, him I call a true cartman. Wrath is never stilled by wrath, but only by meekness. That is the eternal principle. Watchfulness is the path of immortality; neglect leads to death. It is better to live one day of powerful exertion than a hundred years of weak indolence. Strive to be watchful. Guard your heart. Tear yourself from the world as the elephant struggles out of the swamp in which it was sinking. He who sees that the world is a bubble, an illusive picture of the fancy, he does not fear the angel of death. What pleasure, what joy is there in life? Observe man's changing form, how it is dissolved by age. See man's sick body, how it ulcerates and decays. 'I have sons and treasures; here will I live in the winter and there in the summer;' so says the fool, and does not see the obstructions. He who is anxious about his sons and his treasures, he is the man with his heart in chains, he is torn away by death, as the sleeping village is swept away by the mountain torrent. Sons and kinsmen can then render him no service. Let everyone hasten to do good, and turn his thoughts from evil, for he who is not zealous for the good, his mind enjoys itself in the thought of evil."[1]

On his death-bed, Buddha, addressing his disciples, said:[2] "Ye then, my followers, who know so well the perfect law, remember! the end must come; give not way again to sorrow. Use diligently the appointed means. Aim to reach the home where separation cannot come. I have lit the lamp of wisdom; its rays alone can drive away the gloom that shrouds the world. The world is not forever fixed! Ye should rejoice therefore, as when a friend afflicted grievously, his sickness healed, escapes from pain. For I have put away the painful vessel. I have stemmed the flowing sea of birth and death, free forever now from pain. For this you should exult with joy. Now guard yourselves aright. Let there be no remissness. That which exists will all return to nothingness. And now I die. From this time forth my words are done. This is my very last instruction."[3]

SEC. 263. *Siddhartha's Death.*—Siddhartha died in the village of Kusinagara, after an illness that had lasted for several weeks. When only a few hours of life remained to him, he requested Ananda, his favorite disciple, to inform the villagers that his end was near. "And when they had heard this saying of Ananda, the Mallas [villagers] with their young men and maidens and their wives were grieved, and sad and afflicted at heart. And some of them wept, disheveling their hair, and stretched forth their arms and wept, fell prostrate on the ground, and rolled to and fro in anguish at the thought,' 'Too soon will the Blessed One die! Too soon will the Happy One pass away! Full soon will the light of the world vanish away!' . . .

"And the venerable Ananda caused the Mallas of Kusinagara to stand in groups, each family in a group, and so presented them to the Blessed One, and said, 'Lord! a Malla of such and such a name with his children, his wives, his retinue, and his friends, humbly bows down at the feet of the Blessed One.' And after this manner, the venerable Ananda presented all the Mallas of Kusinagara to the Blessed One in the first watch of the night."[1]

The last of the villages having been dismissed, the Blessed One, in the presence of the bikshoos, addressed the venerable Ananda, and said: "It may be, Ananda, that in some of you the thought may arise, 'The word of the Master is ended, we have no teacher more.' But it is not thus, Ananda, that you should regard it. The truths and the rules of the order which I have set forth and laid down for you all, let them, after I am gone, be the teacher to you."[*]

The Buddha inquired whether any of the brethren (a number were present) had any question about the doctrine or discipline of the church, but there was no response. " And the venerable Ananda said to the Blessed One: 'How wonderful a thing is it, Lord, and how marvelous! Verily, I believe that, in this whole assembly of the brethren, there is not one brother who has any doubt or misgiving as to the Buddha, or the truth, or the path, or the way.' To these Buddha replied: 'It is out of the fullness of faith that thou hast spoken, Ananda! But, Ananda, the Tathagata knows for certain that in this whole assembly of the brethren, there is not one brother who has any doubt or misgiving as to the Buddha, or the truth, or the path, or the way! For even the most backward, Ananda, of all these five hundred brethren, has become converted, and is no longer liable to be born in a state of suffering, and is assured of final salvation.'

"Then the Blessed One addressed the brethren, and said: 'Behold now, brethren, I exhort you, saying, Decay is inherent in all component things. Work out your salvation with diligence.' This was the last word of the Tathagata.

"Soon afterwards Buddha became unconscious, and then the venerable Ananda said to the venerable Anuruddha, 'O my lord, O Anuruddha, the Blessed One is dead.' 'Nay! [was the answer] Brother Ananda, the Blessed One is not dead. He has entered that state in which both sensations and ideas have ceased to be.'"

During the last thirty years of his life, and especially towards its close, Siddhartha was treated with extraordinary deference by his disciples. After his death, the Ceylonese Buddhists said of him: "He is the joy of the whole world; the helper of the helpless; the Brahma of the Brahmas; the only deliverer; the teacher of the three worlds; the father and helper of the world; the universal friend; the nearest relative of every man; stronger than the strongest; more merciful than the most merciful; and more beautiful than the most beautiful." We are also told of him that "even as we desire to give peace to our children, so did he long to give rest to the world."

SEC. 264. *Councils.*—Within two weeks after the death of Siddhartha, his chief disciple, Kasyapa, summoned five hundred of the bikshoos to meet with him at Rajagriha, for the purpose of adopting a statement of their ecclesiastical doctrines and rules. These had not yet been reduced to writing, and some of them were perhaps only partially or incorrectly known to many bikshoos. It was important that they should now be fixed in the memory of numerous persons, so that there should be as little discord as possible; and they were recited in the council by those persons who possessed in the highest degree accuracy of memory, and had enjoyed long and intimate acquaintance with Siddhartha. To recite the law or doctrine, Kasyapa selected Ananda, who was Siddhartha's nephew, and a favorite companion and early disciple; and when Ananda had finished a recitation, the whole council chanted it after him. Precisely how often or in what manner the chanting was done, we do not know, but it was doubtless in accordance with the ancient Hindoo system by which the Vedas and other sacred compositions had been handed down for centuries. The recitation purported to give the precise words of Siddhartha and nothing more. These were the only authority. Neither criticism nor dissent was suggested, and if suggested would not have been tolerated in such an assemblage. After Ananda delivered the first of Siddhartha's sermons—that on the kingdom of righteousness—Kaundinya, one of the oldest bikshoos and earliest converts, rose and said: " Venerable Kasyapa, I heard this sermon; it was preached for my benefit. It dried my blood, and the ocean of my tears. I left behind the mountain of bones; it closed the door of perdition, and opened the door of heaven."[1]

The recitation of the disciplinary rules was the task of Oopali; and of the metaphysical sermons and sayings was the task of Kasyapa. It is supposed that the bikshoos of the council were divided into sections, each of which made itself thoroughly familiar with some portion of the ecclesiastical code, so that each country, district, and vihara, if it had enough representatives in attendance, should possess the correct authority in reference to every question. Some doubt has been expressed whether this council was ever held; but the clear tradition of its proceedings, their reasonableness, and the lack of direct adverse evidence, are strongly in its favor.

Although the art of writing was certainly known at this time in Hindostan, and was probably familiar to many of Siddhartha's disciples, there is no statement that it was used in taking down the dogmas and disciplinary rules which were to be preserved. Among Buddhists as well as Brahmins it was a general custom until long after the beginning of the Christian era to trust to tradition and memorizing in preference to books, for a knowledge of the sacred text.

About a hundred years after the death of Siddhartha, a council, called the second general council of the Buddhists, met in the city of Vaisali for the purpose of considering the conduct of several viharas, which allowed their inmates to receive gold and silver, and to eat salt meat. King Kalasoka, in whose capital the council was held, though not a Buddhist, treated the bikshoos with respect, provided a building for their meetings, and, influenced by his sister, a bikshooni, espoused the cause of the orthodox party, who triumphed in the council by a large majority. It is said that 10,000 schismatic bikshoos were condemned. This council consisted of seven hundred members, and remained in session seven months under the presidency of Yasas. The only subject of dispute before it related to discipline. If differences of faith had arisen, they provoked no public controversy.

The third and most famous of the general councils of the Buddhist church was held in 242 B. C., the tenth year of the reign of King Asoka, in his capital of Pataliputra. One thousand bikshoos, selected by the bikshoo Tissa, participated in the council, and they remained in session nine months. At the opening of the council, the monarch delivered an address in which he said: "My faith in Buddha, his law, and his congregation, are well known. Nothing has been well said save what was said by the blessed Buddha. It is necessary, gentlemen, to declare what are the authorities of the law and the congregation, and thus their influence will be permanent. Such declarations seem to me necessary in reference to the subjects embraced in the law, including the discipline, the supernatural faculties of the Ariyas, the dangers of the future, the stanzas and the sutras of the hermit, the doctrine of Outapatissa, and the teaching of Rahoula, rejecting false doctrines."[2]

Several heresies were condemned, and arrangements were made for sending out missionaries in various directions.

SEC. 265. *Asoka.*—It was probably after this council that the great missionary activity of Asoka's reign began. He took an active part in it. He sent embassies to Egypt, Cyrene, Macedonia, Epirus,[1] and presumably to many other and less distant countries, inquiring whether Buddhist missionaries would be received and protected. Such expeditions suggest the probability that in his time the faith of Siddhartha was preached in Western Asia and Greece. Mahinda, the son, and Sanghamitta, the daughter of Asoka, Buddhist ascetics, went with letters from their royal father, and with bikshoo and bikshooni companions, to Ceylon, where they were favorably received by the king, who, with many of his subjects, joined the church of Siddhartha.

When the words of Buddha were written down we do not know, but there is evidence that the Dhammapada, as a record of his language, was in existence as early as 250 B. C.[2]

Asoka was grandson of the monarch Chandragoopta, known to the Greeks as Sandracottus. He was the first monarch who made Buddhism a state religion. His zeal for gaining proselytes to his faith by peaceful means has no equal among kings; and his edicts are unparalleled among governmental documents for the inculcation of kindly sentiment. His inscriptions sound as if love incarnate had at last become dominant on earth. The following are extracts from edicts of Asoka, inscribed by his order on public monuments:—

"And this is true religious devotion, this is the sum of religious instruction, that it shall increase the mercy and charity, the truth and purity, the kindness and honesty, of the world." "I pray with every variety of prayer for those who differ from me in creed, that they, following my proper example, may with me obtain eternal salvation." "There is no higher duty than the salvation of the whole world. My whole care is directed to the discharge of my debt to all creatures, that I may make them happy on earth, and that hereafter they may gain heaven."[3]

"King Piyadasi [Asoka], beloved of the gods, desires that all the sects should dwell at liberty in all places."[4] "Piyadasi [Asoka] the king, beloved by the angels, now in the tenth year of his reign, has learned the perfect wisdom of Buddha, and the only excursions now enjoyable to him are those of the law, including visits and benefactions to anchorites and monasteries, the inspection of his dominions and his subjects, instruction in the law, and advice to obey it."[5]

"The observance of the law is now witnessed for the first time in the course of ages. Abstinence from bloodshed and from malice, obedience to parents, and respect for the old, these virtues and others commanded by the law, are now practiced."[6] "It is my command that the love and practice of the law shall increase hereafter as they have increased in the hearts of all my subjects. Let all my people, the highest and the lowest and the middle class, obey this order and execute it diligently. Let my greatest ministers remember that this kingdom is to be governed according to the law, that the general prosperity is to be gained by the law, and that all are to be protected under the law."[1]

Sec. 266. *Growth.*—The trustworthy facts by which we can measure the growth of Buddhism are very few. The Essenes of Judea and the Therapeutæ of Egypt, while retaining many points of their hereditary Jewish faith, had adopted the Buddhistic code of morals, and some of the bikshoo discipline, in the IInd century B. C. Two centuries later the faith of Siddhartha obtained a firm foot-hold in China,[1] and it had probably at some earlier period become dominant in Burmah and Siam. Three generations after the reign of Asoka, Buddhism was introduced into Thibet, where, in the time of Charlemagne, it was not yet dominant, though the bikshoos there had adopted the peculiar sacerdotal organization which afterwards enabled them to control the government and to establish a peculiar theocracy.[2]

In 630 A. D. a Chinese bikshoo, Hiouen Thsang, made a journey by way of Samarcand to Hindostan for the purpose of studying his religion in the country of its origin, and of getting copies of the sacred books as there preserved. He was absent from his native land for sixteen years, and returned with six hundred and odd different Buddhist books, enough to load twenty-two pack-horses. The remainder of his life, eighteen years, was spent in translating these books, and he died at the age of sixty-eight, highly honored by the emperor and his ministers, who were Buddhists, and lamented by the people. He was a sincere, unselfish, faithful, and efficient intellectual laborer.³ When he returned from Hindostan, many of the three thousand seven hundred viharas in China were deserted, the bikshoos having been slain in civil wars, and the buildings having gone to decay; but, stimulated by the missionary and his scriptural treasures, the emperor ordered all these viharas to be re-established, and provided for the ordination of at least five bikshoos for each vihara, making more than eighteen thousand bikshoos at one installment.

In regard to Hindostan, Hiouen Thsang gives little comprehensive information in explicit language, but he conveys the idea that Buddhism in his time was prosperous in every part of the peninsula, which was then divided into more than seventy kingdoms. He spent more than five years in a vihara which had ten thousand bikshoos, in the kingdom of Magadha, the king of which was a Buddhist. He studied in five cities and visited a dozen Hindoo kingdoms in which Buddhism was "honored,"⁴ a phrase which does not convey a very definite idea of the extent of its prevalence. In Khotan he found the population full of respect for the law of Buddha, and he heard of Buddhists in Persia, but he did not visit that country. He found a hundred viharas in Bactria, and as many in Cashmere. In Turkestan he was treated with distinction because of his missionary character. In Samarcand he found two deserted viharas, and he there ordained some bikshoos. Among the Ugoors he found a vihara and a Buddhist khan who was anxious to keep the Chinese pilgrim to instruct his people in their religion. Ceylon, according to report, in his time had 50,000 bikshoos.

After the middle of the VIIth century, under the influence of persecutions by Brahmins and Mohammedans, Buddhism in Hindostan began to decline; and finally it entirely disappeared throughout the peninsula, south of Bhotan, Nepaul, and Cashmere, in which three provinces it still exists.

At the present time Buddhism is the dominant religion in China, Japan, Thibet, Corea, Burmah, Siam, Anam, and Ceylon, and it is found in Cashmere, Nepaul, Bhotan, Kashgar, Yarkand, the Kirghiz and Kalmuck region (about six hundred miles square north of the Caspian), Sumatra, and Java. The total number of Buddhists is estimated at 500,000,000, or four-tenths of all the people on the globe,[5] and considerably more numerous than the Christians, and more numerous than either the Brahmins or Mohammedans by more than sixty-six per cent. About a thousand years ago, several emperors of China were outspoken adherents of Buddhism, but in recent centuries all have been followers of Confucius, though many have treated Buddhism with much respect and attention, and have contributed to the maintenance of Buddhist viharas and temples. In 1662 A. D. a proclamation called the Sacred Edict was issued by the emperor, blaming the Buddhists for fabricating groundless tales about future happiness and misery for the gain of the bikshoos, and ordering that a certain passage denouncing this superstition should be read publicly at the new moon and full moon in every city of the empire.[6]

Buddhism has had no general council, that is, no council including representatives of different nationalities. Its discipline has no arrangement for active and systematic ecclesiastical intercourse among the countries in which it has been extensively accepted. Travel and letters have brought the Buddhists of Hindostan, Ceylon, Siam, Burmah, Thibet, China, Japan, and Manchooria, into communication with one another, but as individuals, not as authorized representatives of national churches. The consequence has been a great divergence in faith and discipline. The Southern Buddhists, who include those of Ceylon, Burmah, Siam, and Anam, numbering in all 30,-000,000, have departed least from the teachings of Siddhartha. They do not worship ancestors, nor pray to gods or spirits, nor believe in a conscious life and an endless heaven and hell after the cessation of transmigration; but those heresies, besides many others, prevail among the other Buddhists, who are described as belonging to the northern division.

Thibet has a Buddhistic discipline different from that of any other country, with many ceremonies and equipments similar to those of the medieval Christians, and presumably copied from them. It has the cross, the censer suspended by five chains, holy water, bells, candles, chaplets, miters, dalmatics, hymns with two choirs, exorcisms, benedictions with the right hand raised over the head of the laymen, the worship of saints, and a chief priest, who not only rules the church, but in theory at least is entitled to absolute temporal power.

What were the causes of the great and enduring success of Buddhism? That is a question to which every history of culture should offer some reply. The one here offered is that Buddhism was the first universal religion, and is better suited to the wants of an ignorant, superstitious, and peaceful people than the Brahminism, Confucianism, or spirit worship, with which it had to contend in Eastern and Southeastern Asia. It could not have taken its start and obtained a wide dominion among such conquering nations as the Greeks, Romans, or Teutons. The hardships of the struggle for life, in densely-crowded and unwarlike communities, like those of Hindostan and China, prepare the people to look with favor on such a pessimistic tone as that which predominates in the teachings of Siddhartha. All barbarous nations are extremely greedy for fictions of the supernatural. If only one supernatural creed is offered to a people, they accept it; if several, they select the one that harmonizes best with their intellectual condition. Many of the Hindoos preferred Buddhism to Brahminism, because the latter was objectionable in its caste regulations, and weak in its sacerdotal organization. In China, Buddhism came into competition with Confucianism, which has no priesthood and no doctrine of supernatural beings. To triumph over such enemies was not difficult.

In the last ten centuries, Buddhism has gained only by the increase of populations in countries where it had been previously established. It has lost its missionary zeal and its confidence in its own strength. It has few learned men, and not one author eminent in the literature of our century. Its adherents in China and Japan, which countries contain more than four-fifths of all its believers, belong to the most ignorant class. Their number is imposing, but their general intelligence is not great, and their knowledge of the tenets and history of their religion is not respectable. Buddhism does not promise to gain strength in the future by their help. It may long continue to exist by the aid of inertia and tradition; otherwise it has no importance for coming centuries. It is an outworn superstition.

Sec. 267. *Hindostan's Place.*—The Hindoos have not been eminent in industry. So far as is known, they never made an important improvement in agriculture, mechanics, mining, or navigation. The cultivation of rice and the spinning-wheel had their origin in Southeastern Asia, possibly in Hindostan. After the XIth century B. C. the Hindoos exchanged their products by sea, and after the VIth century by land, with the countries bordering on the Mediterranean, but the owners of the caravans, and the owners, builders, and mariners of the ships engaged in these branches of traffic, were natives of other lands. Hindoos of the present day show little capacity for the organization and management of extensive business. The leading manufacturers, ship builders, railway contractors, merchants, and bankers in their country are not of their blood. Among 200,000,000 Hindoos there are not so many first-class bankers and merchants as among 100,000 Parsees. When we compare the Hindoos with the Chinese as to industrial achievements, we find that the latter are far superior. The Chinese had the magnetic needle, the navigable canal, printing, and gunpowder for centuries before the Hindoos knew of them. The Hindoos made no valuable contributions to medicine or surgery except, perhaps, the discovery of inoculation, which was known to them and to the Chinese from very remote times.[1] They understood the art of polishing gems and of cutting stone, but they had no architecture until after the appearance of the Persians and perhaps the Greeks in their country. They worshiped the cow but did not harness the horse. The brute used more than any other for transportation was the elephant, and that could be kept only by princes or persons of great wealth. Cotton was spun in very fine thread and woven into extremely light cloth, but in the clothing of the common people there was no superior excellence. No great roads were made or bridges built before the Mohammedan conquest.

In their polity, the Hindoos have never shown much capacity. They have never tried a republican government. They have had no influential aristocracy. They have had no deliberative council that exercised control over a large territory. They have contributed no valuable institution to constitutional government. They have had no strong and durable monarchy ruling over their whole peninsula. Usually their country was divided into threescore or more petty states, under tyrannical dynasties that had no permanence of tenure. The administration has been notoriously and shamefully inefficient and corrupt. The military discipline was poor. The army was little better than a mob.[2] The country never produced a great conqueror, never sent an invading army into a foreign country, and never made any creditable resistance to an invader. It has not now one first-rate regiment of Hindoos officered by Hindoos. The Persians, the Greeks, the Arabs, and the British, conquered the Hindoos with relatively insignificant forces, and had little difficulty in holding their conquests. Under Hindoo rulers of Brahminical faith, division, discord, tyranny, rebellion, and massacre were common events.

The unquestionable inferiority and inefficiency of the Hindoos as rulers, generals, soldiers, administrators, merchants, bankers, manufacturers, ship builders, contractors, and managers of extensive business enterprises, must have a cause. It is not the climate, for the Parsees have dwelt in Hindostan for more than twenty generations without losing their industrial talents. It is not the food, for the

Parsees have nearly the same diet. The chief cause is caste, which hampers the education, the habits, the opinions, and the industry of the people in many ways.

A comparison of Hindostan with China suggests many interesting thoughts. Each is a great country with clearly-defined natural boundaries which serve to protect it against hostile invasion. Each is the home of a great nationality, one with 200,000,000 and the other with 400,000,000 people. Each had made much progress in agriculture and other peaceful arts 4,000 years ago or more. But here the similarity ends. China achieved political unity, devised a meritorious system of government, originated an ethical religion without mythology and without priests, kept careful historical records, invented paper, printing, canal navigation, the magnetic needle, and gunpowder, and, though several times subjugated by aliens, compelled the conquerors to accept their language, laws, customs, and religion. In all these points Hindostan failed completely or was much inferior, but, on the other hand, it produced the greatest amount of literature claiming divine authorship, and the earliest grammar, dictionary, algebra, and fairy tales.

Three notable religions have been developed among the Aryan Hindoos, Brahminism, Buddhism, and Sikhism. Of these Brahminism and Buddhism are important in their ideas and the multitude of their adherents. Sikhism, which does not possess any remarkable original feature, had its origin in the XVIth century of our era, and has perhaps one million believers.[3]

CHAPTER XVI.
THE ANCIENT PERSIANS.

SECTION 268. *Land and People.*—Modern Persia has an area of 650,000 square miles, extending eight hundred miles from north to south and as far from east to west. Lying between the twenty-fifth and fortieth parallels of latitude, its climate is temperate in the northern districts and subtropical in the southern, but not equable anywhere, the range from heat to cold being relatively large, especially in the northern and more elevated districts. Over much of its territory the rainfall is scanty, and more than 100,000 square miles of its area are desert. It has few large rivers, and none large enough to be navigable to boats driven by steam or sail. Its numerous mountain chains inclose many beautiful and fertile valleys.

In early antiquity, different portions of this region were occupied by Aryan tribes known as Persians, Medes, and Parthians, nearly related to one another in language, customs, and religion, and long independent of one another politically, but after 700 B. C. brought under a common dominion. Of these three branches of the Iranian blood, the Persian is the best known to us, because it founded a greater empire than either of the others, and is the only one that originated a great religion recorded in a sacred book preserved in part at least to modern times. The near relationship of the Zend, the tongue of the ancient Persians, with the Sanscrit, proves that the Iranians and the Hindoos remained together after their ancestors had separated from the other Aryans.[1]

Although there are linguistic and mythological evidences that the Iranian and Hindoo stocks separated from each other as early as 3000 B. C., the first contemporaneous historical mention known to us of any Iranian tribe is of the Medes, made about 850 B. C.,[2] in the Assyrian records. The Persians do not appear until a hundred years later. It was not until 605 B. C., when Assyria was finally overthrown, that the Iranians became a great national power in Asia. Then Media suddenly rose into prominence, with Persia as a subject province. In 558 B. C. Persia gained the supremacy, and the government was known as that of the Medes and Persians.

Cyrus, the founder of the Persian dynasty, a man of rare capacity and energy, was soon at the head of the greatest empire the world had ever seen. He ruled over Persia, the basin of the Euphrates, Armenia, Asia Minor, Syria, Judea, Afghanistan, and part of India, with, it is supposed, 70,000,000 subjects. Although there were many successful generals and conquerors before him, he surpassed all his predecessors in the combination of military genius with political wisdom. To most of his alien subjects he gave a better government than they had had under the absolute rule of princes of their own blood; and thus he secured relative peace and permanence to his authority. His victory and his government were gentle as compared with those of earlier Asiatic conquerors. The people were so rude, national animosities were so bitter, and methods of administration were so defective, that revolts against his authority were frequent, but in most cases they were neither extensive nor difficult to suppress. He deserves to be considered the first emperor, the first monarch, who ruled quietly over many subject provinces of alien blood. With him the political history of mankind ceases to be a collection of records of separate nationalities; with him it assumes a character of international or human relationship which rapidly expands until it includes vast areas and immense multitudes of people.

The Persian Empire lasted two centuries and was overthrown by Alexander, who brought against it a military organization far superior to any previously seen in Asia. The Greeks in Persia were too few to maintain themselves, and after a generation they gave way to a dynasty of Parthians who held the dominion for about four centuries and a half, and were succeeded by a Persian dynasty which reigned until the Mohammedan conquest in 636 A. D., since which year the religion of the ancient Persians, and many of their customs, have almost disappeared; the Aryan blood of the people has been much corrupted by Arabic and Turanian admixture; and the population and prosperity of Persia have diminished.

The Iranians were the most energetic and martial of the Asiatics. They were eminent as organizers of political, military, and ecclesiastical institutions. The Persians excelled in war, and the Medes in agriculture. Neither Persians, Medes, nor Parthians were eminent in mercantile pursuits, navigation, mechanical labor, the ornamental arts, or secular literature. Rawlinson tells us that they have left us "no statues, no modeled figures, no metal castings, no carvings in ivory or wood, no enamelings, no pottery even."[3] But from the ruins at Susa and Persepolis, we can see that they built extensive and elegant palaces, and that they could transport enormous masses of stone. The largest stone block in their ruins is fifty feet long, nine wide, and six thick. The main hall of the Persepolitan palace was two hundred and twenty-five feet square and the roof was supported by a hundred columns, each at least thirty-five feet high.

George Rawlinson thinks that the palaces at Persepolis and Susa "must have been among the fairest creations with which human art ever embellished the earth," and that beyond a doubt they "compared favorably with any edifices which, up to the time of their construction, had been erected in any country by any people. It was in these glorious buildings that Iranian architecture culminated; and there is reason to believe that from them the Grecian architecture gained those ideas which, fructifying in their artistic minds, led to the best triumphs of Hellenic constructive art, the magnificent temples of Diana at Ephesus and of Minerva on the Acropolis of Athens."[4]

SEC. 269. *Persian Government.*—In regard to the social customs of the Iranians, we have little precise information of interest. Among the wealthy, the women were kept in seclusion. Polygyny was common, but the first wife was superior in political rights and in social dignity to the others. Her sons could not be deprived of their position as the main heirs of their father and as the custodians of the family worship.

The administration of the Persian Empire was much improved by Darius. He divided it, according to ethnographical boundaries, into twenty provinces, each of which was permitted to retain its hereditary language, customs, laws, religion, and local officials; and some of them were allowed to have a native governor. The satrap, or provincial ruler, had his own treasury and army, with unlimited power over the lives and property of his subjects; but he was responsible to the emperor for the peace and general prosperity of his province, for a definite annual tribute to the imperial treasury, and for contributions of men, arms, transportation, and food supplies to the imperial army. If the satrap was ordered to take part in a military expedition beyond his province, he could choose a substitute to rule during his absence. A treasurer appointed by the emperor was established in every provincial capital with instructions to make frequent reports to his master.

At strong strategical positions, such as passes, bridges, fords, and the junctions of great roads, fortresses were built in every province, and were garrisoned by Persians, under trusty officers. Great roads, with post stations at intervals of fifteen miles, and mounted military messengers, gave facilities for sending governmental dispatches rapidly from end to end of the empire. The main road from Ephesus to Cabool was more than twenty-five hundred miles long. An annual visit was made to every province by the emperor or by an imperial inspector, who made a report of his observations.

The favorite weapon of the Persian soldiery was the bow; but the spear was also used. A large proportion of the army was mounted, and the cavalry was considered superior to that of any other country. When the armies of Darius and Xerxes invaded Europe, the chief care of the Greek commanders was to select positions in which the Persian cavalry could not be used to advantage; and it was by their cavalry that the Persians inflicted several crushing defeats on the Romans. Of Persian war chariots, we read very little.

Sec. 270. *The Avesta.*—For our knowledge of the religion of the ancient Persians, we are mainly indebted to their sacred book, the Avesta, the composition and publication of which are ascribed to Zoroaster, spelled Zarathustra in the Avesta and Zerdusht in some later Persian books. He was also called Spitama, or spiritual chief. It is uncertain when he lived, but some parts of the Avesta seem to have their origin as early as 1500 B. C. The term Zendavesta, often applied to the book, is incorrect; Zend means commentary, and Zendavesta means the Avesta and its commentary. Zend had much importance to the later Persians, but it has relatively little for modern scholars.[1]

In the time of Darius, the sacred book of Zoroaster comprised twenty-one divisions with eight hundred and fifteen chapters; but in the middle of the IVth century A. D., the old book was revised so as to be included in three hundred and forty-eight chapters; and of these only two have been preserved to our time. One of these, the Vendidad, relates to purification, and the other, the Yasna, relates to worship. These two chapters make up the Avesta as now known to us, and in their contents bear more resemblance to a prayer-book than to any other ecclesiastical book used among Christians.[2] "The greater part of the prayers and thanksgivings [in the Avesta] are without religious feeling or poetical fervor, and very far removed from the richness and abundance, the beauty and freshness of conception, which streams through most of the hymns of the Veda."[3]

The Avesta contains about 60,000 words, and purports to consist mainly of replies to questions addressed to Ahura Mazda by Zoroaster. This composition suggests one method of telling fortunes common among many savage and barbarous nations, of ancient and also of modern times. The Chinese temples in San Francisco now have wooden blocks so made that when thrown up and allowed to fall at random on a table, they must come to rest on one of two sides, one of which means yes, and the other no, to any question which the worshiper asks, either silently or audibly, when he throws the block. Before appealing to the divinity for his decision, the devotee should make an offering; and in cases of great importance, he employs a priest, or person reputed to possess superior ecclesiastical knowledge, to make a solemn offering and throw the block. This method of procedure is based on the theory that the divinity controls the fall of the block, and when properly propitiated, and addressed, will control it so as to reveal the future to the questioner. If the reply should not be satisfactory, the question may be asked again the next day, and the next. The query should be framed so that it may be solved by a simple yes or no, and if one response is not sufficient to give all the information needed, a succession of others leading from general to particular points may be asked.

Something of this kind was customary among the ancient Jews: " Saul asked counsel of God, 'Shall I go down after the Philistines? Wilt thou deliver them into the hand of Israel?' But He answered him not that day. And Saul said, 'Draw ye near hither all the chief of the people.' . . . Then said he unto all Israel, 'Be ye on one side, and I and Jonathan, my son, will be on the other side.' And the people said unto Saul, 'Do what seemeth good unto thee.' Therefore Saul said unto the Lord God of Israel, 'Give a perfect lot.' And Saul and Jonathan were taken. And Saul said, 'Cast lots between me and Jonathan my son.' And Jonathan was taken."[4] In that case, the method of casting the lot is not described, but the divinity refused to reply to the first question, and Saul understood this refusal to mean that some Israelite had committed a sin, and had deprived the nation of a right to a reply. The lot decided who committed sin, and Jonathan confessed that it was true.

A similar proceeding for the discovery of sin is recorded in the book of Joshua.[5] There we read that when the Hebrews attacked the town of Ai, they were badly beaten, because some unknown one of their number had sinned. The sinner was discovered by lot. The first lot fixed on the tribe of Judah; the second fixed on Zerah among the sons of Judah; the third designated Zabdi among the sons of Zerah; the fourth picked out Carmi among the sons of Zabdi; and the fifth reached the offender Achan among the sons of Carmi. Achan confessed and was slain.

We may imagine that Zoroaster obtained his revelation by lot. He may have asked a series of questions to which the dice replied, as he understood them, yes or no; and when he communicated his doctrines to others he may have changed the forms of the queries and responses, so that the divinity would appear to more advantage than if he had no chance to say anything save yes or no. The probability that Zoroaster received his revelation in this manner, is suggested not only by the question and answer in the Avesta, but also by the statements that he is "the publisher of the words of Ahura;"[6] that his law is the answer given to him by Ahura; and that the Persian declares his faith in the word of Zoroaster, in his law and in the oracles received by him.

SEC. 271. *Ormuzd.*—The main idea of the Avesta is that two great spirits, one good and the other evil, are contending for the control of the world; that neither can now entirely overcome the other; that the good spirit will finally triumph; and that all devout men should side with the good spirit and aid him by their worship and by virtuous actions. The good spirit is named Ahura Mazda, Ormuzd or Spento Mainyas; the evil spirit is Ahriman or Angro Mainyu.

Ahura means lord, and Mazda omniscient; Ahura Mazda or Ormuzd is the all-knowing lord, the lord of high knowledge or the lord who bestows intelligence. The sun and fire are regarded as his sacred symbols, and all the more important acts of religion are done in the presence of one or the other, and with the face turned towards it, but without the thought of paying any worship to it, any more than the Christian worships the altar before which he kneels.

Every beneficent thing in the world was created by Ormuzd; and everything came from his hand in a condition of perfect purity. Among his works are life, light, truth, virtue, food, fire, air, earth, water, the horse, the dog, the cow, the sheep, the eagle, the vulture, and man. Ahriman, the evil spirit, created death, disease, decomposition, temptation, crime, vice, poison, smoke, the serpent, and every form of evil. To every good thing made by Ormuzd, Ahriman attached an evil accompaniment. He created darkness to resist light, and falsehood to resist truth; to life he attached death, and to fire, smoke.

The following is an extract from the Avesta[1]:—

Now will I speak and proclaim to all who have come to listen,
Thy praise Ahura Mazda and thine O Vohumano.
Asha, I ask that thy grace may appear in the light of heaven.

Hear with your ears what is best, perceive with your minds what
    is purest,
So that each man for himself may, before the great doom cometh,
Choose the creed he prefers. May the wise ones be on our side.

These two spirits are twins; they made known in times that are by-gone
That which is good and evil in thought and word and action.
Rightly decided between them the good: not so the evil.

When these two came together, first of all they created
Life and death, that at last there might be for such as are evil
Wretchedness, but for the good a happy, blest existence.

Of these two, the one who was evil chose what was evil;
He who was kind and good, whose robe was the changeless heaven,
Chose what was right; those, too, whose works pleased Ahura Mazda.

They could not rightly discern who erred and worshiped the Devas;
They the bad spirit chose, and having held counsel together
Turned to rapine, that so they might make man's life an affliction.

But to the good came might; and with might came wisdom and virtue;
Armaite herself, the eternal, gave to their bodies
Vigor; e'en thou wert enriched by the gifts that she scattered, O Mazda.

Mazda, the time will come when the crimes of the bad shall be punished;
Then shall thy power be displayed in fitly rewarding the righteous,
Them that have bound and delivered up falsehood to Asha, the Truth-god.

Let us then be of those who advance this world and improve it,
O Ahura Mazda, O Truth-god, bliss conferring!
Let our minds be ever there where wisdom abideth!

Then indeed shall be seen the fall of pernicious falsehood;
But in the house where dwell Vohumano, Mazda, and Asha,
Beautiful house—shall be gathered forever such as are worthy.

O men, if you but cling to the precepts Mazda has given,
Precepts which to the bad are a torment, but joy to the righteous,
Then shall you one day find yourselves victorious through them.[1]

The idea of dualism lies at the foundation of Mazdeism. Zoroaster thought that the existence of evil proved that his deity was either not perfect in goodness or not unlimited in power. But the goodness was to him more desirable than power in a deity; and therefore he represented Ormuzd as anxious but unable to overcome Ahriman. The promise of a victory to be achieved after a lapse of thousands of years, does not protect man from misery in his earthly life; he, like his creator, has a hard and long struggle. The Avesta recognizes various inferior beneficent divinities, and also the divine ancestral spirits or Fravashis, so that it is decidedly polytheistic. The following is an extract from the Avesta: " We worship the deified spirits [Fravashis] of all the holy men and holy women whose souls are worthy of sacrifice and invocation! We worship the Fravashis of all the holy men and holy women, our sacrificing to whom makes us good in the eyes of Ahura Mazda; of all those we have heard that Zarathustra is the first and best as a follower of Ahura and as a performer of the law. . . . We worship Zarathustra, the lord and master of all the material world, the man of the primitive law, the wisest of all creatures, the best ruling of all, the brightest of all, the most glorious of all, the most deserving of sacrifice, of prayer, of propitiation, and of glorification, and as worthy of sacrifice and prayer as any creature can be in the perfection of his holiness."[3]

Morality has a prominent place in the Mazdean religion. Truthfulness, justice, purity, and devotion to productive, and especially to agricultural, labor, are among the chief duties of its followers. To irrigate dry soil, to drain wet soil, to plough the ground, to sow grain, to plant trees, and to feed and care for domestic animals so that they shall thrive and increase, are meritorious acts before Ormuzd, and honorable to every rank of society. Without devotion to some serious and beneficent occupation, no one can enjoy the favor of Heaven. Idleness is a great sin; faithful toil is better than any ceremonial observance.[4]

The Mazdeans believed in a future life, with heaven for the good and hell for the bad.[5] They had a final judgment, with a resurrection of the body. The final triumph of Ahura over Ahriman will be aided by the Sosidch or Soshyos, a semi-divine redeemer who will be born of a virgin and will aid men in obtaining salvation.

"The pure Zoroastrian worship consisted of prayers and hymns (such as the gathas), both to Ahura Mazda and to his councillors and angels. For though the former was the only object of supreme adoration, a sort of inferior worship was rendered to the Amshashpands [angels] and Yazatas [spirits], and to all creatures superior to man, among the rest to the heavenly bodies. . . . With these prayers and hymns were combined the maintenance of the sacrificial fire and the curious ceremony derived from the highest Aryan antiquity of offering the juice of the plant called the Homa, the Soma of the Vedas, where the rite is much more developed and Soma becomes the moon-god in association with Mithra, as the sun-god. The ceremony consisted in the extraction of the juice of the Homa plant by the priests, during the recitation of the prayers, the formal presentation of the liquid extracted to the sacrificial fire, the consumption of a small portion of it by one of the officiating priests, and the division of the remainder of it among the worshipers."[6]

The modern Parsees, who number about 100,000, of whom the great majority are in Hindostan, and not more than five thousand in Persia, are the descendants of the Zoroastrians, and preserve their ancient religion; but whether their faith is the same as that of the companions of Darius the Great is doubtful. Cyrus and Darius were buried in tombs, and the modern Parsees have no tombs. The magi were an order of hereditary priests who took charge of the Zoroastrian worship while the Medes were dominant; but whether their claims of sacerdotal authority were justified by the Avesta in its ancient completeness, is not now ascertainable. There are reasons for believing that the Median, the Persian, and the Parthian division of the Iranian people had each its religious peculiarities; but as to the amount of the differences between them, and as to the influence of the different divisions upon the religion of the modern Parsees, our information is unsatisfactory.

A peculiar feature of Zoroastrianism is its rule that the corpse shall be exposed where wild birds or quadrupeds shall eat the flesh. Death is the work of Ahriman; it is a defilement of the life given by Ahura Mazda. The dead body, being corrupt, must not be brought into contact with earth, fire, or water, all of which are pure, as they were created by the beneficent deity. Every community of Zoroastrians should have a "tower of silence," or dead house, on the roof of which the corpse may be exposed to the vultures. The most notable building of this kind is at Bombay, where it is one of the wonders of the city. Numerous vultures visit the place daily, and within an hour they leave nothing but the skeleton. When the bones are clean, they may be buried.

CHAPTER XVII.

THE BABYLONIANS, ETC.

SECTION 272. *Chaldea.*—Babylonia, called also Chaldea, the fertile valley land in the basin of the Euphrates, south of latitude 34°, has a length of three hundred miles and a width of perhaps fifty. The summers are long and oppressively hot; the winters mild and brief, with light frosts and very rare snows. The soil is fertile, but for cereals requires irrigation. The chief crops are dates, wheat, barley, millet, lentils, apples, pears, olives, and grapes.

In a remote antiquity, Chaldea was a populous, wealthy, and powerful nation. It had numerous cities, great irrigating canals, highly developed mechanical arts, famous products of cloth, leather, metal, and glass, an extensive maritime commerce centering at ports on the Euphrates and the Persian Gulf, and numerous caravans that transported freight across Asia. Its people excelled all contemporaneous nations in their systems of measuring dimensions, time, weight, and the circle, and in their knowledge of arithmetic, geometry, and astronomy.

According to the tradition of Western Asia, recorded in Genesis, Babylon was the oldest of cities; and in the Vth century B. C., it was the largest and most splendid. It was ten miles square, and its walls were at least seventy feet high and thirty thick. No smaller measurements are given by any ancient author; and these are only about one third of the figures given by Herodotus, who tells us that the area was fourteen miles square, including nearly two miles square occupied by the royal palace and grounds, and also including many private fields and gardens. The Euphrates ran through the middle of the city, and the banks of the river were lined with high walls, with gates at the ferries, and at the one bridge which connected the opposite sides of the city. There was also a tunnel fifteen feet wide and twelve high under the river.[1] The straight and wide streets crossed one another at right angles.

Babylonia was the first country to engage extensively in commerce with distant nations, differing greatly in this respect from China, Egypt, and Hindostan, which never had much foreign trade, and by their situation or ecclesiastical policy were isolated for thousands of years. The first extensive and systematic commercial intercourse among many nations was that established by Babylon; and hers was also the first great accumulation of commercial wealth. Isaiah[2] considered Babylonia "the glory of kingdoms;" Jeremiah[3] spoke of her as "the praise of the whole earth," and Ezekiel[4] as "a land of traffic." To the author last named[5] the capital was "a city of merchants," and her shipping was the chief subject of her "cry" or boast. Babylon has no fluviatile or maritime commerce now, and is badly situated for it in modern times; but with ancient boats she was conveniently accessible. Her ships traded to all the coasts of the Indian Ocean. Babylon was the head of navigation on the Euphrates for sea-going ships. It was the place where merchandise was transferred from boat to camel on the way between Phœnicia and Hindostan. The Phœnicians as well as the Jews were the descendants of emigrants from Mesopotamia; they inherited their mercantile talents from a remote ancestry. Although Xerxes had a vast number of other sailors in his fleet collected to attack Greece, he also had many from Babylon.⁶ Besides its marine trade with the coast of Hindostan, it had an extensive caravan traffic with Afghanistan, the Punjab, Bactria, Persia, and China.⁷ Thus it became the commercial, industrial, and intellectual center of barbarous antiquity; and it continued to be a great city until a cheaper and more expeditious route for the transportation of merchandise between Hindostan and the Mediterranean was opened, about the beginning of the IVth century B. C.

SEC. 273. *Chaldean Buildings.*—The chief building material was adobe, the surface of which in elegant edifices was lined and faced with burned bricks, enameled tiles, or slabs of stone, either plain or sculptured in relief. In high walls of adobe, at intervals of ten or fifteen courses, there was a layer of reeds or mats in bitumen, which prevented the spread of moisture and protected surfaces exposed to the rain. Stone was scarce and rarely used save in temples and palaces. These were erected on artificial terraces, or mounds, which sometimes reached an elevation of five, ten, or even more yards above the natural surface. Adobe being a material which absorbs water and has no strength when wet through, great care was taken to protect the lower parts of the walls from moisture. Foundations were made with burned brick, and the mounds were supplied with channels and underground drains to carry off water. The principle of the arch was known in a remote antiquity, though it was rarely used, as it is not suitable for application in adobe walls, unless over narrow openings. It was employed however in the masonry supporting the Hanging Garden, in the tunnel under the Euphrates, and in some sewers or drains. The Babylonians made excellent lime mortar for use with stone and burned brick; and they applied bitumen extensively in damp ground.

The wall of Babylon was one of the seven wonders of the ancient world; and another was "the Hanging Garden," as it was called, though a better name would have been "the Elevated Garden." It was a garden four hundred and fifty feet square, seventy-five feet above the surface of the ground, sustained on columns and arches. A deep, rich soil, supplied with an abundance of water, was covered with luxuriant vegetation, including some large trees.

One of the most remarkable buildings of Babylon was the temple or observatory of Baal. It was two hundred and seventy-two feet square on the ground, and consisted of seven stories, the six upper stories being each forty-two feet less each way than the one below it. The three lowest stories were each twenty-six feet high, and the four above each fifteen feet. Each story was dedicated to one of the seven sacred planets, and each was painted externally with a distinctive color, beginning at the ground with black, and ascending through orange, red, purple, yellow, blue, and white to the top. The astronomical observatory at the summit was one hundred and fifty-two feet above the base. Much of the building was a solid mass of adobe masonry, with facings of brick, but there were internal halls and arches, as well as staircases.

SEC. 274. *Chaldean Learning.*—Instead of writing on papyrus or parchment, or cutting or painting their inscriptions on the walls of temples, tombs, and palaces, as did many other ancient nations, the Babylonians impressed theirs on clay tablets, which were preserved with or without burning.

In the later period of Babylonian independence and prosperity, the writing was syllabic. There were about one hundred groups of cuneiform or wedge-shaped marks for as many syllables containing one consonant; and about two hundred marks for syllables each containing two consonants. Alphabetic characters did not come into use until Babylonia became part of the Persian Empire. With the syllabic character, the older word signs were often mingled, and the preservation of these implied that there was a time when word signs were used exclusively in Babylonia for writing.

The Chaldean erudition had its origin in very remote times. As early as 3800 B. C., there was a library at Agadé; and among its books was an extensive treatise on astronomy.[1] They had a work resembling that of Euclid in scope, and it is probable that he used much Chaldean material in his work. It was mainly because of their superiority in arithmetic, mathematics, and astronomy that in the VIIth and VIIIth centuries B. C., the Babylonians were reputed to be the most learned of nations. In their arithmetic, much prominence was given to the number sixty; and they had simple and complex multiplication tables. Of the latter, one gave the squares and another the cubes of all the numbers from one to sixty. They divided the day into twelve hours, the hour into sixty minutes, and the minute into sixty seconds. They divided the ecliptic into three hundred and sixty degrees, presumably adopting that number because it was the product of twelve multiplied by thirty, those multipliers being "the nearest numbers to the lunations in a year, and to the days in a lunation."[2] They divided the lunar month into four weeks of seven days each, assigned a day to each of the seven planets, and called the last day of the week the sabbath, or rest of the soul.

They made maps and catalogues of the stars, divided them into groups, distinguished planets and comets from fixed stars, understood the relative distances of many planets from the earth, recorded occultations of planets by the sun and moon, observed the revolution of the stellar system, traced the track of the sun round the firmament, and divided its course into twelve sections, giving to each its constellation, name, and distinctive sign. It is from them that modern civilization has derived its zodiac and its divisions of the circle, of the day, and of the year. These measures must have been devised by scholars who had profited by the experience and the lessons of many centuries; and after adoption by the scholars, they were legalized by the government, superseding older and ruder standards. Of the many wonderful achievements of the Babylonians, one of the most difficult was the tracing of the sun through the sky, along a path which in the day is hidden, by the glare of light, and at night is discoverable to the reason and not to direct vision. Different languages were spoken in the Euphrates Valley, and these were studied with the aid of dictionaries and grammar.

Their astronomical observations were continued for at least nine centuries, and their records for so long a time were used by Ptolemy the astronomer, in the middle of the IInd century A. D. Aristotle said that their astronomical observations ran back 31,000 years.[3] They invented the astrolabe to measure the altitude of stars above the horizon. They recorded lunar eclipses, and by their tables found that these phenomena recur in cycles of two hundred and twenty-three lunations or periods of about nineteen years. They measured with approximate accuracy the solar day, the lunar revolution, and the solar year. The last, according to their calculations, was about three hundred and sixty-five days and a quarter. They invented two kinds of sun-dials for the measurement of time,—the vertical pillar and the more precise rectangular triangle with its hypothenuse pointing to the pole-star. They also invented the water-clock, to measure time, and with this they calculated the speed of the sun's movement and the diameter of its disk in relation to the length of its orbit. "At the moment when the sun was seen in the sky on the morning of the equinox, a jar filled with water was opened. From this the water was allowed to run into a second small jar, till the orb of the sun was completely visible; then it ran into a third and larger jar till the sun was again seen on the horizon on the following morning. They concluded that the diameter of the sun must stand in the same proportion to the cycle it passed through as the water in the small jar stood to the water in the large one. Hence they found that the diameter of the sun was contained seven hundred and twenty times in its course."[4]

"There can be no doubt that the Babylonian astronomy was more truly scientific than the Egyptian, and that it reached the highest perfection attainable without the aid of optical instruments. The Chaldeans knew the synodic period of the moon, the equinoctial and solstitial points, the true length of the year as dependent on the annual course of the sun (within a narrow limit of error), and even the precession of the equinoxes. But as might have been expected from their want of accurate instruments, they made a mistake in the amount of the precession and calculated it at thirty seconds instead of fifty. Hence their great cosmical year—that is, one complete revolution of the equinoctial points among the fixed stars—was made too long in like proportion, namely, 43,200 solar years instead of 26,000, to use round numbers.[b]"

SEC. 275. *Chaldean Government.*—We know little of the social, political, and military institutions of the Babylonians. The government was despotic and rested on the submissiveness much more than on the affection of the people. In proportion to the number and wealth of its subjects, its military power was not great. The Chaldeans were no match in an open field for the Assyrians, Persians, Medes, or Parthians; and they never won a great victory over a superior or equal number of enemies. That many of the people were slaves is manifest from the magnitude of the public works, which must have required the labor of many thousands of men employed for a long succession of years. The erection of the wall of Babylon was a greater enterprise than an Egyptian pyramid; and it was something that could not be finished in a generation, and to which the common people would not willingly devote a whole life-time. We have no description of a Babylonian palace, but immense mounds still remaining on the site of Babylon are the remains of vast buildings. One of these mounds is half a mile square and fifty feet high, and another is about a third of a mile square.

SEC. 276. *Chaldean Religion.*—The Babylonians were a devout people. One of their chief gods, of whom they had a multitude, was El, and from him their city was named the Gate of El—Babel. They used the titles of their divinities El, Baal, Beltis, Nebo, Merodach, Nergol, Shamas, and Asshur, in many of the names of their cities, kings, nobles, and common people. Belshazzar, Nebuchadnezzar, Nabopolassar, and Shalmaneser, are a few monarchs who remind us of the popular and official piety.

Nearly every name of which the signification is known to us, has a religious meaning. Among them we find such as these [1]:—

Belshazzar—Bel protects the king.
Belteshazzar—Bel guards secrets.
Belipni—Bel has made him.
Nebuchadnezzar—Nebo protects landmarks.
Nebuzaradan—Nebo has given the offspring.
Nabonassar—Nebo protects me.
Nabopolassar—Nebo protects my son.
Nabonahid—Nebo protects me.
Nabusallim—Nebo makes perfect.
Nabubilsami—Nebo is the lord of names.
Merodachbaladan—Merodach has given a son.
Abednebo—The slave of Nebo.

Temples were numerous in Chaldea, and so were the priests. The gods were worshiped with sacrifices of brutes and human beings, with offerings of flowers, fruits, and bread, with instrumental and vocal music, dancing, and prayer. There was one temple in Babylon where every maiden, before she could marry, was required to sell herself to some stranger, and to give the money to the treasury of the temple. After that time she must be chaste.

The Babylonians were Semites. Theirs was the first great monarchy of Western Asia. For more than a thousand years they were the most powerful and wealthy of nations. About 1300 B.C. they were conquered by their Assyrian neighbors and kindred, and they remained tributary to the Assyrian Empire until 637 B.C., when they regained their independence, which they lost again, and finally when they were conquered by the Persians. Their language, blood, political and ecclesiastical institutions, and great city, have disappeared forever.

Here is one of the Babylonian prayers: "Oh Lord, may the anger of your heart be allayed! Oh Lord, who knowest that I sinned in ignorance, look upon me kindly! Oh Goddess, who knowest that I knew not, be conciliated! I eat the food of wrath and drink the waters of anguish! . . . Oh my God, my transgressions are great. . . . I transgress without knowing it. I sin and know it not. I feed on transgressions and know it not. I wander in wrong paths and know it not. The Lord in the wrath of His heart has overwhelmed me with confusion. . . . I lie on the ground and no one reaches out a hand to me. I am silent and in tears, and no one says a cheering word. I cry out, and nobody hears me. I am exhausted and oppressed, and no one helps me. . . . My God, who knowest that I knew not, be merciful to me. . . . My Goddess, who knowest that I knew not, be merciful to me. . . . How long, O my God, must I wait for your mercy? . . . How long, O my Goddess, must I wait for your mercy? . . . Lord, thou wilt not repulse thy servant. In the midst of the stormy waters, come to my assistance, take me by the hand. If I commit sins, turn them into blessedness. If I commit transgressions, let the wind blow them away! My blasphemies are many; rend them like a garment! . . . Oh my God, who knowest that I knew not, my sins are seven times seven,—forgive my sins."[2]

The following prayer indicates a belief in seven great evil spirits: "They are seven! They are seven! Seven they are in the depths of ocean. Seven they are, disturbers of the face of heaven. They arise from the depths of the ocean, from hidden lurking-places. They spread like snares. Male they are not; female they are not. Wives they have not; children are not born to them. Order they know not, nor beneficence. Prayer and supplication they hear not. Vermin grown in the bowels of the mountains, foes of mankind, they are the throne-bearers of the gods; they sit in the roads and make them unsafe. The fiends! The fiends! They are seven! They are seven; seven they are. Spirit of heaven, be they confused. Spirit of earth, be they confused."[3]

They believed in sorcery. Here is a sorcerer's prayer: "As this onion is being peeled of its skins, thus shall it be with the evil spell. The burning fire shall consume it. It shall never be planted in the field. The ground shall not receive its root; its head shall bear no seed; it shall not be an offering at the feast of a god or king. The man who cast the evil spell, his eldest son, his wife, the curse, the lamentations, the transgressions, the written spell, the blasphemies, the sins, the evil in the victim's body, in his flesh, in his sores, may they all be destroyed like this onion; and may the burning fire consume them this day! May the evil spell go far away; and may light and health return."[4]

Not one of the Babylonian mounds has been examined with care and thoroughness; and there is reason to hope that large additions will be made, within a generation or two, to the present stock of Chaldean literature. Until the archæological explorations in the valley of the Euphrates shall have come to an end, any statement of the culture of the Babylonians must be incomplete.

Sec. 277. *Assyria.*—Assyria, a hilly region, three hundred miles long and two hundred wide, in the northern part of the Tigris basin, had no promise of natural greatness in its geographical features. It had no great natural advantages over adjacent countries in fertility of soil, navigable waters, or productive mines. Its inhabitants had no strong stimulus to national pride in the exclusive possession of a distinctive blood, tongue, industry, polity, or religion. But they did have a superior military discipline. For seven centuries they were the best fighters in Asia. Before the rise of Rome, they maintained a dominion over many alien provinces during a longer period than any other nation. Duncker says that no state of the Orient, " beginning with a region so small, and provided with such scanty material means, rose so high as Assyria, attained a wider supremacy, or maintained it so long and so vigorously."[1]

The Assyrians were predominantly Semitic in their blood, and regarded Babylonia as the country from which their ancestors came. For a long period they were subjects of Chaldea, but about 1300 B. C. revolted, established their independence, and conquered Babylonia, which, with occasional seasons of rebellion, remained subject to them nearly seven centuries. The Assyrian Empire included Armenia, Media, Persia, Babylonia, Syria, Phœnicia, Judea, and Egypt.

The first capital of Assyria was the city of Asshur, on the western bank of the Tigris, about latitude 35° 30′. Calah, about twenty miles farther north, on the western bank of the river, was the second capital, and the last and greatest was Nineveh, on the eastern bank, in latitude 36° 21′. It had a circuit of ten miles, within a brick wall a hundred and fifty feet high and fifty feet thick,

Some adobe was used in Assyria, but stone, of which a good quality could be obtained in the hills, and brick, were the preferred materials for building; and therefore the architectural remains are more interesting and more abundant than in Babylonia. As in Chaldea so in Assyria, the important public buildings stood on mounds, usually about thirty feet above the level of the valleys. The Koyunjik mound at Nineveh covers one hundred acres, and is ninety feet high; and the Nibbi Yunus mound is nearly half as large. The former of these mounds must have required the labor of 10,000 men for at least twelve years to complete it.

The royal palaces were large and splendid. The mound of Koyunjik is the ruin of a royal palace and temple with their grounds. The walls were adobe, with facings of thick limestone. Some of the blocks of stone weighed twenty-five tons each. The palace had several large courts. The walls were fifty feet high, and the larger halls one hundred and twenty feet long by thirty feet wide. The roofs were of timber, and were flat and used as a part of the house. The floors were covered with hard tiles, about fifteen inches square and two inches thick. The walls in the larger halls were lined with alabaster slabs covered with low reliefs, of which there were about seven thousand yards of surface. Twenty-four pairs of colossal winged bulls with the heads of men stood at the doorways. The sculpture does not indicate high artistic taste, but it is evidently the work of a great number of men who had been carefully trained to their business.

The Assyrians rivaled their predecessors and masters, the Babylonians, in literary activity. They kept full records of their public business, they accumulated libraries, they prepared grammars and dictionaries, and they evidently had a large number of persons who spent their lives in study and in writing. Thousands of their clay tablets, which have been dug out from the ruins, make up a considerable literature, and it is hoped that many more will be obtained hereafter. Centuries may elapse before archæological and historical investigation will exhaust the materials now buried in the Assyrian ruins.

Among the Assyrian writings preserved to modern times are ancient myths (including some similar to certain narratives in Genesis), private letters, governmental dispatches, geographical, zoölogical and botanical descriptions, laws, legal decisions, contracts, conveyances, tribute and tax lists, assessment rolls, hymns, prayers, lists of the gods, with their titles and attributes, astronomical tables, grammars, and dictionaries. The literary activity of the Assyrians was greatest about the middle of the VIIth century B. C. The Assyrians showed their enterprise in many different directions. They were bold builders and engineers as well as hunters and warriors. They built numerous grand palaces, and they decorated them with fresco painting, enameled tiles, and with sculpture in the round and in relief. Their statuary shows a close study of nature, and the power of representing its leading features with spirit and accuracy. They had schools of sculpture with numerous students who had acquired a skill obtainable only by long practice. Such schools must have contributed to the alabaster slabs carved in relief for the walls of the Koyunjik palace. These were sufficient to cover more than two thousand yards of wall to a height of nine feet. The colossal human-headed bulls of Nineveh are the largest, but not the most artistic, productions of Assyrian sculpture. The Khorsabad palace was an immense structure, and its walls inclosed an area a mile square. The Assyrians supplied water to Calah by a tunnel. Indeed, though upon many points our information is defective, we can scarcely get a clear glimpse into the life of the Assyrians in any direction without seeing that they were an extremely energetic people.

SEC. 278. *Assyrian Polity.*—The Assyrian army consisted of about 200,000 men, drawn probably from 3,-000,000 people. Not often, however, were more than 100,000 employed at a time. It was the policy of the government to keep these men at home in time of peace; they were not distributed over the country in garrisons. The provinces were left to themselves so long as they paid the required annual tribute. If the native king was slain or carried away as a captive, some man of the royal or of a princely family was placed on the throne. The laws, the priests, the town authorities, and the local usages were not disturbed. If the king failed to pay, he was dethroned; if the people rebelled, they were conquered and plundered. Their cattle were driven off, their temples despoiled, the walls of their cities destroyed, a considerable number of their boys and girls taken as slaves, and perhaps many families deported to some remote district, the vacant lands being given to settlers of different blood, religion, and tongue. A province, thus supplied with a considerable number of alien colonists, was crippled in its military efficiency, and not likely to organize a revolt until after several generations had elapsed. The Assyrians were the first conquerors who adopted the policy of deportation.[1]

They did not expect and perhaps did not wish their empire to be peaceful. They ruled harshly and cruelly.

Their army needed a campaign every year to keep up its efficiency, and at some place within a month's march from their capital. Western Persia and Palestine were as far away as they could go conveniently. Egypt and Parthia were too remote. The best places for military practice were in Media, Persia, Babylonia, Armenia, Northern Syria, Phœnicia, Samaria, or Judea, and in one or the other of these provinces some insurrection broke out nearly every year.

Sec. 279. *Assyrian Religion.*—The doctrines and ceremonies of religion in Assyria were very similar to those in Babylonia. The chief god of the nation was Asshur. " His place," as George Rawlinson says, " was always first in invocations. He is regarded, throughout the Assyrian inscriptions, as the tutelary deity both of the kings and of the country. He places the monarchs upon the throne, firmly establishes them in the government, lengthens the years of their reigns, preserves their power, protects their forts and armies, makes their name celebrated, and the like. To him they look to give them victory over their enemies, to grant them all the wishes of their hearts, and to allow them to be succeeded on their thrones by their sons and their son's sons to a remote posterity. . . . They represent themselves as passing their lives in his service. It is to spread his worship that they carry on their wars. They fight, ravage, destroy in his name." [1]

Speaking of an inscription of Tiglath Pileser I., about 1100 B. C., the same author says: " The long and solemn invocation of the great gods with which it opens, the distinct ascription to their assistance and guardianship of the whole series of the royal successes, whether in war or in the chase; the prevailing idea that the wars were undertaken for the chastisement of the enemies of Asshur, and that their result was the establishment, in an ever-widening circle, of the worship of Asshur; the careful account which is given of the erection and renovation of temples and the dedication of offerings; and the striking final prayer—all these are so many proofs of the prominent place which religion held in the thoughts of the king who set up the inscription, and may fairly be accepted as indications of the general tone and temper of his people. It is evident that we have here displayed to us, not a decent lip service, not a conventional piety, but a real hearty, earnest religious faith. . . . The king glorifies himself much; but he glorifies the gods more. . . . The whole tone of his mind is deeply and sincerely religious; besides formal acknowledgments, he is continually letting drop little expressions which show that his gods are in all his thoughts, and represent to him real powers governing and directing all the various circumstances of human life."[2] In another passage, pursuing this train of thought, the same author says: "Even when bent on glorifying himself, the monarch is still 'the illustrious chief who, under the auspices of the sun-god, rules over the people of Bel,' and 'whose servants Asshur has appointed to the government of the four regions.' If his enemies fly, 'the fear of Asshur has overwhelmed them.' If they refuse tribute, 'they withhold the offerings due to Asshur.' If the king himself feels inclined to make an expedition against a country, 'his lord, Asshur, invites him' to proceed thither. If he collects an army, 'Asshur has committed the troops to his hand.' When a people, not previously subject to Assyria, is attacked, it is because the people 'do not acknowledge Asshur.' When its plunder is carried off, it is to adorn and enrich the temples of Asshur and the other gods. When it yields, the first thing is to attach it to the worship of Asshur."[3]

Many of their prayers and hymns have an elevated tone. An Assyrian hymn says: "In heaven who is high? Thou alone art high. In earth who is high? Thou alone, thou art high. As for thee, thy word in heaven is declared; the gods bow their faces to the ground. As for thee, thy word on earth is declared; the spirits of the earth kiss the ground." Another hymn says: "O Lord my transgressions are many; great are my sins. The Lord in the anger of his heart has confounded me; God in the strength of his heart has set himself against me."[4] Of their curses the following is an example: "Whoever shall abrade or injure my tablets . . . may Anu and Vul, the great gods, my lords, consign his name to perdition! May they curse him with an irrevocable curse! May they cause his sovereignty to perish! May they pluck out the stability of the throne of his empire! Let not his offspring survive him in the kingdom! Let his servants be broken! Let his troops be defeated! Let him fly vanquished before his enemies! May Vul in his fury tear up the produce of his land! May a scarcity of food and of the necessities of life afflict his country! For one day may he not be called happy! May his name and this race perish!"[5]

An Assyrian legend tells how the goddess Ishtar went down to the world of spirits. It says: "The daughter of [the moon-god] Sin, fixed her mind to go to the house where all meet, the dwelling of the god Iskalla; to the house which men enter but cannot depart from; by the road which men travel but never retrace; to the abode of darkness and famine, where earth is their food and clay their nourishment; to the place where light is not seen, but in darkness they dwell; where ghosts, like birds, flutter their wings, and on the door and the door jambs the dust lies undisturbed." The queen of the lower world, offended by the intrusion of Ishtar, imprisoned, despoiled, and insulted her; and men and gods, deprived of the influence of the queen of love, fell into confusion and misery until the queen of the lower world had released the captive and allowed her to return to the domains of life and light.[6]

SEC. 280. *Phœnicia.*—Phœnicia was a strip of land about one hundred and forty miles long and twenty wide, extending from the thirty-third to the thirty-fifth parallel of latitude, and from the shore of the Mediterranean to the summit of the Lebanon Ridge, which may have an average elevation of 6,000 feet. Along a considerable portion of this coast, there is no plain, the hills coming down to the sea. The soil is fertile, and the climate, except high up in the mountain, warm and equable.

The people may have numbered 2,000,000 when the country was in the height of its prosperity. They belonged to the Semitic family, and their earliest ancestors of whom they had any tradition, dwelt in the southern part of the Euphrates Valley. As early as 2400 B. C. they had four wealthy cities, Tyre, Sidon, Aradus, and Tripoli.

In agricultural resources, Phœnicia was so poor that it imported much of its food from other countries. Its people were skillful gardeners, bakers, cooks, weavers, dyers, fishermen, and workers in wood, stone, copper, bronze, iron, silver, and gold. Then purple dye, known as the Tyrian purple, was unequaled elsewhere, and was a source of large profit to them.

In regard to the social condition of Phœnicia, our

information is scanty. The women seem to have enjoyed more freedom than in most other ancient states, and to have been treated with much respect. The governments of the Phœnician cities were aristocratic. The political power was nearly all in a senate consisting of the nobles or the heads of the noble clans. In Tyre and Carthage, the nobles were divided into three tribes, each consisting of ten clans, and the heads of the clans were called princes or nobles of the highest rank. These princes formed the little senate of Carthage, and the large senate of the same city comprised three hundred members, including one hundred from each of the three tribes. There was also a senate of three hundred members in Sidon and Aradus. Tyre was a double city, situated on two islands, which, after having been separated for many centuries, were united by a mole. Before the connection each island had, as its chief official, a judge elected for life; afterwards, there were two judges in the one city, one being a check on the other, somewhat as the consuls were in Rome. The senior judge was the political and military head of the government, under the control of the senate. In Carthage, there were two judges who were elected for life and held the chief political, judicial, and military power. The Phœnicians undertook no aggressive war upon people equal or nearly equal to themselves in culture. They looked to trade, not to conquest, for their aggrandizement. Tyre and Sidon, after becoming subject to Assyria, Persia, and other empires, had to fight for their masters; and Carthage, in self-defense, was compelled to send armies to fight the Romans in Sicily, Spain, and Italy. They knew how to fight but they always preferred peace with security.

The Phœnician religion was similar to that of Babylon,

in its polytheism, its idolatry, its sacrifices (including human sacrifices, which were frequent in Carthage), and its doctrines. It had a written revelation, which has not been preserved. Each of several great gods had a temple with its own hereditary priests, who were not necessarily related in blood or connected in discipline with those of any other shrine. El, Yah, Baal, Melkarth, Adonai, Astarte, and Tanais, were among the prominent divinities, and not unfrequently a temple would have the idols of three gods in its sanctuary.

After Tyre had been conquered by Alexander and Carthage by Rome in the third Punic war, the political independence of the Phœnician states came to an end, and the literature, sacred books, and the people as a distinct nationality, disappeared forever. Their tongue was near akin to that of the Hebrews. Even after Carthage had been conquered in the second Punic war, it was the largest city on the Mediterranean. It maintained the customs and institutions of Tyre, but paid more attention than did the mother city to tillage, the breeding of domestic animals, political dominion over alien subjects, and war. Situated in the midst of an extensive coast, where the earlier inhabitants were much inferior in culture to her citizens, she gradually extended her authority over a large region on the mainland, and also over the islands of Sardinia, Corsica, Malta, Majorca, and Minorca, and over part of Sicily. But all these conquests were held as alien possessions; their people were not admitted to share in the government of the chief city, nor to hold the highest provincial offices. The power of Carthage was not based on the affection of her subjects, and yet her wealth and the enterprise, intelligence, and number of her citizens, made her for a long time the greatest power in the Western Mediterranean. She was mainly a naval power; and those of her citizens who adopted arms as a profession preferred service at sea. Their land forces consisted mainly of alien mercenaries, who were often turbulent and treacherous. The third Punic war closed in 147 B. C., with the destruction of Carthage, and a few centuries later nothing was left on its site, of the Semitic blood or of the superior industrial skill which had filled it with wealth and splendor.

SEC. 281. *Phœnician Commerce.*—The Phœnicians were prominent in ship building, navigation, and commerce. They had the best merchants of antiquity, and in the number and excellence of their mariners, ship builders, and merchant ships, they surpassed all other nations. They also had an unequaled supply of conveniently accessible ship timber. The proximity of their forests to places where ships could be built and launched was perhaps the chief inducement for the first settlement of Babylonians, who may have traded in the Persian Gulf and then come with caravans to the Mediterranean.

The Phœnician mariners were familiar in a remote antiquity with all the shores of the Mediterranean and Black Seas, with the coast of Africa to the Gulf of Guinea, with that of Europe to the Baltic, with the shores of the Persian Gulf and the Indian Ocean.[1] From Hindostan they brought spices, silks, cottons, ivory, precious stones, pearls, and gold; from Northern Europe, amber; from Britain, tin; and they furnished nearly all the foreign products needed in the seaports of the Mediterranean.

The Greeks acknowledged the superior sailing qualities of the Phœnician ships and the superior skill of the Phœnician mariners. The latter steered at night by the north star, for centuries before other nations became familiar with it. The Greek sailors for their guide took the Great Bear, and as that is twenty degrees from the pole, and changes to as far on the other side within twenty-four hours, it did not give accuracy of direction. Phœnician mariners, however, and to a still greater degree the Greeks, and later the Romans, preferred to keep within sight of land, and the pilot was expected to be familiar with the coasts, so that by their appearance he would know his position. When out of sight of land, and in doubt as to where he was, the shipmaster released a dove, which flew up to get a view, and if it saw land went to it, and if not, returned to the ship.

The Phœnicians invented the leading classes of merchant ships known to the ancients, such as the pentekonter, the bireme, and the trireme. The pentekonter had fifty rowers, twenty-five on each side, all on the same level. The bireme had a hundred oarsmen, on two different tiers, twenty-five in each tier on a side. The trireme had three tiers, with twenty-five on a side in each tier. The three patterns were of about the same length. All these boats had sails, but as the hulls were not deep enough to carry much sail, and as the art of rigging ships so that they could sail against the wind was not well understood, war ships almost exclusively, and merchant ships often, depended on their oars for propulsion. The rowers were slaves, sometimes chained to the bench, and the expense of rowing was not so much of a consideration as it would be in modern times. The ships were laid up during the three months of winter, when the sky was usually cloudy, and the weather cold and stormy. While not in use, the ships, instead of being left at anchor, were drawn up on the beach, out of reach of the waves.

For centuries the Phœnicians had no competitors in the foreign or international trade of the Mediterranean. Transportation brought other business to them. It gave them opportunities for becoming money changers, money lenders, slave traders, mine owners, and contractors for furnishing all kinds of supplies. They accompanied fleets and armies to buy and to sell whatever was offered or demanded. They needed resident agents in regions where the culture was much ruder than their own, and they established colonies at many places on the Western Mediterranean, on the shores of the Black Sea, and the Red Sea, in the British Isles, and on the Atlantic coast of Africa. They worked mines of silver and lead in Spain, and had numerous colonies there, including several cities. Their most prosperous colony was Carthage, which became one of the great powers of antiquity. In many cities of Greece, Italy, Asia Minor, Egypt, and Mesopotamia, the Phœnicians had resident traders, who had a separate district or quarter for their occupation. They were extensively interested in the caravan trade between Syria, Asia Minor, and Egypt in the West, and Arabia, Mesopotamia, Persia, and Hindostan in the East. Before 950 B. C., most of the caravans had their western terminal point in Phœnicia, but after that time, in Asia Minor.

SEC. 282. *Phœnician Letters.*—The Phœnicians were the first people who established extensive international relations in the basin of the Mediterranean, and who carried the arts of one country to the people of many others. They gave indirect lessons in ship building, navigation, irrigation, mining, metallurgy, and in writing, to the rude tribes of Northern Africa, Southern Russia, and Western and Northern Europe. One of their most valuable services to culture was their dissemination of the alphabet. As we have seen, the Egyptians invented the alphabet, but as they had first done all their writing with word signs, and had afterwards supplemented these with syllabic signs, and had used these word signs and syllabic signs on their monuments and in their sacred literature, their priests were compelled to study these three kinds of signs. Besides, their conservative habits made it fashionable to continue the employment of all these different symbols, of which a thousand must be familiar simple sound symbols, taking only one for each sound, in cases where the Egyptians had several. The Phœnicians not only copied the idea of the alphabet, but they copied its details with modifications, so that the imitation of the forms of the letters is distinctly traceable. The Greeks, Latins, Jews, and Goths copied from the Phœnicians, and modern Europe copied from the Latins. Thus it was that after Egypt had invented the alphabet, she derived comparatively little benefit from it. A magnificent opportunity to introduce a great reform in writing was offered to the Phœnicians, and they seized it.

The weights and measures of the Babylonians were copied by the Phœnicians and by them introduced into all the countries bordering on the Mediterranean. Wherever any industrial art was exercised with superior skill, in the range of their observation, they learned it and practiced it in their cities and colonies; and from these it extended to other nations in the vicinity. Thus for many centuries they rendered unsurpassed services to culture.

CHAPTER XVIII.

THE TEUTONS, ETC.

SECTION 283. *Teutonia.*—When first known to the Romans, about 200 B. C., the Teutons occupied nearly the same regions now inhabited by the Germans and Scandinavians. The Teutons were the ancestors of those two modern nationalities, and also of the Goths, Visigoths, Ostrogoths, Vandals, Lombards, Burgundians, Anglos, Saxons, and Normans, who conquered Gaul, Spain, Portugal, and Italy, in each of which countries half the blood of some provinces is Teutonic, and England, in which the blood is nearly all Teutonic. They settled Iceland, which may be considered purely Teutonic in blood. They also conquered Carthage and the adjacent provinces in Africa, but little trace of Teutonic blood is left there. Their descendants preponderate in the United States, Canada, and Australia, and exercise a large influence in Spanish America. Since the overthrow of the Roman Empire, the Teutons and their offspring have been the leading conquerors, legislators, authors, and artists.

In the time of Cæsar, a large part of Germany was covered with marsh and forest; and the population was far less dense than now. Life was rude and violent. The dwellings in summer were of wattle daubed with clay; in winter, pits covered with earth supported by logs. In lakes and swamps, villages were built on piles. Edge tools of steel were costly; a few of bronze and of stone were preserved from earlier times. The food of the people consisted mainly of grain, sour milk, pork, and game. Flax and various cereals were cultivated; and among the domestic animals were sheep, cows, horses, and pigs. Beer and mead were common beverages. The only garment of the poor was a mantle of linen or skins, without arms, reaching from the neck to the mid calf. It was worn over the left shoulder and under the right arm. The rich had an under-garment of linen. Clothing was rarely washed, and soap was unknown. The people were divided into nobles, commoners, freedmen, serfs, and slaves. The liberated slave or serf was a freedman, as was his son; his grandson became a commoner. Neither serf nor slave was permitted to testify against a commoner or noble. The great nobles had large estates in land; the commoners in the villages owned their tracts in common.

Woman enjoyed a high degree of social freedom and influence. More frequently than in other Aryan nationalities, she was allowed to inherit the regal office, to be a priestess, and to control her property and her children. Custom recognized only one wife, but the nobles had concubines, and traces are found of an earlier condition, in which the sexes lived together promiscuously. It is mainly to their ancestry that the modern nations of Teutonic blood owe the liberality with which they treat their women. Deformed children were exposed to die; and in times of scarcity and migration, persons helpless with age or disease were abandoned or slain.

The Teutons were divided into tribes, each governed by a council of nobles. Clan organization had either disappeared or had become much weaker than among the contemporaneous Celts. There were no national laws, courts, revenues, or monarchs. Justice was administered by local councils or by feud between villages or families. There were no governmental records, and the art of writing was known to few.

SEC. 284. *Teutonic Army.*—They were a martial people, and as early as 50 B. C. many of them were enlisted in the Roman armies, of which they were a valuable portion. Many of these men, familiar with the best soldierly training of their time, returned to their native land with information about the wealth, the genial climate, and the sunny fields of Italy and Gaul, and of the oppression, discontent, and military inefficiency of the people. The ambition for the conquest of the countries of Southern Europe became a national passion among the Teutons. It was their chief hope in life, and was transmitted from generation to generation, leading to a succession of invasions, continuing at short intervals for four centuries, until they had become the masters of all the Roman provinces of the West.

An invading army began its organization by the election of a commander or king, who was surrounded by a council of nobles. The adventurers took their wives, children, and herds with them, and staked everything upon success. They must conquer or be exterminated. They had the advice of experienced drill masters, who had served in the Roman armies, and a discipline superior to any they had before known was introduced among them. If the invaders conquered a province and established themselves in it, they must be prepared to defend it. This required the continuance and improvement of their discipline, and the maintenance of political unity and subordination. They rapidly improved in the arts of war and government. They kept a firm hold on the regions they had conquered; they became the nobles, while the previous inhabitants were reduced to serfdom and slavery.

Most of the invaders were footmen armed with spears; but there were also cavalrymen. As they had no strongholds to which they could flee, and no familiarity with hiding places near them, and no friends among the country people in the Roman provinces, they fought with great desperation, which was called by the Romans "the Teutonic fury." It was better to die in battle than to be slaughtered as captives, or sent to distant regions as slaves. Long before the Germans succeeded in conquering any portion of the Roman Empire, they were recognized as its most dangerous enemies. Tacitus, who wrote about 100 A. D., said that they had been fighting against Rome for two centuries; that they were more formidable than the Samnites, Carthaginians, or Gauls had ever been, and that in their dissensions lay the chief hope for the safety of the imperial city.

SEC. 285. *Teutonic Religion.*—The religion of the Teutons was polytheistic without a definite creed. Great gods, local divinities, and ancestral spirits were worshiped with hymns, offerings of food and fermented drinks, and sacrifices of beasts and men. The greatest of the deities was Odin, or Wodan, whose home is the sun or the heaven, and after whom Wednesday is named. Frigg, his wife, the goddess of the home, and Thor, or Donar, the god of Thunder, made with Odin a triad of superior dignity among the gods. Tuisko, who gave his name to Tuesday, was the god of war. There was an evil spirit named Loki, and his assistants were demoniac giants. A multitude of fairy-like beings inhabited forests, caves, mines, rivers, and lakes.

In most of the Teutonic nations, there was neither a hereditary priesthood, nor any extensive or powerful ecclesiastical organization. The sacerdotal profession did not require long study, nor confer much wealth or power. There were almost as many priestesses as priests, and the chief sacerdotal occupation was divination. Every noble made the offerings to his ancestral divinities. There were no temples and not many idols. When beasts were sacrificed, the meat was eaten by the nobles, who were thus admitted to the communion of the god, and were bound to be faithful to one another. There was a future life, in which spirits had ranks, honors, occupations, and feelings, similar to those of this life. The highest rewards there were for military efficiency here.

The dead were buried with much ceremony. The wife, the concubines, some slaves and horses, were slain at the grave of the great noble; and not unfrequently some dependent freemen would sacrifice themselves to keep him company. When a hut was built, a dog was buried under the doorway so that his spirit should guard the inmates; and under the influence of a similar superstition, a lamb was buried under the doorway of a church by the early converts to Christianity in Germany.

Although the priests were not a prominent and influential class among the Teutons, the people had an elaborate and highly poetical mythology, much of which was preserved until modern times in the Icelandic Edda, which may be considered the sacred book of the Teutonic religion. Some myths are also preserved in the national epic of the Niebelungen Lied.

This may seem a brief account of an ethnological family, which unquestionably occupies the first place in the history of culture, and which for the last eight centuries has far surpassed all others in the sum of valuable contributions to progress; but it must be remembered that not until after the Teutons had been brought under the influence of Rome, did they show their great capacities, and begin to exert a strong influence on other nationalities. Their glories belong to a later period.

SEC. 286. *The Celts.*—The first Aryan settlers in Gaul, Spain, and Britain were Celts, who arrived there probably not later than 3000 B. C., and found an earlier population, small in size, dark in color, and Turanian in blood, who were called Iberians in Central and Southern Spain, Basques in France, and Ligurians in Northwestern Italy. These Turanians were everywhere subjugated, and in Central, Northern, and Eastern Gaul, and in Britain, they were almost exterminated; in Spain and in Southern Gaul, they gradually mixed with the Celts, and greatly modified their blood, and in Spain modified their institutions.

It was not until the Ist century B. C. that the Celts were observed by authors, from whose books we can form a definite idea of the Celtic culture. At that time the population in Western Europe was about one fifth as large in proportion to area as it is at present.[1] The people had been influenced by traffic with Phœnicians since 1000 B. C., and with Greeks since 600 B. C. Every summer, merchants from the eastern and southern shores of the Mediterranean visited the coasts of the Celtic lands and exchanged jewelry, beautifully finished weapons, and cloths with brilliant dyes, for the tin of Britain, the amber of the Baltic, the gold, silver, tin, lead, and slaves of Spain and Gaul.

This traffic stimulated all branches of Gallic industry,

and before the time of Cæsar, the Gauls had developed a high degree of skill in many of the useful arts. They were the first to use large iron bolts in the frames of their ships; the first to build ships depending exclusively on sails for propulsion; the first to use chain cables with their anchors; the first to cover sheets of iron and copper with a coating of tin; the first to make and wear coats of chain armor; the first to manufacture soap; the first to reap grain with a horse machine; and the first to substitute wooden casks for skins and pottery, for storing beer and wine. Their priority and superiority in these respects implies that they made more improvements in industry than any other people of their time; that they held the leading place in the metallurgy of iron; and that their country felt the stimulus of an advantageous situation and of an energetic blood. Ancient Gaul had about the same boundaries as modern France, which is extremely rich in its natural resources. Its soil is fertile; its climate is genial, equable, moist, and favorable to agricultural production and human activity; and its position between Germany and Spain in one direction and between Britain and Italy in the other, fitted it to be a center of traffic, wealth, intelligence, refinement, and political power. Occupied by a homogeneous people, under a wise gov! ernment it could not fail to exercise great influence in European history.

For their food, the Gauls depended partly on game, though they had numerous grain fields and herds of cattle. Much of their country was covered by forest and marsh, which abounded with wolves and wild hogs, and gave convenient opportunities for exciting experiences in the chase. Villages in which the houses were mostly of wood, were numerous, and there were a few large towns. Of the social condition of the Celts we know little. They were divided into clans, organized on the basis of descent in the male line. Polygyny was permitted and was practised by most of the chiefs. In Britain some tribes had a system of promiscuous marriage, in which a number of men were the common husbands of a number of women.

SEC. 287. *Celtic Polity.*—The Celts in Gaul, Britain, and Spain were divided into numerous independent tribes, under chiefs or petty kings who had little power. Under the king or head chief were a number of chiefs, each possessing almost absolute power in his own clan, which included nobles, freemen, and slaves. The nobles and freemen were dependents of the chief and bound to follow and obey him in war; and in return he owed them protection and support. There was a sacredness in the mutual obligation. A man's highest duty was to the head of his clan; and the chiefs were neither loyal to their kings nor peaceful among themselves. The lack of a strong sense of national unity was the great defect of the Gallic polity, and the main cause of their disastrous defeats when they came into conflict with the Romans and Teutons.

The chiefs were the commanders of divisions, and, having reached their office by hereditary right, were generally incompetent. They had never been subjected to strict drill, and they did not know how to discipline their followers. There was no proper sense of subordination among the mass of the soldiers. They were a disorderly crowd. Their bravery and energy made their first onset very formidable, but if they were not immediately successful, they were easily thrown into confusion, and their lack of discipline left them without confidence in one another, and without the means of correcting mistakes. Even when they won a battle they obtained little benefit from it, and in a campaign they were no match for inferior numbers of the better disciplined Romans and Teutons. They had all the elements for a great national success save strength of political organization, which would have brought military discipline with it. For lack of this, there was no united Gaul; for lack of this, they were wiped out from the map of Europe; for lack of this, there is no nation that can now justly claim to be Celtic by a strong predominance in blood; for lack of this, they were unable to resist the Romans; and the Latinized Gauls were unable to resist the Visigoths, the Ostrogoths, and the Franks; and the mixture of Latins, Gauls, and Teutons was compelled to submit to the Normans. The Celts never made a brilliant success in a long campaign except under the command of Hannibal; when the Celtic troops were taken from their hereditary chiefs, and compelled to submit to severe drill they showed what the Celts could do as soldiers.

SEC. 288. *Druidism.*—The inability of the Gauls to unite in one great nation, or even to give a strong political organization to any one of their many kingdoms, appears the more remarkable when we recall the fact that they had a consolidated ecclesiastical system, with jurisdiction extending over Great Britain and Ireland. There was a chief priest holding absolute sacerdotal power over a multitude of priests, arranged in numerous gradations of rank, and held in strict discipline. In unity of management, in thoroughness of ecclesiastical drill, and in completeness of education for clerical purposes, this Celtic priesthood was superior to any other that we have hitherto found in the records of culture, and indeed it never had an equal save in the hierarchy of Roman Catholicism. The chief priest held his office for life, and was elected by a council of priests, who were his advisers. In each kingdom the priests of superior rank formed a sacerdotal council, which had authority to elect a king in case of a vacancy.

The Celtic priests or Druids were not a separate hereditary class, but were selected from the nobles. Their office was highly influential and honorable, and was considered very desirable to those young nobles who had no prospect of becoming the heads of their respective clans. No old man was admitted to the priesthood, and no young man until he had attended a Druid school, and had shown an aptitude for the sacerdotal profession. The Druids were divided into classes of bards, diviners, and sacrificers, and each class had its ranks. An excellent voice and an ear for music were needed for a bard; superior tact, fluent speech, and a dignified appearance, for a sacrificer or diviner; and a good memory, for every position. The diviners were the most influential class. They were the custodians and administrators of the civil and criminal law, the advisers of the kings and chiefs, administrators of the government in case of a vacancy in the royal office, the arbiters of disputed successions to titles, offices, and property, and the spiritual guides who decided whether the omens were favorable for war, peace, battle, or any important enterprise.

Their religion was polytheistic but not idolatrous. They worshiped a number of gods, among whom Esus and Beal or Baal were prominent. They believed in the transmigration of souls, in some cases at least. They believed in a future life with rewards for the good and punishment for the bad. Their ecclesiastical ceremonial was elaborate; and in that and in many points of their religious doctrine, they bore much resemblance to the Phœnicians, from whom they had doubtless learned much, and had taken the names of some divinities. They considered the oak and the mistletoe growing upon it sacred; and most of their ecclesiastical ceremonies were held in oak groves, and in the open air. They had temples in Southern Gaul, and some of these possessed large amounts of precious metal. In Western France and in Great Britain and Ireland there are no traces or traditions of covered Druidical temples.

As among the Phœnicians, so among the Celts, human sacrifices were numerous. In some cases the Celtic victim was slain on an altar; in others, he was burned to death in a large frame of osiers, shaped like a man. He was preferably a criminal, but might be a prisoner of war or a slave.

All the priests were educated in schools, to which none but young men were admitted, and in which all were required to memorize a multitude of songs, hymns, liturgies, patriotic ballads, moral maxims, and formulas of exorcism, which none save a priest might teach, and none save a priest or clerical student might repeat, and none might commit to writing. Many of the priests found that they could not learn all their verses by heart until after twenty years of study. All the higher sacerdotal offices were held by males, but there were also priestesses who devoted themselves to divination. Some of them dwelt on an island on which no man might land. They rowed or paddled to the mainland when they wished to tell fortunes, or to meet their husbands.

The chief priest had not only absolute authority over

all the Druids in Gaul, but also great control over the nobles and freemen. Cæsar tells us that "if any person, either public or private, does not acquiesce in their decisions, they interdict him from their sacrifices. This is among them the severest punishment. They who are thus interdicted are reckoned impious and accursed; all men depart from them; all shun their company and conversation, lest they sustain some misfortune from their contagion; the administration of justice and the protection of the laws is denied them, and no honor is conferred on them."[1]

The Gauls had a confident belief in a future life similar in many respects to the life in the flesh. They buried their dead, and in the graves deposited clothes, weapons, ornaments, and food, and also horses, dogs, slaves, wives, and friends sacrificed for the service of the departed. Every year they set out a feast on the grave for the entertainment of the spirits. They burned letters containing news for their friends in the next world; and they occasionally lent money to be repaid there.[2]

SEC. 289. *Stone Monuments.*—Besides singing hymns at their ecclesiastical ceremonies, the bards recited patriotic songs at public festivals, and accompanied the armies to arouse the enthusiasm of the troops when about to go into battle. One class of priests, probably the diviners, were judges, and had exclusive authority to declare the law. Tradition in Ireland says that the charges of serious crime were tried at Rocking Stones, or Stones of Judgment, as they are called in Gælic.[1] The Rocking Stone, there, is a large rock which is poised on a point in such a manner that it can be tilted from one side to the other, and back and forth, by a child; and in some cases it is very difficult to discover at first sight which way it may be tilted. After it has been pushed to one side, fifty men without machinery can push it no farther in that direction. It is said that in the Druid trials, the accused was taken to the stone and ordered to tilt it, and if he failed at the first push, he was declared guilty. The tradition has been expressed in the following verse:—

> "Behold yon huge
> And unhewn sphere of living adamant,
> Which, poised by magic, rests its central weight
> On yonder pointed rock; firm as it seems,
> Such is its strange and virtuous property
> It moves obsequious to the gentlest touch .
> Of him whose breast is pure. But to a traitor,
> Though even a giant's prowess nerved his arm,
> It stands as fixed as Snowdon."[2]

These rocking stones are numerous in various Celtic districts, including Ireland, England, and Western France. There are none in Scandinavia or Germany.[3] Perhaps the largest one known is in the parish of Constantine, Cornwall. It weighs seven hundred and fifty tons and is sixty feet long. Other notable monuments of this kind are found in the Cornish parishes of Kirkmichael, Kells Balvaird, Kilbrachan and Dron.[4] It is possible that all these rocking stones were deposited in their present positions by glaciers or floating ice, but some authors have supposed that most of them were poised by art.

Besides the rocking stones, England, France, and Ireland have a multitude of rude megalithic monuments, called dolmens, menhirs, and stone circles. These were probably erected by the Druids. In Gaelic traditions, the dolmen is called a stone of the Druids, and a stone circle a place of assembly. The dolmen is a combination of three or more rough stones, one of which rests on and covers the others. In some cases the pillars are

SEC. 289. STONE MONUMENTS. 315

more than sixteen feet high, but rarely more than five or six. At Confalens, France, one of these structures has a cap-stone fifteen feet long, twelve wide, and two thick. In the province of Brittany there are more than six hundred dolmens. They exist also in Germany, Denmark, Sweden, Spain, Portugal, Sardinia, Lombardy, Tuscany, the Balearic Isles, Malta, the Canaries, Algeria, Tunis, Arabia, Hindostan, and the Caucasus, in most of which countries their construction cannot be attributed to the Celts.[5]

A menhir is a rough columnar stone, which has its base planted in the earth. In some cases the height is twenty feet above ground, and the weight several scores of tons. The menhirs are found in England, Scotland, Ireland, Scandinavia, and France, in which latter country the province of Brittany has more than seven hundred. They were called memorial stones by the Northmen. Many places in England and France have great numbers of upright stones planted in lines in the ground, suggesting that they were erected over graves, as perhaps they were. There are more than eight hundred such stones in one field near Carnac, Brittany.[6]

A stone circle is a ring of upright stones surrounding either a level piece of ground or a mound. The largest of these structures are in England and France, but they are also found in Germany, Scandinavia, and many other countries. Brittany has forty, mostly small. The most noted one is Stonehenge, in England. There were thirty rudely hewn pillars from four to eight feet wide, two to four feet thick, and sixteen feet high above the ground, and about three or four feet apart, forming a circle a hundred feet in diameter. Each of these pillars had on its top two tenons which rested in mortise holes cut in a stone architrave connecting each pair of pillars. Most of the posts and architraves have fallen to the ground, but enough remain to show clearly the size and pattern of the structure. An inner circle of stones had ten posts in five pairs, each pair being about ten feet from the one on either side. The material of these posts and architraves is sandstone found in the vicinity; but inside of the second circle there is a third small circle with posts of blue igneous rock, supposed to have been brought from Ireland. The largest of these is seven feet long, two wide, and one foot thick. A large flat stone in the center of the circle is supposed to have been an altar. This ruin at Stonehenge is the most remarkable archæological curiosity of Great Britain. Fergusson says: "In their simple grandeur they are perhaps the most effective example of megalithic art that ever was executed by man. The Egyptians and Romans raised larger stones, but they destroyed their grandeur by ornament or by their accompaniments; but these simple square masses on Salisbury Plain are still unrivaled for magnificence in their own peculiar style."[7]

At Avebury, England, there are two stone circles near together, one three hundred and twenty-five and the other three hundred and fifty feet in diameter, and both inclosed in a circular wall of earth 1,200 feet in diameter. In the center of one of the stone circles there is a dolmen. There are remains of an avenue lined on both sides with upright stones, leading half a mile from the outer wall of earth.[8] France and England have a number of burial mounds dating from Celtic times. In many of them are found sepulchral chambers made with walls and roofs of unhewn or rudely hewn stone, with passages lined and roofed in the same manner leading to the open air.

Some of these mounds have a large central chamber with vault-like small chambers or tombs round their sides.

SEC. 290. *Etruria*.—Etruria was a region of about 7,000 square miles, west of the summit of the Apennines, between the Tiber and the forty-fourth parallel of latitude. It was divided into a dozen independent states, several at the north having an area of 1,000 and several at the south having not more than twenty square miles each. The capital cities were Veii now Isola, Caere now Cervetri, Tarquinii now Corneto, Volsinii now Bolsena, Vetulonia, Falerii, Clusium now Chiusi, Arretum now Arezzo, Perusia now Perugia, Volaterra now Volterra, Cortona and Rusellæ.

Much of our knowledge of the Etruscans has been obtained from the examination of their tombs in this century. Their sepulchers, constructed with much care, in many cases excavated in rock, ornamented with architectural designs, statuary, and paintings, and supplied with vases, jewelry, and armor, are numerous. Their alphabet, their sculpture, their vases, some of their useful arts, the names of several of their gods, and some of their myths, are similar to those of the Greeks, and were probably copied from them. In their sepulchral paintings, the flesh color of the Etruscan man is terra cotta red; that of the Etruscan women, a dull white; a difference that may be due to a conventional rule for distinguishing the sexes, or to a change in the colors under chemical influence.

The population of Etruria was dense. Districts, now desolate on account of malaria, contain many tombs of the Etruscans and ruins of their cities. Veii, which was the capital of one of their small states, had walls more than seven miles in circuit, indicating that the city was as large as Athens in the height of her prosperity.[1] The cemetery of Tarquinii covered sixteen square miles.

SEC. 291. *Etruscan Industry.*—The Etruscans engaged extensively in foreign trade. They had large seaports and many ships. They obtained and perhaps they imported ivory from Africa and amber from the Baltic. They were skillful workers in stone. Remnants of their sewers, tunnels, bridges, city walls, and sepulchers are numerous, and for the age in which they were constructed, remarkable. It is supposed that the main sewer of ancient Rome still in existence, and the tunnel draining the Alban Lake, are their work. In those regions where tufo rock could be had conveniently, their city walls were usually built of that material in blocks about twenty-two inches square and forty-four long, laid up without mortar, the alternate courses being laid crosswise. In some places, however, the stones are polygonal. No mortar has been found in any of the stone work that can certainly be attributed to them. They paved their streets with polygonal stones.

In irrigation, drainage, and agriculture generally, the Etruscans were superior to the other nationalities of Italy in their time. They manufactured glass and enamel, and they were expert smiths in bronze, iron, silver, and gold.

A peculiar kind of jewelry called the Tyrrhene, found in Egypt, Assyria, Phœnicia, and the Crimea, as well as in Etruria, and attributed in its origin to the pre-Etruscan inhabitants of Etruria, is thus described by Dennis: "The [Tyrrhene] style [of jewelry] is easily recognized by its elegant form, the harmony of its parts, and the purity of its design, but chiefly by the marvelous fineness and elaboration of its workmanship. The patterns, which are always simple, yet most elegant and admirably harmonious, are wrought by soldering together globules or particles of gold, so minute as hardly to be perceptible to the naked eye, and by the interweaving of extremely delicate threads of gold, and are sometimes, but sparingly, interspersed with enamels. Tiny figures of men, animals, or chimeras, exquisitely chased in relief or in the round, form another and favorite feature in the ornamentation. On a close inspection, this jewelry astonishes and confounds by its wonderful elaboration; at a little distance, it charms the eye by its exquisite taste and graceful character and harmony of its outlines. In fact, it is the perfection of jewelry, far transcending all that the most expert artists of subsequent ages have been able to produce."

The Etruscans had a literature, with history, poetry, drama, and sacerdotal liturgy, all of which is now lost. They also had schools, to which the ruder Romans, in the VIth and Vth centuries B. C., sent their sons to get a better training than could be had at home. They paid some attention to astronomy, and the length of the tropical year as calculated, or accepted from some foreign source, by them, was three hundred and sixty-five days, five hours, and forty minutes. Their favorite and characteristic amusement was the gladiatorial fight, which was copied by the Romans, as were also their toga, their system of auguries, and much of their military system.

SEC. 292. *Etruscan Polity, etc.*—A notable feature of Etruscan life was that the wife had more freedom, and was treated with more honor, than in Greece. She was educated and accomplished. She sat at meals with her husband; and her children took her name in preference to that of their father.

Tradition, accepted by the Romans, said that the Etruscans arrived in Central Italy about 1100 B. C., and conquered and enslaved the previous occupants of the country. These independent states recognized their community of blood, language, worship, and political interests, and yet could not, or would not, unite in one nation, though they sometimes combined their forces against the Gauls and Romans. Their relation to one another was often discordant, and sometimes bitterly hostile. The governments of all the Etruscan states were aristocratic. A senate or council of nobles had general supervision of public affairs, and selected all the officers, including a chief or president. He held superior authority in sacerdotal, political, military, and judicial affairs. His sacerdotal office was considered the chief source of his dignity, and he was called chief priest or king. The majority of the people were slaves and serfs, and there was a large class of commoners. The nobles owned the land, and were a professional class of warriors.

SEC. 293. *Etruscan Religion.*—The Etruscan states had a common religion under a confederated priesthood, with a national sanctuary at Voltumnæ, the site of which is not now known with certainty, though it was probably about forty miles north from Rome. There the high priests of each of the twelve Etruscan states met at their annual festivals. It seems singular that these high priests, who were also the political and military chiefs of their respective states, did not establish a consolidated nationality, or at least succeed in preventing warfare among their subject communities. The religion was polytheistic and idolatrous. There were twelve great gods; but most of the public worship was paid to deities similar in their attributes to the Jupiter, Juno, and Minerva of the Romans. These three divinities were adored in conjunction. Religion played a very prominent part in the lives of the Etruscans, and their devotions were conducted according to an elaborate liturgy. Sacrifices of beasts and of men were frequent; and before the commencement of any important enterprise, the omens were consulted by the priests. Every noble family worshiped its ancestors, who were represented by clay figures, the male head of the family being the priest in these devotions.

Great attention was paid to the dead. Tombs were excavated in the rock for all the wealthy noble families, and in them were deposited either the corpses or the urns containing their ashes, after cremation. The sepulchral chambers had couches for the dead and seats for the living. Jewelry, arms, clothing, and symbols of office or occupation, were placed with the man or woman in the tomb, and sometimes, also, vases and slabs of stone five feet long and three feet wide, covered with inscriptions giving their names, titles, and pedigrees.

The Etruscan states seemed to have reached the height of their prosperity about 400 B. C., and they not only could not unite to conquer Rome when she was weak, but they did not coöperate cordially and desperately afterwards with the Carthaginians or the Samnites, and the result was that they were not only crushed, but ultimately annihilated, so that no ethnological trace of them remains.

CHAPTER XIX.
HEATHEN BARBARISM.

SECTION 294. *Race and Place.*—Of the barbarous heathen nations, the Aztecs, Quichuans, Chinese, Japanese, Siamese, and Burmese, belong, or belonged, to the yellow race, as did probably the Etruscans. The Semitic Babylonians, Assyrians, Phœnicians, Carthaginians, Syrians, and Sabeans, and the Aryan Hindoos, Persians, Celts, and Teutons, are or were white. The ethnological place of the Egyptians is doubtful; it was perhaps in the Semitic class. Various barbarous heathen nations are passed here without mention, because our information about them is not sufficient to furnish material for separate sections.

In early antiquity—that is, before the Xth century B. C.—the highest culture was limited to portions of a belt extending from the southeastern corner of the Mediterranean to the China Sea. The most advanced countries were Egypt, Phœnicia, Syria, Babylonia, Assyria, Hindostan, and China. Perhaps Saba in Southeastern Arabia, Burmah and Siam should be included in the list.

No nation rose from savagism to barbarism in an isolated position or in a remote antiquity, unless it occupied a region where the winters are mild. All the capitals or central cities of the early barbarians are in subtropical climes, with a mean temperature of not less than 45° in the coldest month. Thebes and Benares, the central cities of Egypt and Hindostan, are in latitude 25°; Woochang, the central city of China, is in 30°; Babylon is in 32° and Tyre in 33°. These are the native homes of the earliest phases of barbarous culture. Nineveh in 36° and Carthage in 37° are later in the date of their origin and prosperity than their mother cities, Babylon and Tyre. The Persians, whose central city of Persepolis is in 30°, were still later; and their tardiness in appearing on the stage of history may be chargeable partly to the high elevation of their country, which, with a subtropical latitude, has a mid-temperate or cold winter. Cuzco in 13° S. and Mexico in 19° N. are higher above the sea than Persepolis, but, being nearer the equator, have much milder winters.

Isolation, that is natural protection by either mountain, desert, or sea against frequent disturbance by hostile incursions, was of great service in guarding the growth of early culture. Such fortunate regions were occupied by the Egyptians, Chinese, Babylonians, Hindoos, Phœnicians, Carthaginians, Aztecs, and Quichuans.

SEC. 295. *Barbarous Industry.*—The possession of bronze tools and weapons, with which barbarism began, implied mining and the smelting of ore with the aid of artificial blast. It led to improved tillage, larger supplies of food in proportion to area, denser population, the moulding and burning of bricks, the quarrying and cutting of stone, the discovery of lime mortar, the construction of durable and commodious buildings, the erection of temples, palaces, aqueducts, and city walls, an advance in marine architecture, and the production of iron. Indeed, it fostered every branch of industry. Under its beneficent influence, barbarians invented the square, level, plumb-line, and carpenters' rule, which are indispensable to accuracy of fit and strength of frame in substantial edifices and large pieces of furniture. They used carts for transporting freight. They manufactured porcelain, glass, and paper; they cut and polished gems; they discovered many beautiful dyes and the mordants needed to give them permanence; they distilled alcohol, crystallized sugar, and sublimated mercury; they made explosive powder and a rude mariner's compass; they dug surface wells and bored artesian wells; they cut ditches for irrigation and canals for navigation; they made paved roads extending thousands of miles, with stations for the shelter of travelers and messengers; they coined money; they established routes for international traffic by ship and caravan; and by the exchange of products they brought distant nations into .regular and friendly intercourse with one another.

SEC. 296. *Barbarous Society, etc.*—Before coming within the range of historical examination, all barbarous nations had outgrown the feminine clan, and had either the masculine clan or consolidated nationality. Most of them gave to woman a much better social position than she had in savagism. They had a higher family organization, a more commodious dwelling, better implements for cooking, and a more regular and varied food supply. Their domestic fire was intimately associated with the ancestral worship, shared its sacredness, and the wife was its custodian. The matrimonial relation increased in importance, and among the Aztecs and Menu Hindoos rose to be a religious contract celebrated before a priest. The Aztecs gave the same social rights to the wife as to the husband.

In barbarism various systems of recording thought came into use, first with knotted cords and then with pictures.

The latter proved to be better adapted to the purpose, and they were employed more extensively. Original systems of hieroglyphics appeared in China, Egypt, and Mexico, and possibly in Babylonia. The peculiarities of their speech prevented the Chinese from developing their hieroglyphics beyond word signs; the Egyptians advanced to signs for syllables and simple sounds; but when they had invented the alphabet, instead of then promptly discarding their older and less convenient symbols, they retained all and mixed together three different modes of writing. The Phœnicians became familiar with the achievements of the Egyptians, perceived the greatly superior value of the alphabet, adopted it exclusively, and gave it to the Greeks and Romans, through whom it became a permanent possession of all the most intellectual nations.

Arithmetic had its origin in the barbarous culturestep. The Egyptians (who were imitated by the Romans), the Aztecs, and the Hindoos, each devised an original method of writing numbers. The Hindoo system, suggested by the abacus, and based on the positional value of the symbols, proved vastly superior to the others, and superseded them in Aryan countries. The Babylonians devised the most complete system of measures for time, space, gravity, and the circle. They divided the year into months, the months into weeks, the weeks into days, each consecrated to its divinity, the days into hours, the hours into minutes, and the minutes into seconds. They observed the ecliptic, divided it into constellations, and used it in measuring the length of the year.

SEC. 297. *Great Achievements.*—If we wish to pick out a few of the greatest achievements of man while in the condition of heathen barbarism, we shall find that they are the production of bronze and iron, the cutting of stone, the invention of the square, level, and plumb-line, the building of cities, the organization of nations, and the introduction of the alphabet. These are worthy successors of speech, tamed fire, edge tools of stone, and tillage, for which we are indebted to the savages.

One of the most important products of evolution is unquestionably the alphabet. In the chapters on the Chinese, the Egyptians, and the Phœnicians, we have traced the development of the art of recording thought, and we have been "met by the same phenomenon which is so conspicuous in the history of language, namely, the fact that there is no such thing as arbitrary invention."[1] The first writing was with pictures, which had literal meanings; these were abbreviated into conventional word signs; figurative meanings were attached to them; symbols for words became representatives of the first syllables, and then of the first simple sounds of the words. Even then, however, the great work was not perfect. The old hieroglyphics still clung to mankind with a grasp that could not be broken until erudition fled to another land, and in crossing the national boundary succeeded in throwing off its oppressive burden.[2] Hieroglyphics were a blessing in early and a curse in later Egypt. In China, progress was aided for many centuries by their mode of writing, and now it is obstructed by the lack of an alphabet. In his early culture man has great need of a pictorial mode of recording ideas; in civilization he requires "some facile, graphic device such as the alphabet by means of which the art of writing can be so far simplified as to become attainable before the years of adolescence have been passed."[3]

SEC. 298. *Barbarous Polity*, *etc.*—Barbarism made much progress in polity. Large kingdoms became numerous; empires made their appearance. The administrative systems became complex and methodical. Public records and written laws became part of the government. Political office was differentiated into many different departments. The Chinese and Aztecs abrogated the hereditary feature of slavery; the former nation abolished the hereditary nobility; the latter elevated commoners and even slaves to the rank of nobles. Private retaliation was limited or abrogated. The administration of justice became the duty of public officials, and in Mexico was intrusted to judges, holding office during good behavior, and drawing salaries, sufficient for their comfortable maintenance, from the public treasury. The independence of the judiciary, the distribution of original jurisdictions among local courts, with appeals to an imperial supreme court on important points, the prohibition of hereditary slavery, the frequent elevation of commoners to the nobility, and the limitation of the sovereign's powers, are original and highly meritorious features in the political system of the Aztecs.

Very different in its constitution, and even more wonderful in some of its features, was the Quichuan government. Its systems of assimilating conquered communities, and of administering public affairs so that there should be no idleness, dissipation, extravagance, pauperism, or professional crime, have never been equaled in civilized states. Almost as remarkable in other points is the Chinese government, with no access to high office save through competitive examination, with a wonderful opening of political career to ambitious talent, and with a democratic system of communal administration.

In military affairs barbarous nations are vastly superior to savage tribes. They have metallic weapons and defensive armor. They have greatly improved discipline. They go into battle in compact masses. They have strong fortifications, long military roads, and regular relays of military couriers. Their large cities, dense populations, accumulated treasures, and systematic governments, give facilities for organizing, disciplining, and maintaining armies.

SEC. 299. *Religious Growth.*—Religion is man's conception of the basis and nature of his duties.[1] It is a part of the mental constitution of humanity. Nearly its whole essence, in some minds, is morality; but for the majority, it includes a belief in supernatural beings and in man's relation to them. It is found among Confucians and Buddhists, as well as among Brahmins and Parsees. It may exist without support from science or history, without aid from a priesthood or a revelation, without the dogma of an omnipotent deity or a personal immortality. The genuineness or fervor of religion does not necessarily increase with the number of dogmas or the multitude of gods. There may be as much religion in a man who denies every theory of supernatural existence, as in one who worships the numberless divinities of Brahminism.

In comparing the ecclesiastical institutions of barbarism with those of savagism, we observe much progress. Ethical conceptions have become more complex and precise; they have been extended to include obligations towards all men; and they are conceived as highly important to the welfare of every man. The Confucians and Buddhists tell us that virtue is indispensable to the enjoyment of this life; the Aztecs, Quichuans, Egyptians,

Persians, and Brahminical Hindoos say it is requisite for the happiness of the life to come.

In barbarous culture, the earlier belief in a world of disembodied souls preserved most of its old features and gained many new ones. The spirits surrounded men and frequently made themselves visible and audible. The persons who were in the habit of communicating directly with the tenants of the other world were not rare; in a district of 10,000 inhabitants, there might be five or ten who were credited with this power, and who really believed they possessed it. Among a thousand of these seers, one might possess occasional clairvoyant perceptions, which, though of no value for the purposes of practical life, had an immense influence on popular belief. The combination of such spirit communication with clairvoyance, dreams, and popular ignorance and credulity, were, among the heathens, the natural basis of belief in a world of disembodied spirits. The Egyptian, the Zoroastrian, the Brahmin, and the Buddhist is each anxious about the welfare of his soul after death, and each says that the method of salvation adopted by all the others is worthless. In Egypt, Hindostan, and Persia we find the bulk of the people accepting the claims of their hereditary teachers to be divinely commissioned to communicate to laymen the commands of the supernatural authority.

To this belief as it existed in savagism, nations, in the next culturestep, added rewards for the good and punishments for the bad beyond the grave. Future retribution forms part of every barbarous religion, which we have so far examined, except that of Confucianism. But while the barbarous creeds generally have a spiritual world, they differ greatly in their conceptions of its constitution, and in their plans of salvation.

The modes of worship changed little from savagism to barbarism. In the former culturestep, as in the latter, we find prayers, hymns of praise, music, dancing, processions, penances, offerings of fruits, flowers, incense, and sacrifices of beasts and men to ancestral spirits at graves and to gods in temples. In barbarism the temples became large and substantial architectural piles; and the rites grew elaborate. Among the Egyptians, Persians, Brahmins, and perhaps also among the Babylonians, Assyrians, Phœnicians, and Carthaginians, the rituals appeared in books accepted as divine revelations. The books of the Confucians and Buddhists are sacred, though not attributed to a divine origin.

The more advanced religions which we have hitherto examined, consist of four parts: theological or ontological creed, ecclesiastical discipline, ethical rule, and mythological lore. All of these parts grow more complex in the periods of early culture, but do not keep equal pace with one another. In one country the mythology, in another the discipline, and in another the morality, takes the lead. Of all these parts, the one that has the least influence on general culture is mythology. It is little more than a decorative trimming, an ornamental fringe to religion, which reaches its highest development in barbarism, as among the Hindoos, Teutons, and early Greeks. Nowhere have we encountered any proof of religious decay. In barbarism as in savagism the changes are progressive. The ruder conceptions disappear or diminish in influence. The priest becomes a scholar; religion is associated with learning; creeds become more definite and more coherent; ecclesiastical organizations are supplied with better endowments and with increased differentiation of occupations; ethical principles receive much development; spirits give way to gods, and a multitude of gods to a Great First Cause, or to dual divinities, who are the respective sources of good and evil. There is no trace of decay in the religions of Egypt, Hindostan, Persia, Babylonia, or Phœnicia: but we do find idolatry and exorcisms in Buddhism, though Siddhartha prohibited them. It is to be observed, however, that such practices should be regarded not as a decline of Buddhist faith but as the adherence, by some of its converts, to their hereditary superstitions. Many converts to Christianity have adhered for generations to pagan customs; and this adherence proved not a decay of Christianity, but its inability to suddenly raise some of its followers to its own level. The same remark applies to Buddhism. Its early converts were considerably above the intellectual level of many of its modern adherents.

SEC. 300. *Religious Comparison.*—Let us now briefly compare the religions of the barbarous heathens, for the purpose of finding their notable differences and characteristics.

The most peculiar features of the Aztec superstition are its multitude of human sacrifices, its deification of some of the victims, and its sanctification of the people by giving them a holy communion in the actual flesh and blood of the deified victims.

The distinguishing doctrines of the Quichuan religion are the divine blood of the Inca dynasty, and the theocratic autocracy of the Inca monarch.

The Egyptians had numerous gods incarnate in beasts; a mummy important if not indispensable to the immortality or enjoyment of the soul in the future life; a final judgment before Osiris; and a ritual describing the precise forms and phrases in which the trial was conducted.

The Aztecs, Quichuans, and Egyptians believed in an immortal future life in a spiritual world, with rewards and punishments to compensate the defects or supposed defects in the moral government of the world. These two doctrines of retribution in a spiritual sphere and individual immortality, are not accepted by the Brahminical Hindoos, who have punishment or purification by transmigration through successive material lives in the forms of beasts or men, ending by the final absorption of the human soul in a conscious pantheistic deity, whose existence is not inconsistent with that of a multitude of other great gods. They consider human existence a source of misery, and they believe that the three twice-born Hindoo castes are the favorites of heaven above all other men, and the Brahmins above the other two castes.

The Zoroastrians have only two divinities, one good and the other evil, who have been struggling, with divided success, through thousands of years, for the control of the world. The Zoroastrian worship is paid to Ormuzd, the good divinity, and to the ancestral spirits, without the aid of temples or idols. A peculiar feature of the Persian religion is that the flesh of the corpse shall be eaten by wild birds or quadrupeds, so that it shall not contaminate the purity of soil, water, or fire.

The religion of Confucius is almost exclusively ethical. He was agnostic in reference to god and immortality. He found ancestral worship universally practiced among his countrymen, and, regarding it as an aid to filial piety and social order, he made no objection to its observance.

The religions of the Babylonians, Assyrians, Phœnicians, Etruscans, Celts, and Teutons, have no peculiar features of much importance.

SEC. 301. *Ecclesiastical Growth.*—The enlightened student, who impartially examines the Avesta, the Rig Veda, the Menu, and the Ritual of the Dead, at first finds it difficult to understand how such compositions could ever have gained extensive credence as the productions of supernatural wisdom. But the religions of barbarism are the natural developments of those of savagism. The popular credulity is the same in both culture-steps. The sacerdotal influence grew with the monarchical power. The early superstitions were strengthened by tradition, ignorance, credulity, and the combined influence of church and state. Sleeman, who lived for years in Hindostan, and studied the popular beliefs and modes of thought, found that the people never ventured to apply their reason to questions of religion. In regard to every matter relating to their ecclesiastical institutions, their minds were in a condition of torpidity. In reference to the sacred Brahminical poem of Ramayana, which is full of absurd mythical stories, Sleeman says: "Ninety-nine out of a hundred among the Hindoos implicitly believe not only every word of this poem, but every word of every poem that has ever been written in Sanscrit. If you ask a man whether he really believes any very egregious absurdity quoted from these books, he replies with the greatest *naïveté* in the world, 'Is it not written in the book; and how should it be written, if not true?' The Hindoo religion reposes upon an entire prostration of mind, that continual and habitual surrender of the reasoning faculties which we are accustomed to make occasionally while engaged at the theater, or in the perusal of works of fiction. . . . With the Hindoos . . . . the greater the improbability, the more monstrous and preposterous the fiction, the greater the charm it has over their minds; and the greater their learning in the Sanscrit, the more they are under the influence of this charm. Believing all to be written by the deity, or by his inspiration, and the men and things of former times to have been different from the men and things of the present day, and the heroes of these fables to have been demigods, or people endowed with powers far superior to those of the ordinary men of their day, the analogies of nature are never for a moment considered; nor do questions of probability or possibility, according to these analogies, ever obtrude to dispel the charm with which they are so pleasingly bound. They go on through life reading and talking of these monstrous fictions which shock the taste and understanding of other nations, without once questioning the truth of one single incident, or hearing it questioned."

A mental torpidity similar to that of the Brahmins when they read their sacred poems, may be observed among modern Christians in reference to omens, witches, ghosts, and spirits. Everywhere round us we find people who fear to undertake any important enterprise on Friday, to sit at a table in a party of thirteen, or to accept any cutting instrument from a cherished friend. The same credulous tone of mind, the same disposition to accept a statement without the least evidence, the same tendency to hereditary faith, led the heathens to follow their false priests.

Judging from what may be seen in modern times and in Christian countries, we may infer that the Egyptian, Hindoo, Persian, Babylonian, and Celtic priests generally believed their own creeds; but supposing their faith to be beneficial, they did not neglect opportunities to increase its credit by falsehood, trickery, concealment of the truth, diversion of attention from damaging adverse evidence, and strenuous efforts to fix the public mind upon favorable facts of minor value. Besides we may assume that whenever they found the people suffering from some great general calamity, or under any influence that prepared them to be frightened and excited by talk about divine wrath, the opportunity of plundering them was never neglected. In such cases large sacrifices were ordered, pilgrim parties were organized, public penances imposed, and other methods adopted for filling the ecclesiastical purse and exalting the sacerdotal power. In the interest of social order the Polynesian priest poisoned the violator of a taboo; in the interest of the true faith, the medieval monk forged lives of saints and relics of martyrs; and in innocent piety the heathen priest wrote from his own fancy the revelations of Thoth, Ormuzd, and Brahm.

The only heathen religion established by preaching was Buddhism, and that was of relatively late origin, all the others having been founded and gradually expanded in their territorial jurisdictions, and some of them in their ecclesiastical systems, as the tribes grew into nations. The dogma and discipline were in most cases easy and natural developments of those accepted in higher savagism.

The introduction of the art of writing contributed much to strengthen some of the barbarous religions. Letters seemed to be productions of superhuman wisdom in those early ages when the separation between divinity and humanity was slight. The book, written as a compilation of ancient history or philosophy, might be accepted in a succeeding generation as inspired; and words might be interpolated here and there attributing the statements to Ormuzd, Thoth, or Brahm; and finally the copies not so interpolated might be declared spurious and destroyed.

SEC. 302. *Natural Causes.*—At the close of the first volume, we examined the causes of man's advance in savage culture, and we found nothing save his mental constitution developing itself under natural laws. His industrial arts, his social institutions, his speech, his government, his military system, his belief in sorcery, omens, powerful disembodied spirits, and his gods, and his modes of worship by offerings, sacrifices, hymns, and prayers;—all these were considered, and not one of them could be traced to any supernatural source. We could not find conclusive proof nor direct testimony nor presumptive evidence that any god had ever appeared among the savages of Africa, America, or Polynesia, to teach them the arts of building boats, burning pottery, weaving cloth, tilling the ground, taming useful beasts, organizing families, clans, or tribes, leading them in war, or teaching them modes of worship. We did find that in many countries savage priests claimed to have divine commissions, to be in daily communication with the gods, and to interpret omens, to perform their sorceries, to curse the violators of taboos, and to sacrifice beasts and men in accordance with direct instructions from the deities; but we discovered that all these claims were made without good foundation. We concluded that man's observation, judgment, imagination, wants, and fears, and the conditions of external nature, had been his only guides in all his achievements while in the savage culturestep.

In tracing the advance of culture among the barbarous heathens, we have found no influences at work save those of natural laws. Man and his innate capacities deserve the praise for all the good and the blame for all the evil that we have encountered in his actions. Literary and metallurgical art, temples of cut stone laid in mortar, and pyramids as enduring as the hills, extensive empires and vast cities, political institutions wisely planned to secure the happiness of the people and the permanence of the government, and civil and ecclesiastical codes represented to be divine revelations, all these we have found among the barbarians, as the products of man's natural capacity. Everything has grown slowly; nothing has been created instantaneously in a state of complex perfection.

Natural law has reigned without interruption in the domain of the heathen religions as well as elsewhere. The Rig Veda, the Code of Menu, the Avesta, and the Funeral Ritual, notwithstanding their claim to divine authorship, are evidently human productions. All show the marks of natural growth, the traces of savage superstition, the effects of sacerdotal greed, the weakness of human ignorance, and the inconsistency of barbarous logic. All of them are text-books of national religion, and nationality is inconsistent with one of the fundamental principles of religion, as conceived by the more enlightened modern mind. The priests, who claimed commissions from national gods to teach and guide, to curse and to bless, to mediate and to absolve within limits bounded by certain ethnological or topographical lines, had an authority based exclusively on human invention. · No god spoke through them any more than through the Congoese, Carib, Choctaw, Maori, or Tahitian priests. Their ecclesiastical systems cannot be traced to any source save delusions, and conceptions of private and public interest.

SEC. 303. *Departmental Values.*—Industrial art exerted

more influence than any other branch of culture on the life and progress of the nations studied in this volume. It supplied metallic tools and weapons, built substantial dwellings and large cities, maintained dense populations, divided labor into many separate occupations, laid the foundation for higher military discipline, and made a demand for extensive international commerce, and for public records. It led, indirectly, to the establishment of extensive empires, and to the development of the art of writing.

Improved social and political institutions were consequences rather than causes of the general advancement, in which they were prominent features. In every culturestep, good government is of vast importance; but in barbarism, as in savagism, it can be traced directly to superior industry, and to superior military art.

In barbarism, religion did not contribute much to the development of any other branch of culture. It did not greatly stimulate industrial art, beneficent social institutions, or military discipline. In Egypt it called for grand temples and tombs, and while it thus led to some architectural progress, it impoverished and oppressed the people, and obstructed improvement in other respects. It was the ally of despotism, ignorance, and superstition. The invention of hieroglyphics in the valley of the Nile is intimately associated with the sacerdotal profession; and yet the Chinese laymen were as successful in writing with original ideograms as were the Egyptian priests. The latter did not complete their work, or clearly understand the value of the alphabetic signs they had invented; they left the finishing touch to the keener perceptions of the Phœnician merchants.

Heathen religion did not make any nation great. It

did not contribute perceptibly to the organization or wealth of Egypt, Babylon, Assyria, or Phœnicia. It gave aid to the political rulers, but took much else from them. It had little influence among the Chinese, and seems to have been a source of weakness to the Menu Hindoos, to the Celts, and to the Etruscans. It helped the Persians, but they owed their military and political successes, which were the most important achievements of their nation, mainly to their soldiers and kings, not to their priests.

Some of the barbarous nations have been distributed in pairs so as to suggest comparisons. Among these are Persia and Media, Assyria and Babylonia, Germany and Gaul. In each of these cases the country which was subject to the less sacerdotal influence had the better political and military system. Media was more priest-ridden than Persia, Babylonia than Assyria, and Gaul than Germany. Hindostan had a powerful priesthood, and its people have been compelled to adopt the official language and institutions of the Persian, Arab, Tartar, and British conquerors. China has a weak sacerdotal class, and its Mongol and Manchoo conquerors have accepted the language, religion, laws, and institutions of their subjects. The ancient Egyptians had a strong sacerdotal system and a weak army. The general rule has been the same in ancient as in modern times,— the stronger the church, the weaker the state; the richer the priesthood, the more degraded the laity. Religious liberty is important to the self-respect of the people and the dignity of the government. The Phœnicians and Carthaginians, though not priest-ridden, were overthrown; they had narrow bases in territory and population, and yet were wealthy and powerful states for centuries, and maintained their independence as long as did other nations of their time, with much larger and more populous dominions.

Although religion is credited here with less influence than industrial or military art, yet its consideration occupies the greater part of this volume. A relatively large space is given to it because, in the barbarous culturestep, ecclesiastical systems are most numerous, and receive their greatest relative development. Besides, our information is much more abundant about the religion than about the other branches of culture in heathen barbarism. Most of the books preserved from early antiquity were written by priests about their sacerdotal affairs.

SEC. 304. *Change of Scene.*—Although we have studied the Chinese, Japanese, Aztecs, and Quichuans, who belong wholly or largely to modern times, and have considered the Celts and Teutons, who became prominent about the beginning of the Christian era, and have not yet taken up the Jews and Greeks, whose activity dates back to a period before the rise of Persia, yet, notwithstanding these inequalities in the chronological lines, the general story of human progress has now been brought down to 500 B. C.

As in the first volume the black tribes passed out of sight, so now, at the close of the second, we take leave of the yellow nations. Their stories have been told so far as concerns the present, though there is reason to hope that their future achievements may furnish abundant material to the historians of later ages. In my coming volumes I shall have to tell how the Aryans, who became dominant when Persia conquered Babylon in 539 B. C., held the leadership of progress until it was contested again by the Semites, and how these two branches of the white race struggled through many centuries for the mastery in arms, letters, and arts, until at last the Aryan triumph became complete and incontestable.

The scene of the most important action is now about to change from Southern Asia and the basins of the Euphrates and the Nile to Syria, Asia Minor, and Europe. The character of the action will lose its predominantly national character and become mainly international; it will gain vastly in depth as well as in breadth, in brilliancy as well as in intensity. Its motives and its judgments will be more in harmony with civilized thought and emotion.

APPENDIX.

A list of the books cited or considered worthy of the reader's especial attention, is given at the end of this, as of the preceding volume. The Bible, Menu, and Avesta are cited by chapter and verse, other books by volume and page unless chapter is plainly indicated. Some of the citations cannot be understood without reference to the books mentioned as authorities.

NOTES.

SEC. 159. *Barbarism.*—[1] Webster.

That culturestep which I call barbarism, when considered in contradistinction to savagism, is called by Waitz and some other German authors the "Kulturzustand," or condition of culture. The barbarians are styled "Kulturvoelker," or culture-people, as opposed to the "Naturvoelker," or nature-people, of savagism. These terms of Waitz imply that every phase of culture above savagism is unnatural, and that the barbarian has outgrown the natural condition of humanity. Metallurgy and letters are undoubtedly very important achievements in culture, but so also are speech, the taming of fire, the invention of edge tools, tillage, weaving, pottery, and canoe building.

The savage, even the rudest known to civilized observation, is no longer in the same cultural condition as were the first men on the earth. They are not without art. They are no more in an exclusive state of nature than is an infant. Intellectual growth in the race is as natural to man as physical growth in the individual. Savagism, barbarism, and civilization, the main steps in advancing culture, are the natural phases in the development of humanity, as the sprouting acorn, the sapling, and the full grown tree are the natural phases in the growth of the oak. It would be as proper to assert that an acorn is an oak in a state of nature as that a savage is a man in a state in nature. Art sprouts out from man, not he from art. The arrow is made consciously, voluntarily, and with a set purpose. Culture is not artificial in the same sense. It is, to a large extent, the result of unconscious and irresistible impulses, the tendencies of which were not even dreamed of among men until they had lived on the earth for many thousands of years; and remote and high tendencies hidden now from the most learned and wise, may become perceptible to the multitude who are to succeed us after the lapse of five or ten centuries more.

SEC. 160. *Bronze Tools.*—The leading authorities in regard to the tools of the Bronze Age are Evans B. T., Worsaae, Lubbock P. T., and Tylor E. H. [1]Chabas says the Egyptians had iron in 3000 B. C. Mariette contradicts this statement. Evans B. T. 6, 7. [2]*Ib.* 18. [3]*Ib.* 10. [4]Max Muller S. L. ii. 247. Beck, i. 206, says that in a later edition Max Muller admitted that he was wrong in asserting that iron was unknown to the primitive Aryans. [5]Deut. xxvii. 5, 8. [6]Evans B. T. 23, 95. Lubbock P. T. 5, 220. Tylor E. H. 206. Keller L. D. 174, 402. [7]Lubbock P. T. 391. [8]Evans B. T. 460-463. [9]Lubbock P. T. 15. [10]*Ib.* 38. [11]*Ib.* 60. [12]Keller L. D. 15. [13]Evans B. T. 425. [14]*Ib.* 469. Numerous engravings of articles in bronze may be found in the books of Evans, Lubbock, and Keller.

SEC. 161. *Superiority of Iron.*—[1]Beck (i. 40, 41) says the melting point of copper is about 2,100° Fahrenheit, and of cast iron about 2,250°; but iron will settle down from its earthy material in the furnace at 1,300°. He thinks the ancients could not produce a heat greater than 1,300°. Evans (B. T. 472, 473) thinks bronze appeared in Britain about 1400 B. C., and iron in 500 B. C. Except in China, there was no cast iron before 450 A. D. Beck i. 3.

SEC. 162. *Anahuac.*—The best comprehensive authorities in regard to the culture of the Aztecs are Prescott C. M., Waitz iv., and Bancroft ii. [1]Waitz iv. 190. Prescott C. M. i. 405. In the time of Cortes, Tlascala was as large as Granada in Spain; now it has 4,000 inhabitants. *Ib.* i. 473. Cholula had 4,000 inhabitants; now it has 1,500. Waitz iv. 93. Several other cities then as large as Cholula are now mere villages. *Ib.* Yucatan had millions of inhabitants before the conquest, and has now only 100,000. Charnay 232. [2]Prescott C. M. i. 400. [3]Waitz iv. 188.

SEC. 163. *Crops.*—[1]Prescott C. M. i. 137.

SEC. 164. *Weaving, etc.*—[1]Belt 33.

SEC. 165. *Metallurgy.*—[1]Cortes says that tin and bronze were sold in the markets; and that in some provinces small pieces of tin were used as money. When he was in great need of artillery, he collected this tin money to mix with copper for bronze cannon. Three attempts have been made to discredit Cortes; one by Hostmann, who contributes a chapter on the metallurgy of the Aztecs and Quichuans to Beck; one by L. A. Morgan in his "Ancient Society;" and one by R. A. Wilson in "A New History of the Conquest of Mexico;" and all are failures. Articles of bronze have been found in Chiriqui graves, according to the Popular Science Monthly, September, 1888, p. 716. Tylor in his "Anahuac" (139) speaks of seeing bronze hatchets, bells, and needles, made by the Aztecs. Evans (B. T. 166) mentions analysis of Aztec bronze. Humboldt (P. E. iii. 296) knew of tin mines in Mexico. The possession of tin and copper implies the possession of bronze. [2]Prescott C. M. ii. 204. [3]In making this statement, I follow Waitz (iv. 101), but not without desire for more evidence. Cortes (104) said nothing was sold by weight. [4]Waitz iv. 105. Bancroft ii. 474.

SEC. 166. *Stone Work.*—[1]Waitz iv. 95. [2]*Ib.* 110.

SEC. 168. *Social Condition.*—[1]Waitz iv. 124. [2]See Chevalier (82) for address of father to son. [3]Waitz iv. 98. [4]*Ib.* 134. [5]*Ib.* 98. [6]Reville 43.

SEC. 169. *Records.*—[1]Prescott C. M. i. 101. Taylor (i. 24) says: "The systems of picture writing, which were invented and developed by the tribes of Central America, are, however, so obscure and so little is really known about their history, that they must be regarded rather as literary curiosities than as affording suitable materials for enabling us to arrive at any general conclusions as to the nature of the early stages of the development of the graphic art."

SEC. 170. *Astronomy.*—[1]Waitz iv. 178.

SEC. 171. *A Martial Empire.*—[1]Prescott C. M. i. 439.

SEC. 173. *Imperial Office.*—[1]Waitz iv. 71.- [2]*Ib.* 69. [3]*Ib.* [4]*Ib.* 70.

SEC. 174. *Laws.*—[1]Waitz iv. 82. [2]Reville 28.

SEC. 175. *Aztec Gods.*—[1]Waitz iv. 138. [2]*Ib.* 140. [3]*Ib.* 122.

SEC. 177. *Human Victims.*—[1]J. G. Muller 620.

SEC. 180. *Aztec Ethics.*—[1]Waitz iv. 128. [2]*Ib.*

SEC. 181. *Aztec Culture.*—Tylor (Anahuac 263) says: "It is curious that the jackal, or human figure in a jackal mask, should have been an object of superstitious veneration both in Mexico and in Egypt. This, the extraordinary serpent crown of Xochicalco, and the pyramids, are the three most striking resemblances to be found between the two countries; all probably accidental, but not the less noteworthy on that account."

APPENDIX. 345

Sec. 183. *The Quichuan Empire.*—The leading comprehensive authorities in reference to Quichuan culture are Prescott C. P. and Waitz iv. Squier and Tschudi are very good upon numerous special points.

Sec. 184. *Agriculture.*—[1]Squier 442, 467, 475. [2]Ib. 342. [3]Prescott C. P. i. 134. [4]Ib. [5]Ib. 139. [6]Ib. 145. [7]Ib. 140. [8]Ib.

Sec. 185. *Various Arts.*—[1]Prescott C. P. i. 150. [2]Ib. ii. appendix 2.

Sec. 186. *Buildings.*—[1]Squier 154. [2]Ib. 68. [3]Ib. 163, 542. [4]Ib. 407. [5]Ib. 517. [6]Ib. 394. [7]Ib. 436. [8]Ib. 281, 283. [9]Ib. 475. [10]A block 30 feet long, 15 wide, and 6 thick, at Tiaguanaco, must have been carried more than 100 miles. Waitz iv. 416. [11]Squier 279. [12]Ib. 363. [13]The ground plans of many buildings are shown in Squier, and also engravings after photogragh of the ruins. [14]Squier 70, 362, 372. [15]Waitz iv. 442. [16]Ib. 446. Rivero 232.

Sec. 187. *Mining.*—Hostmann, who is mentioned in the note to Sec. 165, argues that the Quichuans had no bronze; and in regard to them fails on that point as he did in regard to the Aztecs. All the eminent archæologists and scientists, who in this century have studied the culture of the Aztecs and Quichuans in their own countries, are agreed that those people had bronze. Among these authorities are Alexander Humboldt, E. B. Tylor, E. G. Squier, J. J. von Tschudi, and M. Chevalier.

Sec. 188. *Social Affairs.*—[1]Waitz iv. 443.

Sec. 190. *Aggressive Policy.*—See Sec. 58 in reference to spear cords. [2]Squier 470. [3]Tschudi 340. [4]Rivero 69, 70.

Sec 191. *Quichuan Religion*—[1]Reville 170. [2]Waitz iv. 459. [3]Ib. 461. The cross was worshiped. Ib. 458. [4]Squier 379. [5]Ib. 531. [6]Waitz iv. 467.

Sec. 192. *Quichuan Temples.*—[1]Prescott C. P. i. 98. [2]Ib. 99, 101.

Sec. 193. *Quichuan Ethics.*—[1]Waitz iv. 466. [2]Prescott C. P. i. 171. ii. 482.

Sec. 194. *Culture and Collapse.*—The population was more dense before the conquest. Bastian G. E. B. 16. Rivero 70. "The influence of Spain in Peru has," says Squier, (543) "been everywhere deleterious; the civilization of the country was far higher before the conquest than now."

Sec. 196. *China.*—The leading authorities to which I have had access are the books of Williams and Davis. That of Williams is the best description of a national culture known to me.

Sec. 199. *Different Arts.*—[1]Williams M. K. i. 274.

SEC. 200. *Manners.*—¹Davis i. 200. ²Rein i. 393. ³Gill G. S. 55.
SEC. 201. *Matrimony.*—¹Davis i. 269, 273. ²Williams M. K. ii. 261. ³Max Muller N. R. 174.
SEC. 202. *Music, etc.*—¹Williams M. K. ii. 165. He gives the notes of several Chinese airs. ²*Ib.* i. 293. ³*Ib.* i. 293., ii. 184. ⁴*Ib.* 249. ⁵*Ib.* 257. ⁶Scherzer ii. 170. ⁷Rawlinson O. N. 269.
SEC. 203. *Speech.*—¹ Max Muller S. L. i. 265. ² Williams M. K. i. 590.
SEC. 204. *Writing.*—¹ Williams M. K. i. 613. ²*Ib.* 589. ³*Ib.* 622. ⁵ Davis i. 276. ⁶*Ib.* 275. ⁷ Felton i. 44. ⁸*Ib.* 43. ⁹ Lay quoted in Williams M. K. ii. 172.
SEC. 205. *Imperial Power.*—¹ Douglas 155. ² Brougham i. 174. ³ Williams M. K. i. 369. ⁴*Ib.* 355. ⁵*Ib.* 376.

"Heaven sees as my people see; Heaven hears as my people hear." Mencius in Amberley ii. 43. "Throughout the Shooking we find great stress laid on the doctrine that the rulers of the land enjoy the protection of Heaven only so long as their government is good." Amberley ii. 50. "Confucius said government should be based on the love of mankind," and "the monarch should govern according to the wish of the people."

Section CCX of the Chinese code provides that "if any officer of government, whose situation gives him power and control over the people, not only does not conciliate them by proper indulgence, but exercises his authority in a manner so inconsistent with the established laws and approved usages of the empire, that the sentiments of the once loyal subjects being changed by his oppressive conduct, they assemble tumultuously and openly rebel, and drive him at length from the capital city and seat of his government, such officer shall suffer death."

Williams (M. K. i. 351) says: "The system of mutually checking the provincial officers is also exhibited in their location. For example, in the city of Canton, the governor-general is stationed in the New City near the collector of customs, while the lieutenant-governor and Tartar general are so located in the Old City that, should circumstances require it, they can act against the two first. The governor has the general command of all the provincial troops, estimated to be 100,000 men, but the particular command of only five thousand, and they are stationed fifty miles off, at Shankingfu. The Tartar general has five thousand men under him in the Old City, which, in an extreme case, would make him master of the capital, while his own allegiance is secured by the antipathy between the Manchoos and the Chinese. Again, the governor has the power of condemning certain criminals to death, but the death-warrant is lodged with the fuyuen, and the order for execution must be countersigned by him; his dispatches to court must also be countersigned by his coadjutor. The general absence of resistance to imperial sway on the part of these high officers for the two centuries the Manchoos have held the reins, compared with the multiplied intrigues and rebellions of the pashas in the Turkish Empire, prove how well the system is connected."

The following is an extract from an imperial decree criticising and degrading high officials. "Kweisan, subordinate minister of the cabinet, is hasty, and deficient both in precision and capacity; he is incapable of moving and acting for himself. Let him take an inferior station, and receive an appointment in the second class of the guards. Yihtsih, vice-president of the Board of Works for Moukden, possesses but ordinary talents, and is incompetent for the duties of his present office. Let him also take an inferior station, and be appointed to a place in the first class of the guards. Narkingé, the governor of Hukwang, though having under him the whole civil and military bodies of two provinces, has yet been unable, these many days, to seize a few beggarly, impish vagabonds. After having, in the first instance, failed in prevention, he has followed up that failure by idleness and remissness, and has fully proved himself inefficient. Let him take the lower station of lieutenant-governor of Hunan, and within one year let him, by the apprehension of San Chingstun, show that he is aroused to greater exertions." Williams M. K. i. 355.

SEC. 206. *Examinations.*—[1] Medhurst 175. [2] Davis ii. 151. Brougham i. 17. [3] Martin 42. [4] Williams M. K. ii. 191. [5] Davis ii. 152.

"There is deeply rooted in the minds of the people a respect for civil merit, by which is meant learning; that is, such learning as they have been taught to consider important and sufficient. Their ambition, stimulated besides by the direct advantages to which learning leads, all points towards this quarter. Their desire is to make their children excel themselves by being better educated. Their hope even is to obtain direct rewards from the progress their children may make. Their recreation after labor is the reading or hearing read some portion of those books which they are accustomed to regard as sacred, though the works of uninspired men; works in which Confucius and his disciple Mencius have laid down the law of the land, and inculcated the rules of moral conduct.

With their respect for learning, their attachment to quiet, peaceful, orderly life keeps pace. They have no appetite for bustle or contention; a great dislike of violence; a great aversion to danger; hence they hate war, and they hate revolution, as much as they love learning and quiet industry. Their proverbial sayings, and no [other] people are so fond of proverbs, bear evidence of these, the prevailing dispositions of their minds. 'Train the mulberry tree while it is yet tender;' 'all men are alike, were it not for education;' 'if families have no sons devoted to learning, whence are the rulers of the country to come;' 'better be a dog in peace than a man in strife.'" Brougham P. P. i. 17.

SEC. 207. *Local Administration.*—[1] Davis i. 372. [2] Douglas 49. [3] Williams M. K. i. 298. [4] *Ib.* 298, 382. [5] *Ib.* 351, 437. [6] *Ib.* 475. [7] *Ib.* 516. [8] Williams M. K. i. 381. [9] Davis i. 261. [10] Williams M. K. i. 384; Douglas 54. [11] Davis i. 223.

"The rulers of China have contrived the system of provincial governments in an admirable manner; considering the character of the people and the materials they had to work with, no better proof of their sagacity in this respect can be required than the general degree of good order which has been maintained for nearly two centuries, and the great progress the people have made in wealth, number, and power. By a well arranged plan of checks and changes, in the provincial authorities, the chances of their abusing position and power, and combining to overthrow the supreme government, have been reduced almost to an impossibility; the influence of mutual responsibility among them does something to prevent outrageous oppression of the people, by leading one to accuse another of high crimes, in order to exonerate himself and obtain his place. The sons and relatives of the emperor being excluded from civil office in the provinces, the high spirited and talented native Chinese do not feel inclined to cabal against the government because every avenue to emolument and power is filled and closed against them by creatures and connections of the sovereign; nor when in office, are they disposed to attempt the overthrow of the reigning family, lest they lose what has cost them many years of toilsome study and the wealth and influence of friends to attain." Williams M. K. i. 437.

"The same tolerance which is shown by the people towards the short-comings and ill deeds of the officials is displayed by these men in the discharge of their duties. Only aggravated cases make them take their pens in hand, but when they do, it must be confessed that they show little mercy. Neither are they respecters of persons; their lash falls on all alike, from the emperor on his throne to the police runners in magisterial courts. Nor is their plain speaking more amazing than the candor with which their memorials affecting the character of great and small alike are published in the Peking *Gazette*. The gravest charges, such as peculation, neglect of duty, injustice, or incompetence, are brought against mandarins of all ranks, and are openly published in the official paper." Douglas 57.

SEC. 208. *Person and Property.*—[1] Williams M. K. i. 321. [2] Davis i. 204, 279.

SEC. 209. *Confucius.*—[1] Douglas 106. [2] *Ib.* 116.

Confucius said (Douglas 103): "In the way of the superior man there are four things, to none of which have I as yet attained,—to serve my father as I would require my son to serve me; to serve my prince as I would require my minister to serve me; to serve my elder brother as I would require my younger brother to serve me; and to offer first to friends what one requires of them." Again Confucius said (Amberley i. 458): "It is the way of the superior man to prefer the concealment of his virtue while it becomes daily more illustrious, and it is the way of the mean man to seek notoriety while he daily goes more and more to ruin." Mencius, elaborating the idea of Confucius, wrote (Amberley i. 457): "The superior man has three things in which he delights, and to be ruler over the empire is not one of them. That his father and mother are both alive, and that the condition of his brothers affords no cause for anxiety;—this is one delight. That, when looking up, he has no occasion for shame before Heaven; and, below, he has no occasion to blush before men;—this is his second delight. That he can get from the whole empire the most talented individuals and teach and nourish them;—this is the third delight. The superior man has three things in which he delights, and to be ruler over the empire is not one of them." [5]

"Wherein lay the secret of the vast influence which has been exercised by Confucius? . . . To this we answer first that, being a Chinaman of Chinamen, his teachings were specially suited to the nature of those he taught. . . . With the idea therefore of a future life still unawakened, a plain, matter-of-fact system of morality, such as that enunciated by Confucius, was sufficient for all the wants of the Chinese.

"Secondly, it was to the interest of both the rulers and the ruled to support his doctrines. The *de facto* ruler found in him a tower of strength; for if the throne was the reward vouchsafed by heaven for eminent virtue, then he who occupied it in place must necessarily have an unassailable right to it; and the constant exhortations to loyalty to be found on every page of the Confucian writings cannot but have been grateful to the ears of sovereigns.

"The ruled, on the other hand, felt that they were supreme in the estimation of the Sage. The promotion of their interests and material well-being was the first duty of the sovereign, and the extent of their loyalty was to be measured by his success in this direction. He recognized no ranks or titles save those won by merit, and thus every office in the state was open to everyone alike. The people were to be well cared for, and in case of neglect or oppression, they had the right of rebellion. . . .

"And, thirdly, the possession of so highly prized a literature at so early a date having suggested its adoption as the curriculum in schools, and the test of scholarship at all examinations, the people, ignorant of all else, have learned to look upon it as containing the quintessence of wisdom, and its author as the wisest of mankind. It might be considered impossible to calculate the effects of the concentration of a nation's mind, century after century, on the study of any given text-book; but in China we have the result worked out before us, and we find that it has amounted to the absolute subjection of upwards of forty generations to the dicta of one man." Douglas 169.

SEC. 210. *No Supernaturalism.*—[1] Pfleiderer i. 178.

SEC. 211. *An Honored Sage.*—[1] Douglas 161. [2] Brougham i. 169.

SEC. 212. *Chinese Ancestors.*—[1] Williams M. K. ii. 269. [2] *Ib.* 270, 275. [3] *Ib.* 270. [4] *Ib.* 266.

Of the Chinese idol worship we read that "the lower people, if after long prayer to their images, they do not obtain what they desire, as it often happens, they turn them off as impotent gods; others use them in a most reproachful manner, loading them with hard names, and sometimes with blows. 'How now dog of a spirit,' say they to them. 'We give you a lodging in a magnificent temple, we gild you handsomely; we feed you well and offer incense to you; yet, after all this care, you are so ungrateful as to refuse us what we ask of you.' Hereupon they tie his image with cords, pluck him and drag him along the streets through all the mud and dunghills to punish him for the expense of the perfume which they have thrown away upon him. If in the meantime it happens that they obtain their request, then, with a great deal of ceremony, they wash him clean, carry him back, and place him in his niche again, where they fall down to him and make excuses for what they have done. 'In truth,' say they, 'we were a little too hasty, as well as you were somewhat too long in your grant. Why should you bring this beating on yourself? But what is done cannot now be undone; let us therefore not think of it any more. If you will forget what is past, we will gild you over again.'" Quoted in Lubbock O. C. from Astley.

SEC. 213. *China's Place.*—[1] Tylor Anthrop, 281. [2] Yeats R. E. C. 328. Williams M. K. ii. 25. [3] *Ib.* 75. [4] *Ib.* 107. For date of silk weaving see Pop. Science Monthly, Feb., 1890, p. 505. Gill says the Chinese have no suction pump (76), no improvement of cattle (77), and no graft (78). Fortune, ch. xvi., and Doolittle, i. 45, say they practice grafting.

SEC. 214. *Japanese Society, etc.*—[1] Rein 1412. [2] *Ib.* 328. [3] *Ib.* 477. [4] *Ib.* 396. In reference to Japanese society the best book is that of Rein. He has also a good volume on the industry of Japan.

SEC. 216. *Japanese Religion.*—[1] Shin. means spirit and To doctrine; and considered etymologically, shintoism means the religion of spirits.

SEC. 217. *Egypt.*—The leading authorities in reference to Egypt are Wilkinson, Kenrick and Brugsch. The Ritual of the Dead is given in Bunsen, vol. v.

SEC. 218. *Egyptian Agriculture.*—[1] Herodotus ii. 14.

SEC. 219. *Handicrafts.*—[1] Wilkinson i. 383. [2] *Ib.* ii. 171. [3] *Ib.* i. 360. [4] *Ib.* ii. 169. [5] Kenrick i. 61. [6] Wilkinson i. 340. [7] Kenrick i. 228.

SEC. 220. *Egyptian Architecture.*—[1] Mahaffy 409. [2] Wilkinson ii. 139. [3] Martineau, chap. 5. [4] Sayce A. E. E. 37. [5] Maspero 195.

SEC. 221. *Pyramids.*—[1] Wilkinson i. 13. [2] Brugsch i. 94. [3] De Rougé quoted in Brugsch i. 202. [4] Fergusson H. A.

SEC. 222. *Egyptian Temples.*—[1] Fergusson H. A. i. 106. [2] Martineau, chap. xvi. [3] *Ib.*, chap. xiv.

SEC. 224. *Egyptian Homes.*—[1] Mahaffy 173. [2] Wilkinson i. 315. [3] Mahaffy 293. [4] Wilkinson i. 45. [5] Renouf 242. [6] *Ib.* 70.

SEC. 225. *Hieroglyphics*—[1] Herodotus ii. 32. Wilkinson i. 176. [2] Taylor A. i. 69.

SEC. 226. *Egyptian Books.*—[1] Mahaffy, 411. [2] Rawlinson E. 45. [3] Sayce A. E. E. 76.

SEC. 227. *Political Condition.*—[1] Wilkinson i. 159. [2] *Ib.* 69, 162.

SEC. 228. *Egyptian Gods.*—[1] Wilkinson ii. 514.

SEC. 229. *Osiris the Mediator.*—[1] Mahaffy 263. [2] Kugler i. 31.
SEC. 230. *Sacred Beasts.*—[1] Wilkinson iii. 306.
SEC. 231. *Kings and Gods.*—[1] Mahaffy 357. [2] Brugsch C. K. i. 412. [3] *Ib.* i. 423. [4] *Ib.* ii. 221.
SEC. 232. *Monotheistic Expressions.*—[1] Renouf 221. [2] Mahaffy 264.
SEC. 233. *Adoration of Ancestors.*—[1] Renouf 137. [2] Brugsch ii. 43. [3] Lippert G. P. i. 421.
SEC. 234. *The Mummy.*—[1] Sayce A. E. E. 66. [2] Bunsen E. v. 135. [3] Wilkinson iii. 67. [4] *Ib.* iii. 465. [5] *Ib.* iii. 449. [6] *Ib.* iii. 450. [7] *Ib.* iii. 468. [8] Renouf 130 altered. [9] Brugsch i. 197. [10] Mahaffy 253.
SEC. 235. *Egyptian Morality.*—[1] Renouf 71. [2] *Ib.* 71. [3] Mahaffy 272. [4] Brugsch i. 157.
SEC. 236. *Egyptian Gospels.*—[1] Lippert G. P. i. 394. [2] Mahaffy 273. [3] Lippert G. P. i. 405. [4] Bunsen E. v. 133. [5] Lippert G. P. 183.
SEC. 237. *Last Judgment.*—[1] Bunsen E. v. 259. [2] *Ib.* v. 258.
SEC. 238. *Egyptian Priests.*—[1] Maspero 107. [2] Wilkinson iii. 425. [3] *Ib.* iii. 345. [4] *Ib.* i. 237, iii. 355. [5] Kenrick i. 37. [6] Wilkinson iii. 359.
SEC. 239. *Egyptian Antiquity.*—[1] Brugsch i. 492. [2] Herodotus ii. 143. [3] *Ib.* ii. 4. [4] *Ib.* ii. 142. See also Rawlinson's Herodotus Appendix Book ii., ch. 4. [5] Herodotus ii. 50. [6] *Ib.* ii. 58. [7] Max Muller N. R. 323.
SEC. 241. *Primitive Aryans.*—[1] Max Muller C. i. 62. [2] *Ib.* [3] *Ib.* ii. 17. The following table shows the words for some leading grades of kin in leading Aryan tongues, from Max Muller C. ii. 21.

ENGLISH.	father.	mother.	brother.	sister.	daughter.
SANSCRIT	pitar.	matar.	bhratar.	svasar.	duhtar.
A. PERSIAN	patar.	matar.	bratar.	ganhar.	dughtar.
GREEK	pater.	meter.	frater.		thugater.
LATIN	pater.	mater.	frater.	soror.	
GOTHIC	fadar.		brothar.	svistar.	dauhtar.
SLAVONIC		mate.	brat.	sestra.	dukte.
IRISH	athair.	mathan.	brathan.	siur.	dear.

Here are the persons of the present tense indicative mood of the verb "to be" from Max Muller C. ii. 71.

SANSCRIT.	A. PERSIAN.	GREEK.	LATIN.	GOTHIC.	ENGLISH.
asmi.	esm.	emmi.	sum.	im.	am.
asi.	ahi.	essi.	es.	is.	art.
asti.	asti.	esti.	est.	ist.	is.
smas.	hmahi.	esmes.	sumus.	syum.	are.
stha.	sta.	este.	estis.	synth.	are.
santi.	henti.	enti.	sunt.	sind.	are.

APPENDIX. 353

And here are the numerals from one to ten.

ENGLISH.	GERMAN.	SANSCRIT.	GREEK.	LATIN.	SLAVIC.
one.	eins.	eka.	eis.	unus.	jedin.
two.	zwei.	dua.	duo.	duo.	dwa.
three.	drei.	tri.	treis.	tres.	tri.
four.	vier.	chatuar.	tessares.	quatuor.	chetory.
five.	fuenf.	pantchan.	pente.	quinque.	piat.
six.	sechs.	chash.	ex.	sex.	chest.
seven.	sieben.	saptan.	epta.	septem.	sedm.
eight.	acht.	ashtan.	okto.	octo.	osm.
nine.	neun.	navan.	ennea.	novem.	deviat.
ten.	zehn.	dasan.	deka.	decem.	desiat.

For discussions of the home of the Primitive Aryans see Pictet i. 69. Morris 38–50, 79. Lippert G. P. ii. 344. Max Muller S. L. i. 212. Latham V. M. Sayce I. S. L.

In regard to the order in which the different Aryan nationalities left the land of their Primitive Aryan ancestors Max Muller (C. i. 62) says: "It is more difficult to prove that the Hindoo was the last to leave this common home, that he saw his brothers all depart towards the setting sun, and that then, turning towards the south and the east, he started alone in search of a new world. But as in his language and in his grammar he has preserved something of what seems peculiar to each of the northern dialects singly, as he agrees with the Greek and the German where the Greek and the German differ from all the rest, and as no other language has carried off so large a share of the common Aryan heir-loom,—whether roots, grammar, words, myths, or legends,—it is natural to suppose that though perhaps the eldest brother, the Hindoo was the last to leave the central home of the Aryan family."

SEC. 243. *Vedic Hindoos.*—[1] Max Muller C. i. iii. [2] Pictet iii. 520.

Pictet (ii. 506) says he has examined some Hindoo astronomical tables which in his opinion must have been compiled in 3100 B. C. He mentions nine tables and formulas which when first made known in Europe could not have been prepared fraudulently, because there was not enough astronomical knowledge to make the calculations backwards with accuracy.

SEC. 244. *Vedic Religion.*—[1] Duncker iv. 62. [2] Rig Veda i. 113. [3] *Ib.* i. 65. [4] Amberley i. 30.

SEC. 245. *Vedic Hymns.*—[1] Williams H. 29. [2] Veda Mandala i. 121. [3] *Ib.* x. 129, Williams' translation. [4] I have substituted "spirit everlasting" for "the eternal man" in accordance with Williams' note that the latter phrase might be translated the "everlasting spirit." [5] Williams H. 28. [6] Max Muller C. I. 71. [7] *Ib.* 26.

SEC. 246. *Hindoo Literature.*—[1] Felton i. 37.   [2] *Ib.* 37.   [3] Max Muller C. i. 17.   [4] Mill H. I. ii. 47.   [5] Max Muller N. R. 335. The Mahabarata is spoken of by Talboys Wheeler, quoted in Bose (198) as "that grand epic poem which still continues to exercise an influence on the masses of the [Hindoo] people infinitely greater and more universal than the influence of the Bible in modern Europe."

"At all festivals and fairs, at the marriages of the wealthy, episodes from one of the two poems [Mahabarata and Ramayana] are recited to eager crowds of assembled hearers ; the audience accompany the acts and sufferings of the heroes with cries of joy or signs of sorrow, with laughter or tears." Duncker iv. 109. [6] Tylor A. 315.   [7] Hunter I. E. 119.   [8] Fergusson I. H. 104.   [9] *Ib.* 90.

"In contrasting the two Indian poems with the Iliad and the Odyssey we may observe many points of similarity. Some parallel passages have been already pointed out. We must expect to find the distinctive genius of two different people (though both of the Aryan race), in widely distant localities, coloring their epic poetry very differently, notwithstanding general features of resemblance. The Ramayana and Mahabarata are no less wonderful than the Homeric poems as monuments of the human mind, and no less interesting as pictures of human life and manners in ancient times, yet they bear in a remarkable degree the peculiar impress ever stamped on the productions of Asiatic nations, and separating them from European. On the side of art and harmony of proportion, they can no more compete with the Iliad and the Odyssey than the unnatural outline of the ten-headed and twenty-armed Ravana can bear comparison with the symmetry of a Grecian statue. While the simplicity of the one commends itself to the most refined classical taste, the exaggerations of the other only excite the wonder of Asiatic minds, or, if attractive to European, can only please imaginations nursed in an oriental school.

"Thus in the Iliad, time, space, and action are all restricted within the narrowest limits. In the Odyssey they are allowed a wider, though not too wide, a cycle; but in the Ramayana and the Mahabarata their range is almost unbounded. The Ramayana, as it traces the life of a single individual with tolerable continuity, is in this respect more like the Odyssey than the Iliad. In other points, especially in its plot, the greater simplicity of its style, and its comparative freedom from irrelevant episodes, it more resembles the Iliad. There are many graphic passages in both the Ramayana and Mahabarata, which, for beauty of description, cannot be surpassed by anything in Homer. It should be observed, moreover, that the diction of the Indian epics is more polished, regular, and cultivated, and the language altogether in a more advanced stage of development, than that of Homer. This, of course, tells to the disadvantage of the style on the side of nervous force and vigor; and it must be admitted that in the Sanscrit poems there is a great redundance of epithets, too liberal a use of metaphor, simile, and hyperbole, and far too much repetition, amplification, and prolixity." Williams I. W. 420, 421.

"The myths of the Indian epics are still closely interwoven with present faith. In fact, the capacity of an uneducated Hindoo for accepting and admiring the most monstrous fictions is apparently unlimited. Hence the absence of all history in the literature of India. A plain relation of facts has little charm for the ordinary Hindoo mind." Ib. 433. "The wildest fictions of the Ramayana and Mahabarata are to this very day intimately bound up with the religious creed of the Hindoos." Ib. 432.

SEC. 247. *Brahminism.*—There is no comprehensive treatise on Brahminism worthy of the subject, known to me. The information must be sought through a great number of volumes. The best book is that of Ward published in 1818. [1] Menu ii. 6.

SEC. 248. *Menu.*—[1] Duncker iv. 195. [2] Menu viii. 3–7. [3] Ib. i. 107. [4] James Mills H. I. i. 194.

SEC. 249. *Caste.*—[1] Menu i. 87. [2] Ib. ii. 31. [3] Ib. x. 129. [4] Ib. i. 100. [5] Ib. i. 98. [6] Ib. i. 100. [7] Ib. xi. 85. [8] Ib. xiii. 413. [9] Ib. viii. 112. [10] Ib. viii. 124, 380. [11] Ib. xi. 40. [12] Ib. xi. 6. [13] Ib. ix. 323. [14] Ib. i. 100. [15] Caste divides a people into huge families, each member of which has a right to know everything about his caste brothers, because the whole body might be polluted and degraded by the act of one individual. There is no such a thing as domestic privacy, and no system of espionage devised by rulers could be so complete as that self-imposed by the Hindoos." Burton P. M. 46.

"According to the orthodox views of the Indian theologians, not a single line of the Veda was the work of human authors. The whole Veda is, in some way or other, the work of the Deity; and even those who received it were not supposed to be ordinary mortals but beings raised above the level of common humanity, and less liable therefore to error in the reception of revealed religion." Max Müller C. i. 18.

"Caste can no longer hold its own against necessity and advantage, against railroads and scientific inventions." Williams I. W. xxv. Robertson finds much in caste to commend. He says of it (180, 181): "To this may be ascribed that high degree of perfection conspicuous in many of the Indian manufactures; and though veneration for the practices of their ancestors may check the spirit of invention, yet by adhering to these they acquire such an expertness and delicacy of hand, that Europeans with all the advantages of superior science and the aid of more complete instruments, have never been able to equal the exquisite execution of their workmanship. While the high improvement of their more curious manufactures excited the admiration and attracted the commerce of other nations, the separation of professions in India, and the early distribution of the people into classes, attached to particular kinds of labor, secured such an abundance of the more common and useful commodities as not only supplied their own wants, but ministered to those of the countries around them."

The superior success of the Hindoos in certain branches of industry is perhaps to be attributed to the density of their population as compared with their wealth, rather than to their division into castes. The occupations in which they excelled, and in which they exhibited a wonderful patience of the eyes, and dexterity of the fingers, did not contribute to the cheaper production of the necessaries or comforts of life, and were evidences of extensive abject poverty, not of national enterprise or prosperity.

SEC. 250. *The Brahmins.*—[1] The Celtic, Greek, Roman, Teuton, and Slavonian nationalities have each a peculiar "national character" and "have each one act allotted to them on the stage of history." "Not so the southern tribes [the Hindoos]. They are absorbed in the struggles of thought; their past is the problem of creation, their future the problem of existence, and the present, which ought to be the solution of both, seems never to have attracted their attention or called forth their energies. There never was a nation believing so firmly in another world and so little concerned about this. Their condition on earth is to them a problem, their real and eternal life is a simple fact. Though this is said chiefly with reference to them before they were brought in contact with foreign conquerors, traces of this character are still visible in the Hindoos as described by the companions of Alexander, nay, even in the Hindoos of the present day. The only sphere in which the Indian mind finds itself at liberty to act, to create, and to worship, is the sphere of religion and philosophy, and nowhere

have religious and metaphysical ideas struck root so deep in the mind of a nation as in India. The shape which these ideas took amongst the different classes of society and at different periods of civilization, naturally varies from coarse superstition to sublime spiritualism. But, taken as a whole, history supplies no second instance where the inward life of the soul has so completely absorbed all the other faculties of a people." Max Muller C. i. 66.
¹ Menu iii. 1.   ² *Ib.* vi. 35.   ³ Duncker iv. 181.

"The power of the gods was to them a very real thing. The influence of the stars and the good or ill luck of the days on which the various customary ceremonies were to be performed, or the various businesses of life were to be set on foot, were to them of very real importance. There was indeed very little, if any, of what we should now call prayer. But the gods could be compelled by sacrifices rightly offered, by hymns properly intoned, to favor the fortunate worshiper; and charms rightly recited, horoscopes correctly cast, talismans whose power had been already tested, could insure the results which men had most at heart. The happiness of the soul, too, in the next birth, depended upon the due performance of settled ceremonies; and for all these things the help of the Brahmins was required, and had to be richly paid. It would be useless to attempt to disguise the evils resulting from such a state of things." Davids H. L. 26.

"The Brahminical order . . . delegated to the military class, however formed, the dangers and cares of government, satisfied with ruling from their spiritual throne the despots of mankind. To this single circumstance may, we think, be attributed the feebleness of the Indian governments, and the inefficiency of their armies. In countries where the priesthood forms a separate caste or order in the state, the education which fits a man to be a pagan priest (at least in such a system of paganism as prevails in India), at the same time disqualifies him to a certain extent from comprehending the theory or pursuing the routine of civil business. He belongs to a body more or less distinct from the state, seeking self-aggrandizement at all hazards, actuated by separate interests. His mind, clouded and darkened by a multitude of little passions, contracts itself perpetually, and quickly becomes a scene too narrow for the marshaling and development of grand ideas of public good. . . . If any course of action were proposed which, by promoting the general welfare of India, might incidentally trench, however slightly or remotely, upon the privileges of the Brahmins, the priest, roused like a serpent in his lair, would inevitably oppose the measure to the utmost; and . . . his opposition would be decisive." Knight ii. 229.

"The Brahmins, in all things a shrewd, artful race, have nowhere shown a more signal example of that cunning which Lord Bacon dignifies with the name of 'wisdom for a man's self,' than in creating among their countrymen a deep-rooted belief that their persons were designed by the Deity to be under all circumstances inviolable, and that to deprive them of life, whether by direct violence or by causing their death in any way, is a crime which admits of no expiation. Upon this persuasion is founded a very extraordinary practice, once extremely common at Benares, called 'sitting in dharna,' which may be translated caption or arrest. When a Brahmin desires to gain some particular point which he has found it impossible to accomplish by any other means, he proceeds to the door or house of the person against whom his suit is directed, where he sits down in dharna, with poison, or a poniard, or some other instrument of suicide in his hand, threatening to use it should his adversary attempt to molest or pass him by. This menace completely arrests him. The plaintiff now commences a fast, in which, according to the rigid etiquette, in such cases rarely infringed, he must be accompanied by the defendant; and in this situation they both remain until the former obtains satisfaction. As few have recourse to this desperate step without a firm resolution to persevere, the plaintiff rarely fails of effecting his object; for were the individual thus arrested to permit the Brahmin to perish of hunger at his door, or should he by any harsh measures compel him to make use of his poison or his dagger, the sin would be forever on his head." Knight ii. 9.

SEC. 251. *Suttee, etc.*—[1]Ward ii. 275. [2]Max Muller C. i. 35. Duncker iv. 62. [3]Ward i. 311.

"The widow about to commit suttee, appears at the funeral in her best dress, wearing her jewels, and advancing prays to all the gods, declares that life is nothing to her, and that she wishes to accompany her husband. She gives her jewels to officiating Brahmins, bids farewell to her relatives and friends, and then, addressing the assembled company, says: 'That I may enjoy the happiness of heaven with my husband and purify my ancestors and his, I ascend the pyre in expiation of these sins of my husband, even though he has murdered a Brahmin, torn asunder the bonds of gratitude, or slain a friend. On you I call, ye eight protectors of the world, as witnesses of this action, ye sun and moon, air, fire, earth, ether, and water. Be witnesses my own soul and conscience, and thou Yama [God of Death], day and night and dawn, be ye witnesses, be witnesses! I follow the corpse of my husband to the burning pyre.' She mounts the pile, lies down beside the corpse, throws her arm over it in embrace, and says, 'I pray, suttee, suttee, suttee,' while the flames kindled by her son or nearest male relative swiftly rise and enshroud her." Duncker iv. 512.

SEC. 252. *Brahmin Women.*—[1] Menu ix. 17. [2] *Ib.* ix. 18. [3] *Ib.* 8. [4] *Ib.* x. 147. [5] *Ib.* ix. 23. [6] *Ib.* ix. 94. A family with a daughter unmarried after she has become a young woman, "is considered to labor under the displeasure of the gods; and no member of the other sex considers himself respectable after the age of seventeen till he is married." Sleeman i. 50. [7] Menu iv. 43. [8] *Ib.* v. 157, 160. [9] *Ib.* ix. 81. [10] *Ib.* v. 154. [11] *Ib.* ix. 23. [12] *Ib.* viii. 400. [13] Ward ii. 234. [14] Menu iii. 56. [15] Oman 91. The Hindoo mother lays the child in the sun every day during the first three months of its life. Ward i. 173. This practice suggests the rule in Java that the children of Europeans must be allowed to go naked in their early years; otherwise they do not live to maturity. Bose 86, 208, 238.

SEC. 253. *Brahmin Morality.*—[1] Menu xi. 91, 92. [2] *Ib.* iv. 170–176. [3] *Ib.* v. 4. [4] *Ib.* xi. 238. [5] *Ib.* xi. 242. [6] *Ib.* xi. 236. [7] *Ib.* xi. 228. [8] *Ib.* xi. 262. [9] *Ib.* x. 261. [10] *Ib.* xi. 245. [11] *Ib.* xi. 223. [12] *Ib.* xi. 249. [13] *Ib.* xi. 226. [14] *Ib.* ii. 87. [15] *Ib.* ii. 84. [16] *Ib.* ii. 76.

SEC. 254. *Brahmin Henotheism.*—[1] Menu xii. 87. [2] *Ib.* i. 6–8. [3] *Ib.* xv. 85. [4] *Ib.* xii. 119. [5] *Ib.* iii. 85–89.

Max Muller invented the word henotheism and defines (O. R. 261) it as "a successive belief in single supreme gods;" that is the worshiper addresses one god as supreme and the only divine being and then addresses another in the same way. Muller adds that "in the Veda one god after another is invoked. For the time being all that can be said of a divine being is ascribed to him. The poet while addressing him, seems hardly to know of any other gods. But . . . sometimes in the same hymn, other gods are mentioned and they also are truly divine, truly independent, or it may be supreme." Elsewhere (275) he says: "Each god . . . is felt at the time as a real divinity, as supreme and absolute, in spite of the limitations which, to our mind, a plurality of gods must entail on every single god."

The Brahmins say "God is everywhere . . . but his spirituality perplexes the mind. To collect and fix the ideas on the object of adoration, therefore, an image is chosen, into which image, by the power of incantations, the deity is imagined to be drawn. Hence in dedicating an image they call upon the god to come and dwell in it. . . . God has made himself known in these forms, and directed the various images to be made, that men may be fascinated and drawn to the love of worship. . . . Images are only necessary while men continue in a rude state, and may be laid aside by those who can attain to devotion by means of rational speculation." Ward ii. xxxv.

"Nothing can be more simple than esoteric Hindooism [as conceived by some Brahmins]. It is a creed which may be expressed by the two words—Spiritual Pantheism. A pantheistic creed of this kind is the simplest of all beliefs, because it teaches that nothing really exists but the one Universal Spirit; that the soul of each individual is identical with that Spirit, and that every man's highest aim should be to get rid forever of doing, having, and being, and devote himself to profound contemplation, with a view to such spiritual knowledge as shall deliver him from the mere illusion of separate existence and force upon him the conviction that he is himself part of the one being constituting the Universe." Williams I. W. Intro. xxvi.

SEC. 255. *Transmigration.*—[1] Menu xii. 80. [2] *Ib*. xi. 48–53. [3] *Ib*. xii. 42–50. [4] *Ib*. xii. 73–82.

"It is probable that the idea of transmigration first originated in the curious trick of the memory by which we sometimes feel so sure that sensations we are experiencing have been experienced by us before, and yet we know not how or where." Davids B. 255. He refers to Carpenter's Physiology, p. 430, and Brodie's Psychological Inquiries, second series, p. 55.

SEC. 256. *Krishna.*—[1]Arnold S. C. x. 81. [2]*Ib*. ix. 78. [3]*Ib*. ii. 13. [4]*Ib*. ii. 122. [5]Ward ii. 21, 23. [6]Barth 272.

SEC. 257. *Buddha.*—The best book on Buddhism is that of Kern; and next in interest is that of St. Hilaire. The best in English is David's Buddhism, but it is too brief to give a fair opportunity for the learning and ability of the author. [2] Buddhaghosa Intro. xxxi.

"Early Buddhism had no idea, just as early Christianity had not, of the principle underlying the foundation of the higher morality of the future, the duty which we owe, not only to our fellow-men of to-day, but also to those of the morrow—to the race as a whole, but in the future even more than now. . . . The sense of duty to the race has sprung out of a fact, only lately become a generally received conception—I mean the progressive continuity of human progress." Davids H. L. iii.

"There is no reason to believe that Gautama . . . intended . . . to be the founder of a new religion." Davids B. 151. As Davids is a high authority I quote his opinion, but it seems to me quite plain that Siddhartha did intend to found a new religion.

One of Siddhartha's converts, named Poorna, announced that he would go as a missionary into the district of Sronaparanta. The master said to him:—

"The men of Sronaparanta are passionate, insolent, and cruel, and what will you think, Poorna, when they insult you?"

"Those who do not strike me with their hands or hit me with stones must have kind hearts."

"But if they strike you?"

"If they do not use clubs or swords they must be kind."

"But if they beat you with clubs or wound you with swords?"

"If they do not kill me I will think they are kind."

"But if they should kill you?"

"Then I shall think that they render me a service in delivering me from a body that contains so much impurity."

"It is well, Poorna," said Siddhartha; "with your perfect patience, you can establish yourself in Sronaparanta. Go, then, O Poorna; being yourself saved, help to save others. Having arrived at the other shore, help others to cross. Being consoled, console others. Having become secure of Nirvana, help others to attain it." St. Hilaire 96, 97.

SEC. 258. *Nirvana.*—The theory that Nirvana means annihilation implies that Siddhartha threw away "one of the most powerful weapons in the hands of every religious teacher. If this life is to end in nothing it is hardly worth the trouble which he took himself, or the sacrifice which he imposed on his disciples." Max Muller C. i. 231. ² B. Suttas xi. 248. ³ Beal 86. ⁴ B. Suttas xi. 115. ⁵ Beal 111. ⁶ St. Hilaire 133, 134. ⁷ Davids H. L. 89.

Buddha said, "I do not bid my disciples perform miracles; I tell them, Live so that your good deeds may remain concealed, your errors confessed." Duncker iv. 478.

Buddha says the transmigrated soul is like a flame kindled from another flame. Davids H. L. 101.

"One is the road that leads to wealth, another the road that leads to Nirvana. If the bikshoo, the disciple of Buddha, has learned this, he will not yearn for honor; he will strive after separation from the world." Dhammapada v. 75.

SEC. 259. *Bikshoos.*—[1] I am not fully convinced that the statement of Siddhartha's doctrine in regard to the killing of beasts by his lay disciples is correct, but I follow the authorities. It seems to me inconsistent, impolitic, and not in harmony with his judgment in managing men, that he should have ordered his laymen to abstain from the destruction of any life, while he allowed them to defend their rights, and permitted them, and even the bikshoos, to eat meat. How could people eat meat if beasts could not be killed? And if beasts were killed by unbelievers, was not the purchase of meat from them an encouragement of killing, and an indirect killing? And if the layman could defend his rights in war, why should he not have the consent of his religious teacher to kill the poisonous reptile that threatened his life, or the insect that destroyed his comfort? The people who live on the flesh of their cattle, of fish, or of game, cannot be Buddhists, if they are not allowed to take the life of beasts. I suspect that Siddhartha gave no command to laymen in reference to the killing of beasts; but the authorities are against me. [2] Beal 215.

Kern, vol. 2, gives a full account of the discipline of the bikshoos: "For a part of the year they [the bikshoos] must live in the woods with no other shelter than a tree, and with no furniture but a carpet on which they must sit, and never lie down during sleep." Williams I. W. 58.

SEC. 260. *Laymen.*—[1] Max Muller O. R. iii. [2] Dhammapada i. 2. Buddhaghosa. [3] Beal.

SEC. 261. *Viharas.*—[1] Mills C. D. B. 77. [2] Beal 116.

SEC. 262. *Discourses.*—[1] Pfleiderer i. 215. [2] Asvaghosha. [3] *Ib* .307.

The following is a Buddhist parable: "There was a certain pond, which contained many fish, and had diminished so much in an unusually dry summer that the supply of food for them had run very short, and appearances indicated that before the beginning of the rainy season, many and perhaps all of them would die of starvation. While they were worrying about the great danger of their situation, a crane came to them and told them that there was another and larger pond with abundant water not far off, and as a matter of benevolence, if they wished, he would carry them all to the better place. They listened to him very suspiciously, but finally consented to let the crane carry one of their number, who was old and half blind, to the larger pond, so that he could report. The crane took the deputy fish to the pond, showed it to him, convinced him of its superior attractions as a home for fish, and then took him back. The half-blind fish made a report so favorable that all agreed to move to the new pond. The crane took them up one by one to the edge of the new pond, but, instead of putting them in, he ate them there. When all were dispatched, he took a crab, which consented to follow the fish, but he took care to take hold of the crane's neck with his claw, as he said for the purpose of holding on, but when he saw the pile of fish bones, and the purpose of the crane to kill him, he nipped off the crane's head and walked to the new pond. The shallow pond is the world; the other larger pond is salvation; the crane is the prevalent superstition; the half-blind fish is the priest; and the crab is Buddha." Davids H. L. 117.

A Hindoo apologue, to illustrate the readiness of the ignorant to believe stories told to them by designing rogues, whether in or out of the priesthood, is copied by Max Muller, and repeated by Cox A. M. i. 111. "Three thieves saw a peasant carrying a goat at some distance from his home, and on a lonely road; so they laid a plan to get it. They separated, and one after another met the peasant. Each asked him why he was carrying that miserable cur dog. He answered the first with a curse, the second with a stare, and the third by throwing down the goat and running away. Muller remarks that a man will believe almost anything if told by three different people."

SEC. 263. *Siddhartha's Death.*—[1] B. Suttas. [2] *Ib.* 103. [3] *Ib.* 112.

SEC. 264. *Councils.*—[1] Rockhill 157. [2] St. Hilaire 110.

SEC. 265. *Asoka.*—[1] Duncker iv. 529. [2] Buddhaghosa xx. [3] Duncker iv. 534. [4] Davids H. L. 230. [5] St. Hilaire 108. [6] *Ib.* iii. [7] *Ib.* 112.

SEC. 266. *Growth.*—[1] St. Hilaire 186. [2] Rockhill 221. [3] St. Hilaire 329. [4] *Ib.* 218. [5] Davids. [6] Beals B. C. 96. [7] Asvaghosha xix. 26.

In his Buddhism Davids gives a table of the number of Buddhists as compared with the believers in other religions. According to him there are 500,000,000 Buddhists, 160,000,000 Brahminical Hindoos, 155,000,000 Mohammedans, 152,000,000,000 Roman Catholics, 75,000,000 Greek Christians, 100,000,000 Christians of other sects, 7,000,000 Jews, 1,200,000 Sikhs, 150,000 Parsees, and 125,000,000 others, mostly savages. The Buddhists are comprised in two main classes, the Southern and the Northern. The Southern Buddhists, including those in Ceylon, Burmah, Siam, and Anam, number 30,000,000; the Northern Buddhists number 470,000,000, including 416,000,000 in China, 33,000,000 in Japan, 8,000,000 in

Corea, 6,000,000 in Thibet, 5,000,000 in Manchuria and Mongolia, and 2,000,000 in Loo Choo, etc.

SEC. 267. *Hindostan's Place.*—[1] Ward i. 477. [2] James Mill H. I. i. 180. [3] The Sikh Bible says, "God will not ask man what he is, but will ask what he has done;" and, "To be true belongs to thee; thy success to the Creator."

SEC. 268. *Land and People.*—[1] Max Muller C. i. 81. [2] *Ib.* i. 371. [3] Rawlinson F. G. M. iii. 332. [4] *Ib.* O. N. 104.

SEC. 270. *The Avesta.*—[1] Vendidad Intro. xxx. [2] Darmesteter Introduction xxxi. [3] Duncker v. 100. [4] 1 Sam. iv. 14. [5] Josh. xiv. 20. [6] Lippert G. P. ii. 324.

SEC. 271. *Ormuzd.*—[1] Vendidad Introduction. [2] Rawlinson R. A. W. [3] Darmesteter Avesta ii. 229. [4] Max Muller C. i. 174. [5] "The good immortal, the wicked destroyed." Whitney O. L. S. [6] Philip Smith (433) adds, citing Rawlinson(iii. 114), "As the juice was drunk immediately after extraction, and before fermentation had set in, it was not intoxicating." Rawlinson evidently does not know the intoxicating qualities of the fresh juice of the ava.

The following extracts from modern publications of the Parsees—confessions of faith and prayer—are interesting as illustrations of the faith derived from the ancient Persians:—

"I believe in the existence, the purity, and the certainty of the good Mazdean faith, in the creator, Ormuzd, and the ampaschands [angels]; in the furtherance of the final reckoning, and in the resurrection with a new body." Then the believer adds, "I repent in word and deed for all kinds of sin, prohibited in the law, done by me in thought, word, or deed." Diercks i. 251.

"In the name of God, the munificent, the merciful, the loving, praise be to the name of Ormuzd, who ever was, ever is, and ever will be, from whom all authority comes, the great ruler, mighty, wise, the creator, the preserver, the refuge, the protector, the doer of good deeds, the overseer, pure, good, and just; at thy command I accept all the good things which life offers to me. In thee I think, and speak, and act. I believe thy true law. I seek forgiveness for all my sins by upright conduct. I observe the pure law by virtuous effort and abstinence from vice. I recognize the duties of using with pure purpose the six powers of thought, speech, action, memory, reason, and spirit." Diercks i. 235.

The modern catechism says: "I believe in one God; in the sublime Zoroaster as his true apostle; in his religion and his gospel, the Avesta, as above every doubt; in the goodness of God; and in our duties to obey every command of the Mazdean religion, to avoid all evil, to strive to do good, and to pray five times every day. We believe that we shall be judged on the fourth day after death, and that justice will be done unto us; that we should hope for Heaven and fear Hell; that we should not doubt that there will be a day of destruction and of resurrection; that we must never forget that God's will has ever been and ever will be done, and that we should turn our faces towards the light." Diercks i. 258.

The commandments accepted by the modern Parsees are these: "To know God as one; to know the prophet, the exalted Zurthost as the true prophet; to believe the religion and the Avesta brought by him as true beyond all manner of doubt; to believe in the goodness of God; not to disobey any of the commands of the Mazdean religion; to avoid evil deeds; to exert oneself in good deeds; to pray five times in the day; to believe in the reckoning and justice on the fourth morning after death; to hope for heaven and to fear hell; to consider indubitable the day of general destruction and resurrection; to remember always that God has done what he willed and shall do what he wills; to face some luminous object while worshiping God." Max Muller C. i. 173.

SEC. 272. *Chaldea.*—[1] Rawlinson F. G. M. ii. 514. [2] Is. xiii. 19. [3] Jer. li, 41. [4] Ez. xliii. 14. [5] *Ib.* xvii. 4. [6] Rawlinson F. G. M. iii. 15. [7] The routes of the caravans are shown on a map in Lindsay i. 1.

SEC. 274. *Chaldean Learning.*—[1] Sayce A. E. E. 167. [2] Kenrick ii. 275. [3] Duncker i. 23. [4] *Ib.* 283. [5] Philip Smith, 400.

SEC. 276. *Chaldean Religion.*—[1] Rawlinson F. G. M. iii. 82. [2] Ragozin C. 178. [3] *Ib.* 155. [4] *Ib.* 162.

SEC. 277. *Assyria.*—[1] Duncker iii. 83.

SEC. 278. *Assyrian Polity.*—[1] Sayce A. E. E. 90.

SEC. 279. *Assyrian Religion.*—[1] Rawlinson F. G. M. ii. 2. [2] *Ib.* 73. [3] *Ib.* [4] Enc. Brit., Article Babylonia. [5] Rawlinson F. G. M. ii. 71. [6] *Ib.* R. A. W. 73.

SEC. 280. *Phœnicia.*—"The Phœnicians indeed were an eminently receptive people. Like the rest of their Semitic brethren, they lacked originality, but they were gifted beyond most other races with the power of assimilating and combining, of adapting and improving on their models." Sayce A. E. E. 184.

"The Phœnicians form, in some respects, the most important fraction of the whole group of antique natives, notwithstanding that they sprang from the most obscure and insignificant families. This fraction, when settled, was constantly exposed to inroad by new tribes, was utterly conquered and subjected by utter strangers, when it had taken a great place among nations, and yet by industry, by perseverance, by acuteness of intellect, by unscrupulousness and want of faith, by adaptability and pliability when necessary, and dogged defiance at other times, by total disregard of the rights of the weaker, they obtained the foremost place in the history of their times, and the highest reputation, not only for the things which they did, but for many that they did not. They were the first systematic traders, the first miners and metallurgists, the greatest inventors (if we apply such a term to those who kept an ever watchful lookout for the inventions of others, and immediately applied them to themselves with some grand improvements on the original idea); they were the boldest mariners, the greatest colonizers, who at one time held not only the gorgeous East but the whole of the then half-civilized West in fee; who could boast of a form of government approaching to constitutionalism; who, of all nations of the time, stood highest in practical arts and sciences; and into whose laps there flowed an unceasing stream of the world's entire riches, until the day came when they began to care for nothing else, and the enjoyment of material comforts and luxuries took the place of the thirst for and search after knowledge. Their piratical power and daring was undermined; their colonies, grown old enough to stand alone, fell away from them, some after a hard fight, others in mutual agreement or silently; and the nations in whose estimation and fear they had held the first place, and who had been tributary to them, disdained them, ignored them, and finally struck them utterly out of the list of nations, and they dwindled away miserably, a warning to all who should come after them." Deutsch 162.

"The Phœnicians were certainly among the most industrious and persevering of mankind. The accounts which we have of them from various quarters and the remains which cover the country that they once inhabited, sufficiently attest their unceasing and untiring activity, through almost the whole period of their activity as a nation. Always laboring in their workshops at home in mechanical and esthetic arts, they were at the same time constantly seeking employment abroad, ransacking the earth for beautiful and useful commodities, building cities, constructing harbors, founding colonies, introducing the arts of life among wild nations, mining and establishing fisheries, organizing lines of land traffic, perpetually moving from place to place, and leaving wherever they went abundant proofs of their diligence and capacity for hard work. From Thasos in the East, where Herodotus saw a large mountain turned topsy-turvy by the Phœnicians in their search for gold, to the Scilly Isles in the West, where workings attributable to them are still to be seen, all the metalliferous islands and coast tracts bear traces of Phœnician industry in tunnels, adits and air-shafts, while manufactured vessels of various kinds in silver, bronze, and terra-cotta, together with figures and gems of a Phœnician type, attest still more widely their manufacturing and commercial activity." G. Rawlinson S. P. 56.

SEC. 281. *Phœnician Commerce.*—[1] Ships built by Phœnicians in the Red Sea brought gold, ivory, almug (sandal) wood, apes, and peacocks to Solomon. 1 Kings ix. 27, 28; x. 10, 22.

SEC. 282. *Phœnician Letters.*—[1] "The advance from one stage in the development of writing to the next, is only attained by the transmission of a graphic system from one nation to another. The transmission of the Aztec hieroglyphics to the Mayas of Yucatan, of the Egyptian hieroglyphs to the Semites, and the thrice-repeated transmission of the Semitic alphabet to the Aryan nations,—to the Greeks, to the Persians and to the Indians,—are instances in point. Each of these transmissions was accompanied by important developments in the art of writing." Taylor A. i. 39.

SEC. 283. *Teutonia.*—In reference to the ancient Teutons, there is no one authority of superior comprehensiveness and accuracy.

SEC. 286. *The Celts.*—The same remark applies to the Celts. [1] Napoleon ii. 26.

Mommsen (i. 419, 420) says the Celtic blood "is deficient in those deeper moral and political qualifications which lie at the root of all that is good and great in human development," and therefore the Celts "have shaken all states and have founded none." This opinion seems to me to be unjust to the character and capacity of the Gauls. As compared with other peoples of their time, I see no serious moral or mental defect. The main reasons why they did not found a great modern nation are that their political organization was weak and they came into conflict with Rome before they had time to ripen in a consolidated monarchy.

SEC. 288. *Druidism.*—[1] Toland vi. 13. [2] "Cæsar brought to Italy so much gold and silver from the Druidical temples that there was a perceptible decline in the value of the precious metals. From one temple at Toulouse he took more than $15,000,000." Lippert G. P. ii. 579.

Sec. 289. *Stone Monuments.*—[1] Toland 313. [2] Mason's Caractacus in Toland 325. [3] Toland 316. [4] *Ib.* 327. [5] Du Chaillu i. 71, 72, 75, 273. [6] *Ib.*, 311, 313, 320, 321. [7] Fergusson R. S. M. 91. [8] *Ib.* 63.

Fergusson, who made a careful study of the rude stone monuments of Western Europe, and gave us the best book about them, came to the conclusion that their builders certainly were not Aryan, but were Turanians after they had come into contact with the Romans not earlier than 100 B. C. While I have great respect for Fergusson's industry and ability, in this instance I cannot accept his conclusion. But works of such magnitude must have been erected by a nationality dominant at the time in the regions where these monuments stand, and we know not only that no Turanians have been dominant in France north of the Loire, in England, Scotland and Ireland where these works are most numerous, but that there has been not even one Turanian village there. Besides, the districts known or supposed to be Turanian—such as Finland, Hungary, Liguria, Etruria and the Basque provinces—have nothing of the kind.

Fergusson thinks the dolmen builders may have been descendants of the cave-dwellers; but how they could have erected these monuments after 100 A. D., without being known to history or tradition, is inexplicable. Besides, he admits (R. S. M. 258) that a stone circle was erected at Stennis in the Orkneys by Northmen; and that menhirs at Carnac commemorate a battle between Britons and Northmen about 500 A. D. (375). He (279, 281) also mentions the facts that the sites of several battles in Norway are covered with upright stones, resembling those of Carnac in their arrangement; and he (282) mentions a burial mound with a circle of stone round it and a dolmen on top in Iceland. Lubbock P. T., ch. v, gives a good summary of information about megalithic monuments. In reference to those in France see Duruy iii. 262–264.

Worsaae (78) thinks the dolmens were raised by men in the stone age. Many writers use the word cromlech as synonymous with dolmen; Fergusson (44) says cromlech has a different meaning. The descendants of the Turanians in France are all south of the Garonne; the megalithic monuments of France are nearly all north of that stream, and in the region bounded by it, the Seine and the Rhone. Duruy iii. 262. For statistics of ancient British graves see Lubbock P. T. 154.

Sec. 290. *Etruria.*—[1] Dennis i. 15.

Sec. 297. *Great Achievements.*—[1] Taylor A. i. 54. [2] *Ib.* 39. [3] *Ib.* 4.

Sec. 299. *Religious Growth.*—Max Muller (C. i. Preface) writes of "the inevitable decay to which every religion is exposed. . . . Wherever we can trace a religion to its first beginnings, we find it free from many blemishes that affected it in its later stages." He does not trace the history of any religion for the purpose of showing its decline, nor does he give reasons why all ecclesiastical systems must become corrupt with time. The best example to sustain his point would be Buddhism; but, when closely examined, it furnishes no proof. Siddhartha was superior in culture to most of his modern followers; their adherence to their ancient superstitions does not prove an inevitable tendency to decay in religion.

Sec. 300. *Religious Comparisons.*—General usage gives the name of religion to the belief of the Confucian and to that of the Buddhist; and therefore the definition of religion must include those beliefs; the common definitions do not. Those who find fault with my definition should give another equally comprehensive or deny the authority of usage in language. Max Muller devotes the greater part of his book on "Natural Religion" to a discussion of the various definitions of religion, and he offers (188) his in these words: "Religion consists in the perception of the infinite under such manifestations as are able to influence the moral character of man." He says that "there is no conceptual knowledge which is not based on perceptual knowledge;" but we certainly do not perceive the infinite. We may infer the existence of the infinite from our perception of the finite; but the inference is a conception not a perception. Roskoff, as cited in Muller (189) defines religion as something that lifts man "above the real world." There are many religions, however, which do not lift him "above the real world," but carry him off in a fictitious sphere of existence. The transmigration of the Brahmin, and the cannibalistic heaven of the Fijian are not "above the real world;" they are on a level with the actual world of the believer, and far below the plane of the enlightened scholar. I quote the following passage from John Stuart Mill to sustain my definition: "The essence of religion is the strong and earnest direction of the emotions and desires towards an ideal object, recognized as of the highest excellence, and as rightfully paramount over all selfish objects of desire. This condition is fulfilled by the religion of humanity in as eminent a degree, and in as high a sense, as by the supernatural religions even in their best manifestations, and far more so than in any of their others. . . . The sense of unity with mankind and a deep feeling for the general good may be cultivated into a sentiment and a principle capable of fulfilling every important function of religion and itself justly entitled to the name." Mill agrees with general usage in recognizing the "religion" of Confucius, Siddhartha, George Eliot, Herbert Spencer, and T. H. Huxley.

SEC. 303. *Departmental Values.*—The chief advocate of mythology as a powerful influence in the development of religion and of general culture is Max Muller, in his "Science of Language," and various other works. Among those who have expressed the opinion that mythology is not a prominent factor in culture are Lippert G. P. ii. 348 and W. Robertson Smith (R. L. 19).

SUPPLEMENTARY NOTE TO SEC. 186.—It deserves remark that while Squier denied the use of lime mortar in the architecture of the Quichuans, he was much impressed by the hardness of a mortar which he called clay. Thus he spoke of "stones laid in a tenacious clay" (87); of "solid rubble walls" (144); of "a compact mass of rubble" (150); of "tenacious clay mixed with broken stones so as to form an indurated mass almost as hard as mortar" (119); of round stones in "a cement or mortar of kneaded clay" (215); of rough stones laid in "a tenacious clay which may have had some intermixture to give it greater cohesion" (152); of "tenacious clay mixed perhaps with other adhesive materials binding together rough stones into one enduring mass of wall" (436); of rough stone "cemented together with a stiff clay" (410); of rough stones laid "in some tenacious material which I have called clay" (518); and of a most compact *mamposteria* (156). The last word is Spanish, and means stone laid in lime mortar. These expressions, scattered about through two hundred pages of his book, describing ruins seen in different portions of Peru and Bolivia, including places a thousand miles apart, and seen at intervals of time separated by many months—these expressions were evidently not compared by their author with one another, for if they had been, he would have seen the necessity of making some comprehensive remark, which he did not make. This Quichuan mortar, much as it looks like clay, is certainly not clay, and it is presumably a mixture which deserves a study that has never yet been given to it. Squier gives engravings showing the ruins of Quichuan buildings with walls thirty feet high of rough stone laid in this clay-like cement, and that have stood without a covering for centuries in the rains of the high Andes. No clay would keep its place under such circumstances, and through such a period of time. We may presume that the same material as that of this clay mortar appeared in the "clay stucco," as Squier calls it, used to cover many of the Quichuan walls of stone and adobe, and still found on the ruins. Its moulded decorations, and the bright colors of its original painting, are still plainly discernible in places which have been exposed to more than three centuries of storm. Such stuccoes are still visible at Pachacamac, Chimu, the island of Coati, the island of Titicaca, and the temple of Viracocha, south of Cuzco.

This clay cement and this clay stucco presumably owed its hardness to the same material which gave their unparalleled and unexplained durability to the Quichuan adobes, which have lasted like stone. Prescott (C. P. i. 156) says that "these adobes possess a hardness insensible alike to the storms and the more trying suns of the tropics;" and he remarks that "Ulloa, who carefully examined these [unburned] bricks, suggests that there must have been some secret in their composition, so superior in many respects to our own manufacture."

LIST OF AUTHORITIES.

Anderson, R. B., Norse Mythology, Chicago, 1884.
Amberley, Viscount., An Analysis of Religious Belief, 2 vols., London, 1876.
Arnold, E., Translator, The Song Celestial (Bhagavadgita), London, 1889.
" Translator, The Secret of Death, London, 1885.
Asvaghosha, Bodhisattva, Life of Buddha. Translated, Oxford, 1883.
Bancroft, H. H., Native Races of the Pacific States, 5 vols., New York, 1876.
Barth, A., The Religions of India, Boston, 1882.
Bastian, A., Geographische und Ethnologische Bilder, Jena, 1873.
Beal, S., Buddhism in China, London, 1884.
Beck, L., Die Geschichte des Eisens, Braunschweig, 1884.
Belt, T., The Naturalist in Nicaragua, London, 1874.
Bible, the Holy, King James' Version.
Birch, S., A History of Ancient Pottery, 2 vols., London, 1858.
Bose, S. C., The Hindoos, London, 1881.
Brougham, H., Political Philosophy, 3 vols., London.

Brugsch, Bey. H., The History of Egypt. Translated, 2 vols., London, 1881.
Buddhaghosa, Parables. Translated, London, 1870.
Buddhist, Suttas. Translated, Oxford, 1881.
Burton, R. F., Pilgrimage to El-Medinah, New York, 1856.
Chabas, F., Antiquité Historique, Paris, 1876.
Charnay, D., The Ancient Cities of the New World, New York, 1887.
Chevalier, M., Mexico, Ancient and Modern. Translated, 2 vols., London, 1864.
Chinese Classics. Translated by J. Legge, London, 1869.
Clarke, J. F., Ten Great Religions, 2 vols., Boston, 1883.
Colenso, J. W., The Pentateuch, 2 vols., London, 1863.
"   "   The Pentateuch and the Moabite Stone, London, 1873.
Cortes, H., Historia de Nueva Espana, Aumentada por F. A. Lorenzana, Mexico, 1770. This volume contains nothing by Cortes save his letters to Charles V.
Cox, G. W., Mythology of the Aryan Nations, London, 1870.
Darmesteter, J., The Zend Avesta. Translated, Oxford, 1880.
Davids, T. R., Buddhism, London, 1886.
"   "   Origin and Growth of Religion, New York, 1882.
"   "   Hibbert Lectures, New York, 1882.
Davis, J., The Chinese, 2 vols., New York, 1848.
Dennis, G., The Cities and Cemeteries of Etruria, 2 vols., London, 1878.
Deutsch, E., The Literary Remains of, New York, 1874.
Diercks, G., Entwickelungsgeschichte des Geistes des Menschen, Berlin, 1881.
Doolittle, J., Social Life of the Chinese, 2 vols., New York, 1865.
Douglas, R. K., China, London, 1882.
"   "   Confucianism and Taouism, London.
Du Chaillu, P. B., The Viking Age, 2 vols., New York, 1889.
Duncker, M., The History of Antiquity. Translated, 5 vols., London, 1877.
Duruy, J., The History of Rome, 5 vols. Translated, Boston, 1883.
Encyclopedia Britannica, Ninth Edition.
Evans, J., Ancient Bronze Implements, New York, 1881.
Ewald, H., The History of Israel. Translated, London, 1876.
Fergusson, J., A History of Architecture, 3 vols., London, 1865.
"   "   The Illustrated Hand-Book of Architecture, London, 1859.

Fergusson, J. A., Rude Stone Monuments, London, 1872.
Forbes, F. E., Five Years in China, London, 1848.
Forbes, Major, Eleven Years in Ceylon, 2 vols., London, 1841.
Fortune, R., Residence among the Chinese, London, 1857.
Gibbon, L., Exploration of the Valley of the Amazon, Washington, 1854.
Gill, W., The River of Golden Sand, London, 1883.
Gray, J. H., China, London, 1878.
Haug, M., Essays on the Parsees.
" " The Sacred Language of the Parsees, Boston, 1878.
Hearn, W. E., The Aryan Household, London, 1879.
Heeren, A. H. L., Historical Researches. Translated, 4 vols., London, 1854.
Helps, A., The Spanish Conquest in America, 4 vols., New York, 1857.
Herodotus, The History of. Translated by G. Rawlinson, 4 vols., New York, 1882.
Humboldt, A., Political Essay on New Spain. Translated, 4 vols., London, 1811.
Hunter, W. W., The Indian Empire, London, 1882.
Johnson, S., Oriental Religions, Boston, 1886.
Kauless, F., Assyrien und Babylonien, Freiburg, 1885.
Keller, Ferdinand., The Lake Dwellings of Switzerland, London, 1886.
Kenrick, J., Ancient Egypt, 2 vols., New York, 1852.
Kern, H., Der Buddhismus. Translated into German, 2 vols., Leipzig, 1882.
Knight, C. (publisher) author not mentioned. History of the Hindoos, 2 vols., London, 1834.
Kugler, F., Geschichte der Baukunst, 5 vols., Stuttgart, 1872.
Latham, R. G., The Varieties of Man, London, 1850.
Lauth, F. J., Ægyptens Vorzeit, Berlin, 1881.
Lenormant, F. and M. Chevalier, Ancient History of the East, 2 vols., Philadelphia, 1871.
Leonowens, A. H., Life and Travel in India, Philadelphia, 1884.
Lillie, S., Buddha and Early Buddhism, New York.
Lindsay, W. S., A History of Merchant Shipping, 4 vols., London, 1874.
Lippert, J., Allgemeine Geschichtes des Priesterthums, 2 vols., Berlin, 1884.
Lowell, P., Choson (Corea), Boston, 1876,

Lowell, P., The Soul of the Far East, Boston, 1888.
Lubbock, J., Prehistoric Times, New York, 1872.
Mahaffy, J. P., Prolegomena to Ancient History, London, 1871.
Maine, H. S., Early Law and Custom, New York, 1883.
" " Early History of Institutions, London, 1875.
Mallet, M., Northern Antiquities. Translated, London, 1878.
Martin, H., Histoire de France.
Martin, W. A. P., The Chinese, New York, 1881.
Martineau, H., Eastern Life, Boston, 1876.
Maspero, G., Egyptian Archæology. Translated, London, 1887.
Mayer, B., Mexico, New York, 1844.
Menu, Institutes of. Translated by W. Jones, and edited by S. G. Grady, London, 1869.
Mill, James, A History of British India, 6 vols., London, 1820.
Mill, John Stuart, Three Essays on Religion, New York, 1874.
Mills, C. D. B., The Indian Saint, Northampton, 1876.
Milne, W. C., Life in China, London, 1857.
Mommsen, T., History of Rome. Translated, 4 vols., New York, 1870.
Morgan, L. H., Ancient Society, New York, 1877.
Morris, C., The Aryan Race, Chicago, 1888.
Moevers, F. C., Die Phoenizier, Bonn, 1841.
Muller, F. Max., Chips, 5 vols., New York, 1872-1876.
" " Origin of Religion, New York, 1878.
" " . Science of Language, 2 vols., New York, 1865.
Muller, J. G., Amerikanischen Urreligionen, Basel, 1867.
Muller, S., Die Nordische Bronzezeit. Translated into German, Jena, 1878.
Napoleon, L., Vie de Cesar, 2 vols., New York, 1866.
Ober, F. A., Travels in Mexico, New York, 1884.
Oman, J. C., Indian [Hindoo] Life, Philadelphia, 1889.
Pfleiderer, O., Die Religion, 2 vols., Leipzig, 1878.
Phear, J. B., The Aryan Village, London, 1880.
Pictet, A., Les Origines Indo-Europeennes, 3 vols., Paris.
Popular Science Monthly, New York.
Prescott, W. H., The Conquest of Mexico, 3 vols., Boston, 1856.
" " The Conquest of Peru, 2 vols., New York; 1848.
Ragozin, A., The Story of Assyria, New York, 1887.
" " The Story of Chaldea, New York, 1886.
" " The Story of Media, Babylonia, and Persia, New York, 1888.

Rawlinson, G., The Five Great Oriental Monarchies, 3 vols., New York, 1881.
" " The Sixth Great Oriental Monarchy, London, 1873.
" " The Story of Phœnicia, New York, 1889.
" " A History of Phœnicia, London, 1879.
" " The Religions of the Ancient World, New York, 1883.
" " The Origin of Nations, New York, 1878.
Records of the Past, 5 vols., London, 1872.
Rein, J. J., Japan, London, 1884.
Renouf, L. P., The Origin and Growth of Religion, London, 1880.
Reville, A., The Native Religions of Mexico and Peru, New York, 1884.
Rivero, M. E. and J. J. von Tschudi, Antiquities of Peru, New York, 1853.
Robertson, Wm., The Works of, 2 vols., London, 1831.
Rockhill, W. W., Translator, The Life of Buddha, London, 1884.
Sayce, A. H., The Ancient Empires of the East, New York, 1884.
" " The Principles of Comparative Philosophy, London, 1874.
" " Introduction to the Science of Language, London, 1880.
Scherr, J., Deutsche Kultur und Sitten, Geschichte, Leipzig.
Scherzer, K., Voyage of the Novara. Translated, 3 vols., London, 1861.
Singh, J. A., The Sakhee Book (Sikh Bible), Benares, 1873.
Sleeman, W. H., Rambles and Recollections, 2 vols., London, 1844.
Smith, G., Assyria, London, no date.
" " The Chaldean Account of Genesis. Revised by A. H. Sayce, New York, 1880.
" " Assyrian Discoveries, London, 1875.
Squier, E. G., Peru, New York, 1877.
St. Hilaire, J. B. L., Buddha, Paris, 1862.
Taylor, I., The Alphabet, 2 vols., London, 1883.
" " Etruscan Researches, London, 1874.
Tennent, J. E., Ceylon, 2 vols., London, 1860.
Tiele, C. P., History of the Egyptian Religion. Translated, Boston, 1882.
" " Outlines of the History of Religion. Translated, London, 1867.

Toland, J., A History of the Druids, with notes by R. Huddlestone, Montrose, 1814.
Tschudi, J. J., von, Travels in Peru. Translated, New York, 1854.
Tylor, E. B., Anahuac (Mexico), London, 1861.
" " Anthropology, London, 1884.
" " Early History of Mankind, London, 1870.
Vinaya Texts. Translated, Oxford, 1881.
Waitz, T., Anthropologie, 6 vols., Leipzig, 1859-72.
Ward, W., The Hindoos, 2 vols., Serampore, 1818.
Webster, N., Dictionary of the English Language, Springfield, 1889.
Westropp, H. M., Prehistoric Phases. Translated, London, 1872.
Whitney, W. D., Oriental and Linguistic Studies, New York, 1874.
Wilkinson, J. G., The Manners and Customs of the Ancient Egyptians, Edited by S. Birch, 3 vols., London, 1878.
Williams, M., Hinduism, London, 1880.
" " Indian Wisdom, London, 1875.
Williams, S. W., The Middle Kingdom, 2 vols., New York, 1883.
Wilson, R. A., A New History of the Conquest of Mexico, Philadelphia, 1859.
Worsaae, J. J. A., The Primeval Antiquities of Denmark. Translated, London, 1849.
" " The Prehistory of the North. Translated, London, 1886.

END OF VOLUME II.

www.ingramcontent.com/pod-product-compliance
Lightning Source LLC
Chambersburg PA
CBHW020258240426
43673CB00039B/638